# Praise for *Your Public Best*

"Eminently practical advice...a notably helpful guide."

*—Publishers Weekly*

"An enormously practical guide to managing your appearance as effectively as you manage your business...Everything Brown discusses comes across in the same intelligent, no-nonsense fashion."

—Mark J. Estren, *The Miami Herald*

"Lillian Brown is a godsend for anyone who plans to meet the public directly or through the media. If you can't have Lillian with you in the dressing room, this book is the next best thing."

—Ann Richards, former Governor of Texas

"There is something of interest here for anyone wanting to improve one's public image."                            —Jane Larkin, *Booklist*

"Lillian's advice helped me look 10 years younger and 10 pounds thinner!"                               —Senator Barbara Mikulski

"The definitive work in a very crucial area—public performance. It should be beneficial to the neophyte as well as the experienced person. I cannot help but believe this will become the standard against which all competing books will be measured."

—Lou Prato, former Director of Broadcasting,
Medill School of Journalism, Northwestern University

"A guide to making successful public appearances. It covers everything from how to deal with a balding head on television (powder it) to handling stage fright (one tip: rehearse, rehearse, rehearse)."

—Sharon Nelton, *Nation's Business*

"Business people at all levels, government officials, teachers, congressional staffers, city council members—all of these people must take to the platform and put their best foot forward. This book will be essential to them."                       —Richard Lesher, former President,
U.S. Chamber of Commerce

"Lillian Brown's coaching is the best in the business. She makes even the most inexperienced amateurs look like professionals."

—James J. Kilpatrick

"*Your Public Best* is essential reading for anyone whose public presentation is key to their personal success...will help make the right impression for just about any audience the reader will face."

—Former Senator Alfonse D'Amato

"Lillian Brown brings to this book the wealth of her experience and the respect of the best people in our business."

—Charlie Rose, *The Charlie Rose Show*

"Lillian Brown is the greatest—the best voice trainer I ever had. I don't know what I would have done without her. Thank heaven she has put it all in a book."

—Dr. Geraldine Cox, Vice President & Technical Director, Chemical Manufacturing Association

"Lillian Brown is a pro! In her popular performance workshop for the top women in state governments throughout the nation—women governors and cabinet secretaries—she gives practical advice about what works at the podium and in front of the camera."

—Meg Armstrong, former Executive Director, Women Executives in State Governments

# YOUR
# PUBLIC
# BEST

**THE COMPLETE GUIDE TO MAKING SUCCESSFUL
PUBLIC APPEARANCES IN THE MEETING ROOM,
ON THE PLATFORM, AND ON TV**

## Lillian Brown

Newmarket Press, New York

Second Paperback Edition 2002

Copyright © 1989 by Lillian Brown and Kristi Brown

This book published simultaneously in the United States and Canada.

10 9 8 7 6 5 4 3 2

Library of Congress Cataloging-in-Publication Data

Brown, Lillian
Your public best: the complete guide to making successful public appearances in the meeting room, on the platform, and on TV/ Lillian Brown. —1st ed.

p. cm.
Includes index.
ISBN 1-55704-541-0

1. Public relations.   2. Public speaking.   3. Grooming for men.
4. Beauty, Personal. I. Title.
HM263.B685    1989
659.2—dc19                                            89-30759
                                                          CIP

QUANTITY PURCHASES
Companies, professional groups, clubs, and other organizations may qualify for special terms when ordering quantities of this title. For information, write Special Sales Department, Newmarket Press, 18 East 48th Street, New York, NY 10017; call (212) 832-3575; fax (212) 832-3629; or e-mail mailbox@newmarketpress.com.

www.newmarketpress.com

Book design and composition by The Sarabande Press

Manufactured in the United States

# ACKNOWLEDGMENTS

I am very grateful to Hy Badler, former Vice-President of Operations and Engineering, CBS Washington, for his invaluable advice on the technical information in the chapter "Appearing on Television."

I would like to thank my daughter Kristi Brown for her contributions to the book, which include editing and typing the original manuscript, and my other daughter, Carla Gorrell, who has worked with me professionally for more than two decades.

# CONTENTS

# CONTENTS

Jokes and the Use of Humor, 95 • Quotations and
Anecdotes, 96 • Saying Something Memorable, 97

Pauses within Your Speech, 101 • Brevity, 102 • Talking
Too Fast, 104 • Eliminating the "Uh," 105

Being Shy, 110

Upward-Turning versus Downward-Turning Body
Language, 117 • Summary of Good and Bad Body
Language, 118

# FOREWORD

## by Edwin Newman

It's a little late in the day for me to be thinking of running for office, or as it might be more pompously put these days, offering my capacity for citywide, statewide, or national leadership. If, however, I did decide to make that leadership capacity publicly available, I would ask Lillian Brown to join my team. Many who have run for office and made it have done just that, and with good reason. Lillian Brown gives them sound advice, often on matters they themselves have never thought of, advice based on decades of experience and also on much wisdom and common sense. (If you want to see what I mean by "matters they themselves have never thought of," just glance at her table of contents.)

It is not that she would recommend anything intended to be misleading. What she does help people do—people in many fields, not only politicians—is to present themselves as they are, but with a degree of confidence and comfort necessary to be at ease before a camera, a microphone, or an audience. She helps make sure they exhibit no distractions, such as a tie of the wrong color, a dress that is too flashy, a gesture that is too large, a delivery that is monotonous or one that is extravagant and overdone, a smile that is too practiced, an earnestness that is excessive, or a detachment that suggests that the speaker himself or herself is not much interested. What she strives for is reminiscent of a line from one of the early television serials: "Just the facts, ma'am," coupled with a still older exhortation: "Put your best foot forward."

I mentioned the word camera. The world in which we live is increasingly a television world. It is, of course, no secret that many disparaging words are spoken about television. During the 1988 election, for example, we were told over and over again how it had reduced the contest to a battle of sound bites. The term "sound bite" was represented as somehow contemptible and was spoken, as often as not, with a sneer.

In fact, the sound bite is not quite that bad. Much depends on how well-chosen it is, how accurate, how revealing. In any case, if the sound bite is the way of the world today, denouncing it is pointless and self-defeating. Learning to live with it—or better, to master it—is a more sensible course.

That is where Lillian Brown comes in. For more and more of us, a tremendous amount depends on how we present ourselves, how well and how convincingly we speak, what impression we convey, whether we get our message across. Why not rely on an expert for help? Why not present our public best?

I met Lillian Brown when I was working on "Modern Maturity," the television program of the American Association of Retired Persons. With Lillian in the makeup room there in the Washington studio, I knew that I would go on looking my best, without looking phony, and so would the guests I was to interview. As these guests came in, I would introduce them to Lillian—when it was necessary. Most of the time it wasn't, because the majority of them had been made up by her before, or had been advised by her, or had appeared on programs she had produced. You see, she is something of a legend in Washington.

And not only in Washington. When I was in some other city for a television program and mentioned her name to the makeup artist, there was instant recognition. Other makeup artists speak of her with something approaching awe.

But *Your Public Best* is not about makeup alone. Far from it. It is about personal appearance; about dealing with the press, with radio, with television; about speaking publicly; and about, as she puts it, surviving life in public. There is a vast amount of good advice in her book, advice which may be broadly applied. For when you stop to think about it, the title *Your Public Best* lends itself to a broad interpretation. You might as well be at your best in small groups, too, or while going about your ordinary day-to-day affairs. After all, there is everything to gain.

# INTRODUCTION
## You, the Public Person

It is often said that people judge you during the first five seconds of simply looking at you, and again during the first five seconds after you begin to speak. These dual aspects of your person—your appearance and your voice and speaking ability—can make a crucial difference in your career and in your life.

Every time you stand up to speak at a business meeting, participate in a panel discussion, address students in a classroom, hold a press conference, talk to reporters, lobby an elected official, make a major or minor speech, or talk into a microphone, you are appearing in public. You are being sized up and judged by your bosses, your professional colleagues, an audience, members of the public who watch television or listen to the radio, reporters, or members of some other group. If your appearance doesn't always inspire respect in those looking at you, or if you are a mediocre communicator, your audience will tune you out. In such a case, you will have failed to get across what you wanted to say not because your message was not a good one, but because there was something about you—your appearance or your delivery—that put up a barrier between you and your listeners.

In today's fast-paced world—where men and women can hold very important professional positions at a very young age, where elected officials can rush into (and sometimes right out of) the public spotlight at an amazing speed, where entire careers can be made or broken by a chance (or intended) remark that ended up at the top of the evening news—you can't afford to be someone from whom others turn away or whose message is unclear, for any reason.

The late Edward R. Murrow is an excellent example of someone who learned early in his career to project himself effectively to the public—first to radio listeners and ultimately to TV viewers. One of the pioneers of broadcast journalism (his protégés include Eric Sevareid, Walter Cronkite, Charles Collingwood, and many others), his distinctive voice reached across the sea during the 1940s to millions of Americans hungry for news from war-torn Europe. Later he made a smooth, seemingly natural transition to TV news, where his image—along with the ubiquitous cigarette—was soon a familiar sight to viewers.

Although he was always known as an outstanding journalist, interviewer, and analyst, Mr. Murrow's success as a broadcaster had just as much to do with his voice, appearance, and body language. While on radio, he developed a very deep and resonant voice and learned how to speak effectively into the primitive microphones of the 1940s. Likewise, his manner of speaking—the way he projected his personality through his voice—captured his listeners' attention and imaginations. His spare and informal speaking style, the way he used short pauses, the thoughtful questions he asked during interviews all made his listeners want to hear more from him. After his transition to television, his simple, low-key gestures and relaxed-yet-alert body language communicated to his viewers a sincerity and earnestness that went along with the voice they knew so well.

Years later, in 1961, Murrow decided to leave TV journalism to become the director of the United States Information Agency in President Kennedy's new administration. I was there in the studio when he gave his farewell speech over closed-circuit television to CBS and its affiliates. (I had done his makeup for the occasion.) The emotions that all of us in the audience felt that day was a clear sign of the power of this man's message and his ability to share it with an entire generation. It was also a symbol of the ending of one era in broadcast journalism . . . and the beginning of another.

# THE NEW POWER OF THE MEDIA

Important as the media has always been, it has grown even more influential in the last ten or twenty years. John F. Kennedy has been called our "first TV president." Since then, our presidents and political leaders use the media and often get abused by it.

Today's press—particularly TV news and the wire services—jumps on any story so fast that news organizations say their reporting of the story was a "triumph" or a "failure" when the story was aired mere seconds earlier or later than the competition. Just look at the "spin doctors" who appeared on every network news program after the 1988 presidential debates to see how the media's interpretation of an event can influence public opinion.

Yet the common denominator through all of this media coverage is still the human dimension—you, the public person. Even though the circumstances of how they are viewed have changed, good communication skills are still essential and universal.

You may never be a great communicator like Daniel Webster, Winston Churchill, Eleanor Roosevelt, John F. Kennedy, and Edward R. Murrow. You may never hold listeners in awe like Martin Luther King, Jr., Lee Iacocca, Mario Cuomo, and others have done. But with a little coaching, you can become an *excellent* communicator, a man or woman whose appearance and speaking skills attract others to you and make them want to listen.

The power of the media has now made it not only desirable, but necessary for the public person to master media skills. All of a sudden, the "public person" has become a "media person." Dealing well with the public and the press is a fine art, especially in this day of instant news. But it is not a difficult art to learn. This is true regardless of what stage of your career you are in or what kind of work you do. *The higher you go in your professional life, the more is expected of you and the more you will need to develop solid communication skills.* And that is the point of this book: to help you improve your appearances before others on the platform, in the studio, or simply speaking at a business meeting.

# BUT ARE YOU A PUBLIC PERSON?

So just who are you, the person who can benefit from this book? Perhaps you have just landed your first job, or you have been working for several years but have just been promoted and are now concerned about how you appear to others. Perhaps you have become so successful in your career that all of a sudden you find yourself being asked to moderate panels, give speeches, present awards, or be interviewed on radio and television. Maybe you are running for public office for the first time or have held public office before and are now running for a higher position and are dissatisfied with some aspect of how you appear on TV.

Maybe you are a radio announcer, a television newscaster, a newly appointed chief executive officer of your corporation, an author on a promotional book tour, a diplomat, a university professor, a lobbyist for a national association, a person on the paid-lecturer circuit, a public relations officer or a spokesman for a company, a physician or lawyer or economist who finds himself or herself invited to comment on TV and radio, or a financial adviser or real estate whiz who keeps getting invitations to speak in public.

Maybe you are an up-and-coming young executive with a company where you hope to make it big. But when you are asked to give an important presentation, you make one or more of the following mistakes: You rush out and get a too-short haircut; you choose to wear a "power-red" tie with your black suit and white shirt; you arrive at the meeting with the body of your report scribbled on a scrap of paper; or you are suffering from acute stage fright and don't know how to relax instantly so that no one notices.

No matter what your present status is, you will find something in this book to help you become a better public person.


## WHY I WROTE THIS BOOK

*Your Public Best is* the distillation of thirty years of experience that I've had helping people in the public eye to improve their personal appearances, their voices and speaking habits, and their media management skills.

I started out in the mid-1950s in the days of black-and-white, live television as the host of three documentary series. Behind the camera, I produced several Emmy award-winning educational television programs, such as "The Other Two Billion" and "Focus on the Law."

For a total of twenty years, I served as the director of radio and television for two major universities in Washington, D.C.—George Washington University and American University. Currently, I'm the producer of a nationally distributed radio program for Georgetown University, also in Washington.

During most of these years, I have also worked for CBS News and other broadcast entities as a television makeup artist, associating with such stars as Dan Rather, Walter Cronkite, Eric Sevareid, Charles Kuralt, and Diane Sawyer. And I've run in and out of the White House as the personal makeup artist to five presidents during their terms of office (Kennedy, Johnson, Nixon, Ford, and Carter).

Over the years, a number of political candidates running for public office from the presidency on down have hired me as a media consultant. This has meant everything from searching through stores for the perfect dress or suit for a crucial speech, going through closets and pointing out what clothes should or should not be worn on the campaign trail, transforming wooden gestures into effective, natural ones, and demonstrating where in the body the voice should originate from.

I've conducted hundreds of workshops and seminars on dealing with the media, improving the appearance, and speaking in public for leaders in business, members of Congress, and many other groups. Some of my workshops are for people who want to learn everything they can about appearing in public. Others might focus on just the voice and/or giving a speech. The seminars that focus on appearing in front of television cameras usually involve making an on-the-spot video tape of each participant and then critiquing the result. Sometimes I simply address small groups on a very specific subject, such as when I advise freshmen congressmen about clothes, makeup for TV, and the use of gestures when speaking in public.

I have also been a voice and diction teacher for international radio broadcasters for the United States Information Agency's "Voice of America," as well as to numerous other groups and private individuals.

During all of these years working in the media, I've observed and experienced firsthand many historical events. I've enjoyed the friendship of presidents, members of Congress, and foreign dignitaries. Perched on top of a network TV truck, I watched Martin Luther King, Jr.'s March on Washington. I've ridden in *Air Force One* and presidential motorcades, stood in the wings at political conventions with Secret Service agents, and watched space shots and moon walks from a network TV news control room.

I wrote this book because in all these years working both in front of and behind the cameras, I have never seen a definitive book that teaches what I teach, that helps people to improve their public appearances in a comprehensive way. The truth is, no matter who you are, you can improve your public persona.

## CAN YOU HELP ME? THE TWELVE MOST-OFTEN-ASKED QUESTIONS

At my seminars and workshops around the country, people ask me the same questions over and over again about some aspect of their public appearances. Often there is just one small thing that is acting as a barrier between the individual and others.

Here are the twelve most frequently asked questions:

1. What kind of clothes should I wear (when I'm giving a speech, making a business presentation, appearing on television, etc.)?
2. What colors are best to wear when appearing in public?
3. When I hear my voice on an audio tape, I don't sound like I thought I would (instead, it sounds high-pitched, harsh, or nasally). Why do I sound like that?
4. My friends (or colleagues) say I talk too fast, or they have trouble understanding what I just said. How can I slow my speech down, or improve my pronunciation?
5. At my age, can I change my voice (lower the pitch, get rid of a regional accent, etc.)?
6. When I stand up to speak before others—even a small group—what can I do to avoid the stage fright I feel? (Once I begin talking, I'm fine, but I still get sweaty palms and so forth beforehand.)
7. How should I sit (with legs crossed or uncrossed, leaning forward or backward, etc.)?
8. What should I do with my hands (put them in my pockets, place them on the conference table or podium, or put them out of sight)?
9. When I'm giving a talk or lecture, how can I organize my thoughts so that I don't ramble?
10. What should I do when I'm asked a question that I refuse to answer (or don't want to comment on or don't know the answer to)?

11. I've been asked to go on television or radio for the first time and I'm nervous about it. What can I expect once I get to the studio, and what should I do once I'm there?
12. I saw myself on TV, and I thought I looked terrible. Why was that? (Was it because I had on no makeup, or because I wore that certain color, or because my hair was too teased and sprayed?)

   This book addresses all of these questions, and many more that you may have.

As you develop your public presence, you must learn to anticipate. When you arrive for a public appearance, it is too late for you to change your clothes, rewrite your speech, or learn how to sit under the lights and in front of the camera lens.

That's why this book takes you step by step through such subjects as what to wear in public (including the best colors to choose), day-to-day makeup for women, TV makeup for men and women, and other aspects of your personal appearance.

You will learn how to improve your speaking voice, how to take care of your voice, the importance of proper breathing techniques, and how to work with a tape recorder.

Another chapter will take you through the process of organizing, writing, and giving an excellent speech, including how to stand at a podium, talk into a microphone, and answer questions from the audience.

You will find out how to deal with reporters and other members of the press and how to hold a press conference. You will also learn about appearing on radio, going on a book tour, and handling difficult media situations and hostile questions from the press.

Another section in this book will take you inside a TV studio, telling you what to expect, what TV lights and cameras do to your appearance, how to dress for the TV cameras, and how to sit and use effective gestures. You will learn how to be interviewed on TV and how to work with a prompter, among many other things.

As a person creating your own public presence, you should strive to be true to yourself in analyzing your own abilities and goals. You don't have to be handsome or pretty to appear successful in the public eye or to make a worthwhile contribution to society. After all, you have special skills, knowledge, and experiences that have put you in the public's unblinking eye in the first place. What matters at this particular point is *what you do with what you have already achieved.*

Look at those who have made the most notable contributions to society in any given field. They come in all shapes and sizes and ages, from different ethnic, racial, cultural, educational, and economic backgrounds, with varying degrees of natural ability. And they all have something special in them—to contribute or teach or communicate— that got them where they are . . . just like you.

Lillian Brown
Washington, D.C.

# ONE

# YOUR PERSONAL APPEARANCE

I'll never forget one day in the mid-1980s when that old saw "clothes make the man" came vividly alive for me.

I was escorting a U.S. senator out of a TV studio where he had just completed a taped interview about ongoing arms control talks with the Soviets for a network news talk show. He was a serious, all-business type of man, and he was dressed that day in clothes typical of senators—a plain, dark-gray suit with a white shirt and a red "power tie."

As we were about to reach the door to the studio, it opened, and down the steps clattered the four members of a punk-rock band.

The two female members of the band were wearing what you might expect—leather jackets painted and studded with rivets and rhinestones, lacy blouses that looked like lingerie, very short skirts, and high-heeled boots painted in bright colors. One had blond and green hair, and one had brown and blue hair. Each had on a dozen pieces of jangly jewelry. Their makeup was heavy and stark, and both were cracking gum.

The two male rockers were dressed similarly, only minus the lace and with somewhat less makeup and jewelry.

As the band squeezed by us on the stairs, the senator stared at them, turned to me, and blurted out, "What do *they* have to do with *arms control?*"

Fighting to keep a straight face, I explained that the show we were taping that day was not a theme show, with all interviews being on one subject, but was instead a mix of subjects, both serious and not so serious.

I sometimes call this little incident "the collision of the clothes"—a rather extreme lesson on the fact that your appearance is important, that you are instantly judged by others on how you look.

In fact, other guests who came into the studio over the next few days to appear on that same talk show included a North African ambassador dressed in his long flowing robes, a Catholic priest in his black suit and white clerical collar, an athlete dressed in her Olympic warm-up jacket, and a Country-and-Western singing star in her bouffant hairdo and glitzy dress. The appearance of all of these people made them readily identifiable.

The clothes *you* wear in public may not be as easily recognizable as these people's clothes were, but they do, nevertheless, say a lot about you.

The choices you make as you create your own image can, if well chosen, transmit a statement about you and about what you think about yourself.


## FEELING GOOD ABOUT YOURSELF

People *do* judge you during the first few seconds of merely looking at you—and before you even open your mouth. Whether you are making a business presentation, giving a speech, or even being interviewed on television, this is especially important for you, a person who is appearing in public or among your peers.

If your appearance is attractive, you can get an audience on your side before you have even said a word. Likewise, you can alienate an audience if your appearance is not quite right.

But there is more to this thing of having an effective personal appearance. It is essential that *you* feel good about yourself, because by doing so you reveal your personal conviction to your audience. When you know that you have taken the time to be well groomed, tastefully dressed, and in reasonably good physical shape, you exude confidence in yourself. When you sense that something is wrong or below your own basic standards, you tend to center your attention on that inadequacy. Even though others may feel that you look fine, *you* know that you may not look your best, and you can unconsciously transmit that negative feeling.

You do not dress to impress members of the opposite sex as much as you dress to please yourself, and for your own self-esteem and satisfaction. You, the wearer, are the important part of this equation.

Certain well-known public figures have been almost transformed when they finally found out what makes them look good.

Barbra Streisand is an example of such a person. Pictures taken earlier on in her career show a rather plain, almost gawky woman whose appearance said little about herself or even that she didn't seem to care how she looked. As she developed as a singer, actress, and movie producer, pictures of her began to show a very different woman—one who learned how to wear her hair and apply her makeup to diminish "faults" (such as her eyes that seemed slightly too close together) and enhance her good points (such as her long neck and her regal—but slightly crooked—nose). Many women's magazines called her "beautiful." She also developed a sense of style in her choice of clothes that was hers alone.

Other well-known people or fictional characters have become famous for certain things they have adapted as part of their appearance—things that became their trademarks.

For example, think of Winston Churchill and his vest with the chain across it; the Sherlock Holmes character and his hat, coat-with-cape, and the shape of his pipe; Abraham Lincoln and his stovepipe hat; or Fred Astaire and his elegant tuxedo and top hat.

One man who has a *very* distinctive personal appearance is Gene Shalit, writer and longtime movie critic for the "Today" show. He is known for his curly hair; wide handlebar mustache; and his large, brightly printed, loosely tied bow ties. His look is unique, to say the least—so much so that he tells a story about how it once affected his career.

Mr. Shalit says that his movie reviews had been appearing mostly in the print media, when in the late 1960s he got a phone call from someone in the broadcasting industry inviting him to come in and talk about a possible on-air job. But when the interviewer *saw* Mr. Shalit, he said something like, "let's talk about a job on radio"—as opposed to television. And sure enough, he went on radio for several years before finally appearing regularly on TV.

The point here is that what you look like and what you choose to wear can have a great effect on what others think of you and on what you think about yourself.

Whether you are a business executive, a lobbyist, or a salesperson, you set the tone for the entire day by your morning rituals and the wardrobe choices you make. That positive feeling can become an "upper," which leads to better performance; and that negative feeling can become a "downer," which starts a cycle of doubt and leads to an inferior performance.

The public person must be prepared to move with grace and dignity from one visual situation to another with total confidence. You must feel that you are "well turned out," and that your advance preparations were adequate.

The classic look always reflects good taste. Your clothes should be graceful, restrained. Simple, understated clothes act as a proper support for you and allow the viewer to notice *you* rather than what you are wearing. You can express your individuality in many subtle ways that tell about your background, who you are, and what you would like to be.

For example, I often run into Senator Paul Simon of Illinois. He looks like a senator. He wears plain, well-cut suits in navy blue and similar colors. He has a good haircut that always seems to be the same length (i.e., he's not one of those people to whom you say, "I see you just got a haircut"). His shoes are always polished. But Senator Simon almost always wears a bow tie. In fact, he seems to be one of the very few of our congressmen or senators who do. On him—a man known for his intellect and his individuality—it looks good; it has become a trademark, part of his persona.

Another senator I know is also always dressed like a senator . . . except that if you examine his appearance closely, you'll notice that he is wearing cowboy boots with his suit. This senator is from a Western state. He has told me that he wears the boots because (1) he's always worn them and sees no reason to change just because he's in Washington now, (2) they're comfortable, (3) they're sturdy and practical, and (4) he *likes* them. If you had the opportunity to inspect the feet of other members of the Senate and House of Representatives, you'd probably find other, similar types of nontraditional footwear paired with those congressional suits.

Women, too, can dress conservatively and simply but also wear something that expresses individuality in subtle ways. I know a woman who owns her own public relations firm. She often wears Gucci silk scarves wrapped around the neckline of her rather plain dresses and suits. She often pairs the scarf with a long string of pearls. In fact, she has a small collection of these scarves. They look great on her, adding a dash of color to a conservative wardrobe. She might take off such a colorful scarf if she were appearing on television, but she usually wears one when she is meeting with her clients or otherwise appearing in public.

Once you are confident that your clothes work for you and fit your own image of yourself, you can forget all about them and focus on the task at hand. That's why we are discussing your personal appearance in the first chapter of this book—to get you well dressed and well groomed and send you out ready to face the public, whether that public means colleagues, clients, reporters, or a national television audience.

In this chapter, we will be referring often to what effect your clothes and other aspects of your personal appearance have when you go on television, since in front of TV cameras you must be particularly careful about how you look. You may never actually go on TV—you may only be seen by customers, clients, or professional associates—but since these days so many successful professionals are eventually asked to make some kind of TV appearance at some point in their careers, you should be aware of the rules of the game.

## YOUR CLOTHES

In this section, we'll be discussing the clothes that work best when you are the person "up front" and all eyes are upon you. In private, you can indulge in your flights of fancy and wear whatever you choose. But as a public person, your choices now have a different focus—they must not attract too much attention to themselves because their role is to allow you to transmit your message. In short, your clothes should work for you, not overpower you.

The right outfit can do wonders for the effect a person's message has, and should be considered a key component of this preparation. Just look at Ann Richards, treasurer of the state of Texas, who was chosen to be the keynote speaker for the 1988 Democratic Convention in Atlanta. As one of her consultants, I was asked to find a dress that would be suitable for such an important occasion. She had already looked at many dresses—some sent to her by well-meaning friends—but had found nothing among them that she particularly liked; they were all too frilly or ornate or severe. In order to choose her dress, I had to keep in mind the following:

- The background color of the podium area was gray;

- The front of the podium was "busy," with a stylized version of the flag in muted colors of red, white, and blue;
- The lights would be susceptible to the blue range, would be "thrown" from a long distance, and would be brought up and down, from bright to dim;
- She would be seen in person by thousands of people from every walk of life, all staring at her and sizing her up. She would also be seen by possibly millions of TV viewers, and the TV cameras being used would be very sensitive and would be focusing from close up to a long distance;
- Members of the live audience would be moving about, dressed in many colors, and would be seen in the TV camera's long shots;
- The photographers would need a color that looked good in black-and-white and color, on video tape and film.

After studying hours of video tapes of Ann, I was aware of her delicate coloring, the halo of silvery hair, her chiseled features, the blue-green color of her eyes, and her strong, vibrant personality.

As I recommend to all my clients for whom I select clothes, the dress shouldn't be red, white, black, boldly printed, or striped. What was really needed here was a plain dress of good design, soft fabric, and in the middle of the color spectrum—possibly near to her actual eye color. I ended up trooping through a dozen or more stores until I found the perfect outfit—a jacket dress with a plain neckline. It was simple and elegant and was of a lovely aquamarine blue.

To see how the dress would look, the day before the convention started we had Ann hold up the dress on the actual podium she would use during her speech. Instead of attracting attention to itself, it enhanced her—the person with the message. After she gave what most agreed to be a dynamic keynote speech, that dress was mentioned in several magazine and newspaper articles as having added to her overall success.

Another client of mine, a near genius in real estate investing, was finding himself more and more in demand as a speaker to a wide variety of business, investor, and consumer groups. A terrific speaker, he lacked self-confidence only in his appearance—particularly in his choice of clothing for his speaking engagements.

When he first came to me for advice, he was accustomed to dressing in the flamboyant manner of some salespersons, including wearing a flashy diamond ring, a bright pocket square, an out-of-style tie, and a striped shirt with a solid white collar. Also, his suits tended to be ill-fitting, unpressed, and made out of synthetic fabrics.

It was obvious to me that his choice in clothes was not on the high level of his business expertise.

By simply telling him the basic points contained in this chapter on dressing well and rather conservatively, he was able to project a professional image to his audiences. He did this by purchasing a couple of good wool suits (one in navy and one in gray), new shirts (solid colored, with no stripes this time around), and ties (in the currently correct width, in subtle patterns only). The diamond ring and bright pocket squares went into a drawer, where they remain until this day.

When you shop for that perfect suit or dress, "photograph" yourself from top to bottom in a full-length mirror. Look at yourself from the sides, front, and back. Be honest with yourself about your good and bad points. From your past experiences, you already know some of the things that work best for you.

Take women, for example. Since you may be sitting as well as standing—on a platform or dais, perhaps—you should wear a skirt that looks good when you sit down. A tight skirt hikes up above the knees and wrinkles across the front. You should have at least an inch of leeway in the fabric on each side of your hips. Also, try to imagine how it will look to your audience, which may be sitting on a level below you. Avoid split skirts that fall open when you are seated, since often no amount of tugging and fussing will pull the slit closed.

Your hemline is a personal thing. It should not move up and down each season with the dictates of fashion. Depending on your height, weight, build, the shape of your legs, and your own personal style, there is a becoming hem length that works best for you. A hemline several inches below the knee is usually the most becoming and has the additional advantage of not going out of style.

Now for the men. Your suit must not only appear to be of as good a quality as you can possibly afford, but it must be of an attractive fabric and color, hang well on your body shape, and be of the proper size. When you sit down, the hem of your pants should not ride up above your socks so that skin is showing. Your shoes should always be shined. Your shirt should fit you and not be too small (heavy-set men, take note—there is nothing worse than a shirt that buckles open between buttons once you sit down). Your tie, if patterned, should be discretely patterned and colored. If you are color-blind, you should have someone else choose ties for you.

Some of these tips may seem obvious to you, but in the space or just a few months not long ago, I observed the following men: a prominent economist giving a speech wearing one black shoe and one brown shoe, neither shined; a U.S. congressman appearing before a group of his constituents wearing socks that were too short and too old (he kept having to bend over and pull them up); a salesman giving a sales pitch wearing a kelly green polyester-blend suit and a green-and-red patterned tie; and a singer performing on stage wearing a black leather jacket decorated with food stains and dandruff.

These rules—among many others—should be the basic good-taste dressing rules for all men. But they bear repeating for the public person just for that reason—because you will be seen and judged by the public.

We will discuss clothing choices for both men and women in greater detail later in this chapter.

## Visual Vibrancy

Certain colors and patterns of fabrics, shiny metal found in jewelry or eyeglasses, and harsh colors found in makeup produce what could be called an undesirable visual vibrancy. It is especially important to be aware of visual vibrancy when you are appearing on TV. Some examples are discussed below that relate to all personal appearances in general but should be especially noted when TV cameras are present.

When you look at your wardrobe and try to decide what you should wear, it is important always to view the article from the standpoint of the vibrancy of its color and pattern. If you are choosing earrings or jewelry, ask yourself if they will sparkle and glitter or dangle or otherwise outshine your eyes. Your eyes assist you in the transmission of your message. Your face is expressive, and we must see *it* first. Therefore, anything that outshines or outsparkles your eyes and face should not be your first choice.

Visualize, if you will, a young woman with frizzled hair down over the eyes, a scarlet line of shiny lipstick, glittery tinted glasses, long dangling earrings, multiple necklaces over a red sequined dress, and an arm full of quivering bracelets. This may be fine for the Academy Awards, but do you see or care who is really under there? Take the same woman, smooth the hair back so it does not obscure eye contact, remove the glasses, subdue the makeup, remove most of the jewelry, make the dress a soft raspberry color—and you will find a naturally beautiful person whose message you can pay attention to. The above is true for public appearances with or without TV cameras present.

If you are appearing on TV, you are dealing with high-powered lenses, and it is difficult for those camera lenses to balance certain colors—in particular, the color extremes of black, white, and red. Red, especially, contains the maximum amount of what you could call visual vibrancy; you see it long before you see the person. Clothes designers who wish their clothes to dominate, love for their clients to wear red. But red is an unstable color that "bleeds" around the edges and defies camera focus. In a group of four panelists, you will pick out the red dress or tie, and not the person. Alternative, middle-spectrum colors will be discussed in detail in the next sections.

Fabric patterns that might shimmer and vibrate on TV cameras include: striped, polka-dotted, iridescent, checked, or multicolored. As a TV viewer, you have probably noticed that strange shimmer effect (called a moiré pattern) when a reporter wears a striped shirt, a plaid tie, and/or a chevron-patterned jacket.

Also to avoid wearing are sequins, which are meant to reflect and dance in the light. On TV, sequins and other sparkling fabrics can be blinding.

It takes courage and discipline to wear plain colors and patterns that don't "do anything." They just photograph beautifully. (Note this short paragraph well; it may make all the difference in the world to your choosing fabrics as a public person.)

A quick trick: Just before you go on for a TV or other public appearance, shut your eyes halfway and look at yourself in the mirror. If some accessory you are wearing outshines you, take it off. Again, what the public must see first is you, plain and simple.

## The Color Spectrum

When you see a beam of light dispersed through a prism, all of the colors are displayed. They are arranged in the order of their wavelengths. You also see these colors in a rainbow, in an artist's or scientist's chart of colors of the spectrum, and even in the "color bars" of the camera test pattern on your TV set. The two extremes of the color spectrum are black and white.

It is difficult for the eye or the camera to bridge the distance between the two. That explains why a still or TV camera can have trouble with a white face with a black dress, or a black face with a white suit, or a bold black and white fabric print.

Dark colors absorb the light and make you look smaller. Light colors reflect the light and make you look larger. Some colors, such as red and orange, are vibrant, harsh, and domineering. Yellow and green tend to reflect a sallow tinge onto the skin.

In my seminars on how to dress for public appearances, I always say that due to these facts, a good basic rule is to wear no bright reds, black, or white.

Rather, when you select colors to be worn on the platform or before the camera, you need to stay in the center of the color spectrum. The closer you come to the middle, the better the colors will look, and the more becoming they will be. Thus, blues, grays, and jewel tones are the most flattering.

Many women like to have a "color analysis" done in order to find what colors are becoming to them. This may work well for the private person, but for the public person the recommended colors often do not look good, especially when viewed through a still or TV camera lens.

**Blue and Purple.** Blue is the most pleasant color of all because it is stable and in the middle of the color spectrum. It is an excellent choice to complement the owner of blue eyes. Denim blue looks good on almost everyone, from cowboys to babies. Pale blue blouses or shirts photograph white. Probably the most beautiful garment on or off camera would be a deep blue suit, with (for women) a blouse either matched to the color of the suit or in a muted, jewel-toned pattern.

Good variations of blue are navy, bright navy, royal blue, marine blue, colonial blue, French blue, Delft blue, slate gray-blue, or cadet blue. Other variations include the teal blues and nonbright aquas that are mixed with green. Periwinkle blue is a good cool color and is about as light as you should go.

The blues to avoid are turquoise blue, bright aqua blue, and solid pale blue.

Many of the purple shades work very well. Mauves, rich royal purple, dark violet, dusky violet, deep lilac shades, purple with red tones, and plum purples are all flattering colors.

**Green.** True Christmas green is too bright to be a good clothes color. The same goes for the brighter variations of kelly green, forest green, and, of course, lime green. However, some shades of green can be very nice. Jade green that contains gray, dark emerald, or soft olive green (close to khaki) are excellent.

**Red.** Red does cheer you up; however, it is an energetic color that dominates you and your surroundings. It should usually be considered a "no-no" for the public person. It is unstable and vibrant and often bleeds outside of its own borders when being photographed.

In a stadium full of people, notice that the one in a red parka is more visible than all of the others and is the one you will notice. You see a red tie long before you see the person. Red can reflect on the whites of the eyes and cast "heat" onto the skin tone.

However, many of the variations of red are excellent choices, including wine, burgundy, rose, and dusty rose.

Pink is a tricky color. Hot pinks, bright pink, and nearly-white pinks should be avoided. If you like pink, select the dusty rose or grayed rose mentioned above.

**Orange.** Orange is a hot, vibrant, glowing color and is generally harsh and unbecoming to all skin tones.

About three years ago, a TV studio where I often work was auditioning a series of applicants for an opening for a newscaster. I'll never forget a woman who came in dressed in an orange suit and blouse with an orangy rouge and lipstick to match. You can easily picture how that looked with her blond hair. She had obviously spent much time assembling that orange look. She wanted to be noticed, and she was! But she didn't get the job.

However, brown-based earth tones somewhat related to orange are good middle-spectrum colors. These include terra-cotta, apricot, brick, or autumn-leaf tones.

**Yellow.** Yellow is a bright color that attracts attention to itself. It tends to reflect onto the face, giving the skin a sallow, jaundiced, unhealthy tinge. It is often said that when a performer comes into a TV studio wearing bright yellow, the technicians can be heard groaning in the background.

**Brown.** Brown should not be your first choice, particularly if the brown has a reddish tone. On the other hand, a deep chocolate brown sometimes looks well with dark hair, eyes, and skin. Lighter shades of brown (such as taupe, rust, or clay) are good neutral colors.

*Gray.* Gray is a quiet color, and for that reason it is one of the best colors the public person—man or woman—can wear in any setting. You should always have one well-cut gray suit in a natural fabric such as wool to fall back on when all else fails. Gray does nothing to attract attention to itself but, instead, flatters you. It makes a strong statement of strength at the same time that it makes you appear approachable. Banker's gray denotes confidence, trustworthiness, success, and authority.

For women, gray can be easily and attractively accessorized with jewelry or scarves or contrasting blouses. It is compatible with many other colors. Luckily, gray pearls and hematite beads are quite fashionable.

High saturations of gray added to other colors make them deeper, richer, and more pleasant. Thus, bluish slate gray is an excellent choice for the person with blue or hazel eyes. Gray is especially flattering for the gray-haired person. For all people, gray forms a soft background and permits you to dominate the visual framework.

Good variations of gray are slate gray, slate blue, dove gray, charcoal gray, steel gray, stone gray, and Oxford gray.

Since it is obvious that I recommend gray so highly as a prime choice in clothing color for the public person, both male and female, I would like to go into a bit more detail with this color to give you some ideas for your own wardrobe.

For men: Imagine yourself in a darkish gray suit (a gray somewhere between steel and charcoal, perhaps), worn with a pale gray shirt and a silk tie printed in a simple paisley pattern of blue and green. Or imagine wearing a textured gray suit with a pale gray shirt and a plain, darker blue tie. You could add a vest, a gold collar pin, a discreet blue silk square in the jacket pocket, or whatever to dress it up or down. But this is an example of a look that is distinguished, flattering, and businesslike, but not at all boring.

For women: Imagine yourself in a dove gray suit made out of a natural fabric such as wool or suede or raw silk or even a synthetic suede, paired with a blouse in a muted print of gray and another color such as pink or a soft blue. Or if you chose a solid-colored blouse, you could wear a somewhat colorful scarf with your gray outfit. You may have added a long chain necklace in a gold tone, or hematite beads, or fake pearls, possibly with matching earrings. You could appear anywhere in this outfit and feel perfect confidence in your appearance.

After a quick perusal of how elegant and restrained you look, your audience will view you with admiration then quickly forget your appearance and concentrate on what you are saying.

*White.* As mentioned previously, white "flares" and makes everything look larger. Hold a sheet of white paper up near your face in front of a mirror, and you will see the paper first, because it is brighter than your face. A white dress or shirt will add pounds to your image. If you could look at a TV monitor or a picture of yourself, you would see a white shirt or blouse look larger than it really is.

Instead of white, choose soft grays or pale pastels; they will "read" as white if you are to be photographed by a still or TV camera. This is especially important for men to remember when choosing shirts. A pale gray or blue shirt is always better than a white shirt.

*Black.* Black makes things disappear. It diminishes anything that it covers, which is why puppeteers wear it when they wish to remain invisible. It also appears harsh against most skin tones. Finally, black can denote mourning and sadness. Think of the stereotype of the Italian or Spanish widow wearing a black dress, hose, and shoes, with even a plain black scarf tied over her head. Black can be a "downer" color that should be avoided by the public person.

Every decade or so, black comes back as a fashionable color for women. (In fact, as a choice of late-afternoon-through-evening, the "little black dress" is one of the oldest and perhaps best-known clichés in the fashion world.) This has once again been the case in the last few years. However, black is still not the best daytime choice for women who appear frequently in public. This is especially true for the woman with delicate coloring, where black looks particularly harsh against the face; and for the woman whose face is starting to show her age, where black's severity can make the face look even older.

## Clothes for Women

Even though you may feel at times that you are working in "a man's world," that doesn't mean you have to dress like a man. An expensive, well-cut suit can be accessorized to look feminine. Be creative to soften and individualize your look.

Obviously, however, a woman who is in business or perhaps is a physician may have to dress more conservatively than one who is speaking before a civic group or a charitable organization or an interior decorator meeting with her new clients.

Inventory the clothes you already own and update them with minor changes or alterations. Get rid of clothes that are hopelessly outdated, too small, or not suitable for your public image. You need only a few good, classic outfits that fit perfectly.

The original financial outlay for what could be called your "in-public clothes" could be considerable; therefore, each piece must be carefully chosen to play a significant role.

Good fit is essential—better a little roomy than too tight. Tight clothes with stretch lines across the front make you look heavier. They also tend to wrinkle more quickly, especially across the front of your skirt.

Another important rule of thumb for the woman appearing often in public is to always wear long sleeves, even in summer, since short sleeves give an informal look. Bare arms attract the eye away from the face because they are lighter in color. Long sleeves slenderize the silhouette and look more professional.

You must feel comfortable in your clothes. Never wear a new suit for the first time in front of your audience. Instead, try it out in private until it feels like an old friend and has no surprises. You need to know that the sleeves are the right length, how the neckline fits, how the skirt falls, and where the pockets are. You need to know in advance how the whole outfit looks when you are standing, sitting, or moving about. Since the same audience seldom sees you twice, you can wear the same tried-and-true things time after time with total confidence. This enables you to forget about what you are wearing and concentrate on your message.

What should you wear if you are going to address a group of truck drivers? Should you dress like they do? The answer, of course, is no—you dress like the person you are, with a few minor adjustments to the circumstances, time, and place. You are brought in as a speaker because you have a message your audience wants to hear. You are an expert in your field, and it would be a mistake to appear in jeans and a plaid shirt. Maintain your own high standard of simplicity and good taste. A plain shirtwaist dress or a well-cut suit will take you anywhere. Since in such a circumstance you will be in the minority and will stand out more, your appearance should be understated and conservative.

Similarly, if you are running for political office, you should dress for the office you wish to fill. In other words, if you are running for the U.S. Senate, dress like a senator.

**Color Coordination.** When putting together a minimum wardrobe for campaigning, book tours, selling real estate, or whatever aspects of your life take place in public, it is possible to coordinate your colors so that you can make multiple outfit combinations. By carefully choosing two basic colors that are very becoming to you, you can create forty different looks out of a dozen or so garments.

For example, buy two expensive suits—one a soft navy blue and one an Oxford gray. The navy suit might have a blazer jacket with dull-finished gold buttons, which could go with different skirts year-round. The gray jacket might be collarless, with a neckline that could be dressed up or down with accessories.

Coordinate blouses, scarves, sweaters, coat, hat, umbrella, shoes, hose, belts, purses, and jewelry with these two colors. Buy several blouses in solid colors that match your basic suits with different necklines. Add complementary-colored blouses with soft, indistinct patterns (such as paisleys, jacquards, foulards, or color-on-same-color patterns) in colors that match both suits. You could also add your own favorite colors such as soft blue, old rose, or plum—all of which look good with both suits.

The navy suit jacket will serve in many capacities. The jacket of the gray suit would look well over the navy skirt and blouse with a colorful navy-gray-rose scarf. You need very little genuine jewelry—a string of pearls, a gold chain, plus possibly a lapis lazuli string of beads for the navy suit and a gray hematite necklace for either suit. The purse and shoes can be black or blue-black navy to go with everything.

If you will be photographed or will appear on camera, choose either suit. For example, with the gray suit, wear your matching gray blouse, small pearl earrings, a pearl necklace, and you will look great.

**Fabrics.** When shopping for your wardrobe, select the fabrics carefully. Men's clothes are often made of good, sturdy materials that hold up well with constant wear. Unfortunately, you have to search for women's clothes of equal quality. As a public person, your clothes need to look good under trying circumstances and to withstand frequent dry cleaning.

Natural fabrics or blends are usually the best choices. Select materials that conform easily to the body. Stiff, shiny fabrics look awkward and add pounds to the silhouette because they are unyielding. The fabric should have little or no sheen or gloss. Look for fabrics that have a "hand," with a soft, dull finish. Thin knits cling and can look sleazy. Double knits, on the other hand, are very comfortable, and they pack well with minimal wrinkling.

Some fabrics are "verbal" and rustle into the microphone.

The newly popular thin woolen fabrics (such as wool challis for dresses and skirts) are also excellent, due to their lovely drape and wrinkle-resistant nature.

Synthetic suedes with a dull finish now come in a lighter, more drapable weight. These synthetic suedes are excellent choices because they can be washed by hand, yet they always look luxurious and elegant and are nearly wrinkle-free.

*Accessories.* The secret of wearing good, basic clothes lies in the accessories you choose to go with them. This gives you the opportunity to express your own personality. Accessories can creatively change a plain suit to fit the various seasons and occasions. Once you have the look you feel is flattering to you, you can change the entire look with belts, jewelry, scarves, a lace collar, or discreet fabric flowers. For example, an extra paisley skirt that matches your suit jacket, a sleeveless jacket-sweater, a blazer, or a soft knitted top all add variety.

For the public person, your purse becomes your home and desk away from home. You have to practically live in it, and depend on it to get you through many varied experiences. Select a purse especially suited to your public appearance, and look at it in a mirror to see if it fits your build, size, and purpose. Choose a solid, dark color that matches most of your clothes. Spend as much as you can afford on one good, plain purse. Make it roomy enough to hold all of your necessities and small enough not to look bulky.

Organize it like a bureau drawer, inside and out, so that you can find your glasses, keys, billfold, datebook, business cards, checkbook, credit cards, and notes—without upending the whole thing as you search in public. Have an outside pocket for plane tickets, boarding passes, or subway tokens, and a special place for change for telephone calls and tips. Assemble a small, private telephone directory containing the critical numbers you will need when away from your desk.

When traveling, label an envelope with the date and city to contain reimbursable taxi receipts, hotel and restaurant charges, airline ticket carbons, etc. There is nothing more difficult than trying to sort out the debris from a week of traveling to different cities with different expense accounts. Soon, the cities, airlines, restaurants, and hotels all fade into one unrecallable blur.

If you change to an evening purse, consider keeping your traveler's checks, cash, and credit cards in a money belt.

Once a week, ruthlessly toss out everything you can possibly get along without, keeping that purse as lean and uncluttered as possible.

Good taste in jewelry should not change with what's currently popular. Similarly, the public person must remember that what looks good in public or on a TV camera does not alter with the changes in fashions.

Your jewelry should enhance your appearance without becoming the main attraction. A few genuine pieces, worn discreetly, are always in the best of taste.

The basic rule is that anything that sparkles or shines too much, dangles in the light (such as earrings), or rattles and makes noise (such as multiple bracelets) will distract attention away from your face and what you are saying. Thus, large surfaces of shiny gold, rhinestones, diamonds, some silver-colored jewelry, and flat white jewelry (such as large fake pearls, white disk earrings, bone or ivory bracelets) are not the best choices.

Big shiny earrings, larger than the eyes, interfere with your eye contact. A strand of oversized beads attracts attention as it migrates back and forth over the chest. No one should hide behind big, gaudy, fake jewelry, which can subliminally transmit insecurity and bad taste.

Better choices for jewelry include:

- Pearls, especially colored pearls such as gray, blue, or beige;
- Dull, satin-finished gold or silver jewelry;
- Filigree pins;
- Cameos;
- Beads in subdued, rich colors, especially semiprecious stones (such as hematite, dark jade, garnet, onyx, tiger's eye, amethyst, lapis lazuli, or amber) or lighter stones (such as pink quartz, coral, or blue-lace agate);
- Colored, semiprecious stones set in pins or earrings, especially in the darker colors such as amethyst, garnet, or dark-blue topaz;

- Antique or antique-looking jewelry;
- Enamel or cloisonné jewelry in rich, jewel-toned colors, such as deep purple disk earrings or pins.

It takes courage to wear plain jewelry, but the public person must never forget that the wrong jewelry can detract from, rather than enhance, a public image. TV correspondents are often seen removing their big jewelry pieces before going on camera, then putting them back on afterward.

I have one client who is the vice-president of a brokerage house. In her private life she wears a plain, expensive suit, but always seems to top it with scarves, a couple of gold chains, and a rope of genuine pearls. On her, it looks wonderful. But when she started doing frequent business-related TV commentaries, she asked my advice about her appearance on camera. Now, when she comes into the TV studio, she unloads all those accessories down to the plain suit. She exchanges her big earrings for small ones. She goes on camera, tapes her "piece," comes out of the studio, and puts everything back on. The reason she does this is simple: After I encouraged her to study her video tapes, she saw and learned to understand what the camera sees.

***Shoes.*** A word about shoes. Show me a woman with pain lines around the eyes, and I suspect that her feet hurt. High heels were never made for walking very far, and I feel sorry for the woman who teeters down the street with the pelvis thrown into an unnatural position. Granted, you can't wear hiking boots on a city street, but these days one sees women striding along in comfortable footwear with the high heels tucked into the briefcase.

As we will discuss in a later chapter, the public person needs to center the body and dig the heels into the floor, whether walking, sitting, or standing. However, high heels throw the body off balance and make it almost impossible to breathe with the diaphragmatic muscle.

Thus, it is important to wear comfortable, well-fitting shoes with heels as low as you can tolerate. Current styles offer attractive yet trendy low-heeled shoes. You will need such shoes since you will probably have to walk long distances or stand for extended periods of time at public functions.

Spend as much as you can afford on a few pairs of plain, good-looking, comfortable shoes, and keep them in perfect condition. Low-heeled pumps are a good choice.

Buying several pairs of good-quality, genuine leather shoes in several solid colors is not only smart, but is a good investment. One pair each in black, navy, medium or dark brown, and even gray could make up a good, basic wardrobe of shoes. Other colors that can look sophisticated when worn with a coordinating dress or suit color are dark purple, royal blue, and charcoal.

Many business, professional, and political women like plain pumps, but "wing-tip" shoes (the kind with the perforated hole-patterns on the toe and around the side areas) and stacked heels can look good as well. Some women like the look of a solid-colored, simple bow on their shoes, or shoes with a simple "T-strap."

Avoid shoes that are brightly colored, bicolored, or have heels in unusual shapes.

To minimize the legs, choose hose and shoes in dark colors. If you are short, wearing shoes and hose the same color can make the leg look longer. For example, you might try beige shoes with beige hose or black shoes with black hose. Can you see how light hose with black shoes could chop up the visual image and make you look shorter?

If you are one of those women who wear tennis or jogging shoes to commute or when you travel, and you are on your way to make a business presentation, give a speech, or otherwise appear in public, change into your dress shoes in the lobby or a ladies' room or even in a taxi before showing up at the actual site of your appearance. It's a bit awkward being seen leaning over to change footwear in a business or public setting.

Also it is a good idea to tuck a plastic bag or cloth shoe protectors (available in luggage shops or through many mail-order catalogs) in your briefcase or large purse to protect the dress shoes from scratches and the contents of your case from shoe dirt.

*Your Travel Wardrobe.* For the frequent traveler—whether you are a business tycoon, an author, or a department store buyer—your travel clothes are a part of your image.

About ten years ago, when I traveled to India with a group of educators, I met a woman on the plane who told me that she carried everything in one carry-on bag. Later I realized that because of this, she didn't have to wait at the baggage claim area with the rest of us. She would sprint on ahead, breezing up the stairs with that bag swinging from padded shoulder straps. The bag also had little wheels so that she could pull it along behind her.

All of the basic pieces in that bag were black—one elegant suit with pants and blouses coordinated. There was something in that bag to meet every occasion, including a light raincoat and tops for warm or cold weather. Apart from these black pieces, she also kept pulling out wonderful colorful scarves, jewelry, and accessories for every occasion from the beach to a concert. Over it all, she wore a huge black cape (which obviously did not fit into the bag) that shielded her from the cold, the rain, and the sun. She slept in it, on it, and under it, on buses and planes.

She always looked wonderful.

I can go around the world with one bag on wheels, but I still have to check it.

When you travel, consider the modes of transportation you will be taking. Is it a native four-wheel-drive jitney, luxury bus, car, plane, or *Air Force One?*

Make a list of the functions you will be attending and be sure to plan in advance to dress appropriately for the opera, the formal dinner, the business conference, the professional breakfast, or the country pub. When and where will you be making public appearances?

But the most important consideration is to travel as light as you can. One learns to eliminate the nonessentials. Once you have packed your bags, repack them, leaving out everything you can do without. (Remember, there are times when you may have to carry your own bag.) When possible, take clothes that are washable, such as knits, polyester, cotton, or synthetic suede. Coordinate your wardrobe and accessories to one color, anticipating the occasions and climates in which they will be worn.

***Emergency Kit.*** Assemble an emergency kit and keep it in a desk drawer or within easy reach in case you have to make an unexpected appearance. It should contain a few essentials such as a toothbrush and deodorant. Add a fresh blouse that will go with most of your clothes, and an extra pair of hose.

Take your individual needs into consideration: extra contact lenses or glasses, a source of fiber, a food bar, or some reading material.

During the years I was the personal makeup artist for several U.S. presidents, I had many an opportunity to use my own emergency kit when I was called to the White House with no prior notice. I remember one time in particular when I was glad that I had a food bar and a magazine with me, because I had to wait in a formal anteroom for three full hours for Gerald Ford due to a sudden scheduling change.

***A Few Additional Tips.*** Reserve low-cut bodices for the Academy Awards.

Your neckline should conform to the contours of your face. You can lengthen the face with a V neckline or soften the effect with a scarf. Scarves can be tied or looped around the neck in many different ways. If you have a short neck, avoid bows, turtlenecks, and collars that sit too high up under the chin.

When making a grand entrance, take off your coat before you enter the room so that you do not have to struggle out of it in public.

Imagine the nation's First Lady entering a crowded hall directly through an outside entrance from where she is going to walk across part of the room to a podium to give the keynote speech at a function. Can you see how her dignified entrance would be spoiled if she had to pause by the door to slip off a coat with the help of an aide?

Or what if you had to face a situation such as going directly from the outdoors on a cold, rainy night into a hotel lobby where you were to meet some business clients? Wouldn't it be better to shake out your umbrella and take off your coat under the awning before entering the lobby?

## Clothes for Men

What do you want your clothes to say about you? What message should they transmit to your peers, clients, or members of your audience? In that brief first impression, they make a lasting judgment about you. Your clothes should be so well chosen that you communicate well-being, confidence, and authority.

You also have to dress for yourself. You, the wearer, must feel good about your appearance, so that you can forget about how you look and concentrate on the message you are transmitting.

Your clothes should be well cut, fit perfectly, and be made of good fabric. It pays to spend as much as you can afford on a few plain, elegant suits. Your wardrobe might include an Oxford-gray suit to wear on television, a dark blue suit for public appearances, plus a navy blue blazer with dull-gold buttons and two pairs of gray pants—one light and one medium gray in color. These few pieces of clothing could be interchanged to take you through various situations. Add a tweed jacket in subdued tones for less formal occasions, and you are all set.

Avoid bold patterns, most plaids, checks, stripes, garish colors, and anything that attracts attention away from your face.

The three-piece suit with a vest is always a good choice.

Since the shoulder line is a part of the setting for your face, your jacket must fit smoothly across the shoulders with the lapel lying in a straight line. To keep the lapels in a smooth line down from the shoulder, unbutton the bottom button when sitting down.

**Shirts.** These days, you never know ahead of time when a TV camera crew will turn up at a public event, so it is important for the public person to be ready to be caught by a TV camera. The savvy public person no longer wears a blinding white shirt or even a "television blue" shirt. He wears a soft gray shirt because, when photographed, it will "read" white but won't blind a camera lens.

Men's shops often stock a variety of plain gray shirts that are perfect for the sophisticated public person. Gray is a flattering neutral color that is soft, inconspicuous, and retiring. It doesn't "do" anything—it doesn't attract attention, and the soft color is more compatible with skin tones. It is also elegant. It looks better with a dark suit because the contrast is not so great. It is excellent with navy, banker's gray, and other colors.

As mentioned previously, white should not be worn on camera. This is not so much because the cameras cannot handle it, but because white is a dominating, blinding color that appears brighter than your face. Shut your eyes halfway and look critically at yourself in a mirror, and you will see the white shirt before you see your eyes and your face. When you look at a black-and-white photograph in the newspaper, the person in white looks twice as large as the person in black. When you hold a piece of white paper under your chin, you will see that the white color predominates.

Also pay a little attention to your shirt's collar. The fit of your collar is important to the overall picture you present to those looking at you because it frames the lower part of your face and neck. If you have wrinkles on your neck, you can wear a collar that fits higher in front to cover the wrinkles to some extent.

Not only is a tight-fitting collar uncomfortable, it can draw lines that make your neck look bulkier than it is.

A button-down collar often bulges from the top down to the button and looks less sophisticated.

A smooth, neat collar that fits perfectly around your neck and under your jacket is your best choice.

**Shoes and Socks.** Always wear long, black socks because bare shins are very unattractive when you cross your legs during a business meeting with no table, on the speaker's platform, or on a television studio's set. Your shoes should be black, well fitting, and plain styled. Since you may have to walk long distances or stand on your feet for extended periods of time, your shoes should be comfortable and previously broken in.

Also it should not have to be stated that you should always wear shoes that are shined. It is amazing how simply wearing a pair of scuffed shoes can spoil an otherwise good-looking set of clothes.

If you are about to make a public appearance and notice that your shoes aren't properly shined, it only takes five minutes to dash into a shoeshine shop. If you are in a strange city and don't know where to get a quick shine, run into any upscale hotel. They usually provide such a service, often in the barbershop. Shoe repair shops will often shine shoes in a pinch.

If you find on your way to a public appearance that your shoes are shined but you have dried mud on the sides of the soles or heels, go into a men's restroom and take the mud off with a slightly dampened paper towel.

**Neckties.** A man's necktie is his one declaration of independence—his opportunity to express himself. Wear anything you like in your private life, but for your public appearances choose a quiet, neutral tie that does not attract attention away from your face. Any man who faces clients, professional peers, or a business group of any kind should think twice about what his choice of tie says about him. Some executives who appear frequently on TV even carry tried-and-true "television ties" in their briefcases. They put them on when they go on camera, and take them off when the program is over. This may be an extreme example, but it shows the care that should be taken in choosing your tie.

Avoid conspicuous patterns, plaids, stripes, polka dots, bright colors, and shiny fabrics. (It is amazing how many car salesmen wear ties that make them look like stereotypical car salesmen.) Also avoid black, most reds, and white. Select a tie made of a soft, dull-finished fabric, in a monotonic, middle-spectrum color.

Regard the selection of a tie as an opportunity to enhance the color of your eyes. The person with blue or gray eyes, for example, should own several plain, slate-bluish-gray ties. Combined with a gray shirt and a dark gray suit, this elegant combination shows off your eye contact first. Darker eyes look best with dark ties—consider such colors as wine, burgundy, slate, or dark blue. There are lovely soft paisleys, foulards, and neutral patterns in monochromatic colors, but it often takes some searching to find them.

Prepare yourself for a possible argument with the salesperson when you look for a quiet tie. He or she may think you have no taste for what's currently popular. You may have to look past the stripes and brights to find a neutral tie with a dull finish. But if you persevere, you will emerge with a few perfect ties you thought you would never wear—until you understood the purpose the tie is to accomplish.

Many men have a dedication to red ties, which they regard as a spot of color. TV cameras had been installed on the floor of the U.S. House of Representatives for several years by the time the senators voted to allow them in the Senate chamber as well in the mid-1980s. At the time, the red "power tie" was just coming into vogue. When the Senate cameras were finally installed, it seemed like everyone was wearing red ties. Many a time I—and probably you—have turned on the television to see a panel of senators or bankers or journalists or whatever sitting in chairs all wearing the "uniform" of navy suits, white shirts, and the ubiquitous red ties—the ties looking like a row of red exclamation points. But the truth is that the red tie attracts too much attention to itself, and we see the brilliant red long before we see *you*.

Also the red tie reflects color under the jaw onto the skin tone and reddens the whites of the eyes. Look at the red ties you see on the street and you will realize that they make their presence known a long way off. The successful businessman or public official should not wear a red tie, in my opinion, but instead express his individuality in something more subtle.

Some very distinguished men like bow ties. With a bow tie, you can't go halfway. You have to decide if it fits the image that you have of yourself, then you have to wear it all the time. A bow tie can be an effective accessory if you have a strong personality and consistently make it a part of your public image as Senator Paul Simon does.

***Pocket Handkerchiefs.*** Many men like to tuck a silk or cotton pocket square into their suit jacket pockets. This can be very chic and fashionable, or it can end up looking cheap and flashy. The rule of thumb is to avoid using a light or brightly colored pocket square in the breast pocket, since it pulls the eye away from the face. Instead, choose one that is of a dark solid or printed color that (1) coordinates perfectly with the colors of your suit and tie, and (2) is well folded and not hanging out too much.

As a voice coach, I sometimes schedule several individual clients in the same day. I remember one such day when I noticed a series of pocket squares and how they worked with the rest of the clothes the men were wearing.

My first client, who was a CEO of an insurance company and gave many speeches, came in wearing very handsome clothes that I could not help admiring: He had on a plain navy suit with a blue shirt and a navy and burgundy-figured tie. Tucked into his suit pocket was a small silk square of plain burgundy that he had folded straight across the top. I remember thinking how distinguished he looked, and that discreet pocket square added just a little bit of dash. In short, he looked like a CEO, but one who was forward-looking and not afraid of being a bit fashionable.

The second client wearing a pocket square was a young man trying to get his first job as a TV correspondent. He wore a nice navy suit, but had on a white shirt, a boldly striped burgundy and white tie, and a white cotton pocket handkerchief that had been carelessly folded and was sticking quite far out of his pocket. His clothes were nearly the uniform worn by many TV anchors (indeed, he was attempting to copy them), but it was all wrong. On camera, or even on a podium, the white in his shirt, tie stripes, and even his pocket square would stand out too much from his navy suit.

The third man I gave a voice lesson to that day was a former salesman who had been promoted to become a public relations spokesperson for a major corporation. He always wore expensive suits, but often with too much jewelry. That day, his suit was a conservative gray with lighter-gray pinstripes, but he was wearing a tie with a paisley pattern of green and white. To make matters worse, he sported a silk pocket square that matched the tie, and he had folded it into points that stuck out quite far from his pocket. If he had just changed his tie and choice of pocket square, he would have looked very distinguished and a suitable representative of his company.

The lesson here is that it's not just your choice of suit (all three of these suits were fine), or even your tie that makes for a tasteful appearance—

your pocket square, small thing as it is, can enhance or detract from the overall image that you are presenting.

If in doubt, it is better to wear no pocket square rather than one that detracts from your appearance.

By contrast, last year I caught a gentleman in a TV makeup room tucking a gray wool thing into his suit pocket before he was about to be interviewed on a talk show. He noticed that I was looking at what he was doing, and he said, "Oh, you caught me. I always wear a pocket handkerchief, and I discovered this morning in the hotel that I'd left them all at home, so I'm using this instead." And he pulled out of his pocket the object, which turned out to be a clean, well-folded . . . sock. (Actually, it looked fine!)

***Jewelry.*** Men should choose any jewelry that they wear very carefully. For example, if you wear a lapel pin that denotes an organization or whatever, it may flash light as you move, distracting your listeners. Also people will constantly be trying to figure out what it denotes, if anything. Thus, it is usually a good idea not to wear such a pin when you are appearing under bright lights.

Watches and rings should not be flashy or diamond-studded. If you like such jewelry, wear them once you are out of public scrutiny.

Avoid wearing necklaces. Even the open-shirt-collar Hollywood crowd and singers should consider not wearing them on TV or before large audiences.

Tie clasps generally look dated and usually flash in the light. If you feel that you need a tie clasp, try a tie tack, such as a single gray pearl, instead. Collar pins, on the other hand, look wonderful on some men.

For those men who sport a single earring, consider taking it off when you appear on TV—unless you're in a rock video!

***Emergency Kit.*** Consider assembling a kit for emergency situations. Pack a pair of long, black socks, a tried-and-true TV tie, a gray shirt, a disposable razor, a comb, and a compact of translucent blotting powder.

## MAKEUP FOR WOMEN

Makeup has only one purpose: to enhance your natural beauty. It should maximize your good features and subtly diminish any problem areas. Your makeup should be a miracle of understatement and should not attract attention to itself. It should be becoming to your hair, skin, and eye coloring, and it should present you at your very best.

In Washington, D.C., where I live, a certain society hostess is well known not only for her wonderful parties, but also for her overdone makeup. She seems to spend a lot of time before a major party putting on several layers of the stuff, which ends up only seeming to cover up and distort what natural beauty she possesses. Other women in town are always talking behind her back about her bad taste in makeup, which includes drawn-in black eyebrows, a too-dark red lipstick, and a thick base that clogs in her forehead wrinkles.

The public should not see blatant, garish makeup first and the real you second. When attention is attracted to just the makeup, it is obviously too much. Some women go into beauty salons and come out looking like someone else. Obviously, this look cannot be maintained under public scrutiny. Makeup cannot transform you into something you are not; it is only temporary.

You don't want your friends to say, "What beautiful makeup. Who did it for you?" or "You look like Greta Garbo." Instead, you want them to say, "You look so beautiful!"

High-fashion makeup follows fads and endeavors to sell new products and "in" colors each season. But your face does not change very much with the seasons (unless you get a tan, of course). One season, the style is to apply white to the browbone; the next season it is rouge wandering up onto the cheekbones and temples; and the next season it is orangy lipstick.

It's best to avoid excessive, attention-getting makeup altogether. Too much makes us wonder what the person is hiding, and we ask ourselves, "What does she look like without it?"

Whether you are an elected official, college professor, a management trainee about to be promoted, or a family finance investment counselor who meets with clients, you should be aware of these guidelines for good makeup. You should work out what is best for you and stick to it, presenting the same becoming, attractive look at all times. The only time you might want to change your basic look is when you are in evening clothes at some formal event.

Makeup is a highly individual thing. It is based on the bone structure and contours of your own face. However, there are some basic procedures involved in selecting and applying your own makeup, and this is what will be emphasized in this section.

As you read the tips given below, remember you are striving to look like yourself. You are enhancing your features, not distorting or obliterating them. You are bringing out your own natural beauty.

The basic procedure for applying makeup whenever you are going to appear in public is as follows:

1) Apply makeup base all over your face.
2) Eliminate the circles (dark shadows or hollows or puffy areas) under your eyes.
3) Contour cheekbones and, possibly, other portions of your facial structure such as at the jawbone.
4) Apply eye makeup.
5) Make up your mouth.
6) Use translucent, oil control-type powder lightly all over your face, concentrating on naturally oily areas such as the forehead and nose.

These steps are covered in more detail in the following subsections.

## Base Color

Carefully choose a main base color that exactly matches or is slightly darker than your own skin tone. Base color that is even a shade lighter than your natural skin color can enlarge and fatten the face. It also makes a noticeable and unfavorable contrast with the true color of your neck and hands. When the color is too light, you can clearly see where the makeup begins and ends. The color must be a perfect match and must also be changed from season to season if your skin color changes. Between summer and winter, you may have to mix two shades together.

There is no such thing as one perfect base color for your face. A professional makeup person may easily mix three or four different tones to match the gradations of color in your skin. Using only one color can give a mask-like, flattened effect all over. Once you have chosen your base color, choose a couple of other colors—one lighter and one darker. Use the lighter shade under the eyes, and the darker one for contouring.

TV makeup artists call the makeup you buy at the department store makeup counters or drugstores "street makeup." Most of these bases come in liquid form, while others come in creamy formulas in little pots. Another type comes in a compact formula, often called a combination base and powder formula. (This type of base is applied with a dry sponge.) Also cake-type bases are available, which are dry and must be applied mixed with water on a wet sponge. Bases can also come in a mousse formula that is released into your hand under pressure, similar to hair mousse.

One other type of base often used by actors, entertainers, and professional TV makeup artists is a creamy type that comes in a hard plastic tube that resembles a large lipstick case. This "stick" makeup is advanced by screwing up the bottom. It is applied with the fingers or a dry makeup sponge.

Generally speaking, the liquid bases, be they water based or oil based, provide the sheerest coverage; the pot-type and compact bases medium-heavy coverage; and the cake- and stick-type bases the heaviest coverage. Choose the type of base that is best for you by personal preference or skin type. And don't be afraid to try new brands and formulas. Formulations are changed and improved upon all the time by manufacturers, and many women who have been using the same type of base for years are surprised at how much better they look in a new color and/or base type.

## Contouring

Contouring is the art of playing light against dark to bring out the interesting or to de-emphasize the not-so-interesting features of your face. When you have chosen a base color, choose a couple of other colors— one lighter and one darker than your base color but in the same color family and of the same base type. Use the dark shade to diminish or blot out something you wish to recede. Use the light shade to increase or brighten something you wish to emphasize.

You can slightly change the shape of your face by defining your bone structure. The idea is to balance your features. If the nose is too long, darken its tip *slightly*. If it is too short or too wide, run a light stripe down its full length, darkening the sides. If you wish to shorten your whole face, darken up at the hairline and the bottom of the chin line, indenting the cheekbones. To lengthen the whole face, darken in front of the ears and lighten the point of the chin and the top of the forehead.

To sharpen the jawline and eliminate the look of a heavy neck run a line of dark base from ear to ear just under the jawbone. Stay two inches away from the collar or a neck scarf, carefully blending toward the base of the neck.

Any contouring you do must be subtle and nearly invisible. Cover the contoured areas with some base and translucent powder.

Contouring can also be done using a bit of blusher on a brush, but this is very tricky and must be done skillfully to be effective. Models, TV correspondents, and the like often use blush in this way—it's usually quicker than using base colors and provides a healthy glow as well. To contour with blush, mix a small amount of powder blush and loose translucent powder on a large, clean, fluffy brush. Try brushing the mixture lightly on the forehead at the hairline area, in front of your ears at the hairline, and even a bit under your chin. When contouring with blush avoid the red shades and keep to the pink or slightly brownish-rose shades (for white skin) and the brown-burgundy shades (for black skin).

## Circles under the Eyes

You may have inherited those circles under your eyes from your grandmother. Even so, you have to do something about them. One reason the circles are so conspicuous is because lights cast dark shadows under the eyes, and you must compensate for that. (TV lights are particularly guilty of this.) The other reason is that when you are tired, tense, worried, suffering from jet lag, your feet hurt, or you have been misquoted in the morning newspaper, it shows under the eyes first.

There are many good products on the market that aid in erasing those circles under the eyes. Try out several of them until you find something that is not chalky but is soft and creamy. I personally recommend the creamy types that come in little pots or tubes rather than the more waxy type that comes in a lipstick-like case.

Select a color one shade lighter than your base. Tap it gently into the delicate under-eye skin until you can no longer see it. Cover it carefully with a little translucent powder, and repeat the process. If you can see little fine lines, the mix is too dry. Keep it soft and fleshlike. Then, use a bit of your base color over all.

If you have puffy areas under the eyes with a circle below, try a slightly darker shade on the puffy areas. For white skin, apply pale ivory in the "ditch" with a fine-line brush, then blend it together by dotting on a little of your base color. With black skin, do the same using whatever color gives the best effect. Avoid using a brand of mascara that tends to flake, depositing black specks under the eyes.

With a little experimentation using these hints, you will soon find a procedure that successfully takes care of those circles.

Finally, whatever cover you select to use under your eyes can also be used to eliminate blemishes, skin discolorations, and age spots.

## Cheek Color

Cheekbones are the most neglected part of your face—and the most attractive when they are given some attention. They mold your face, adding character and distinction. In my opinion, covering the cheekbones with rouge contours them out under most lighting situations.

To emphasize the cheekbones, you need to create an indentation underneath them. To do this, first use a normal base color on both the cheekbones and the jawbone. Find that soft hole between the two and press your finger there, against the upper back teeth. In that exact spot, apply a slightly dark contour color and bring it back toward the earlobe, without getting it on the upper and lower bones. Apply a soft blusher in the same area. Smile, and apply a bit of blusher on the prominent part of the cheek, avoiding the cheekbone itself.

Your colors, especially the dark color, should be blended enough to give a natural look. Try blending with a foam cosmetic sponge or a fresh cotton ball instead of using your fingers or a brush.

Try this several times in a mirror until you achieve the look you want. By indenting the cheekbones and contouring under the jawbone, you can take pounds off your face.

There are several types of blushers on the market. Generally speaking, for dry skin try a cream-style blush (sold in pots); for oily skin, a powder blush; and either type for normal skin. As one gets older, fine lines often appear around the cheek area (near eyes or nose), and powder blush often creeps into these lines. If you have this problem, switching to a cream blush will help.

In choosing a blush color, avoid selecting colors in the orange, bright pink, magenta, or bluey-red shades. Softer colors are more flattering to women of all ages—soft rose (often called "old rose") or rose with a little brown in it are the colors to try for white skin. Soft peach tones are another good choice. With black skin, try richer shades tending toward wine or burgundy; but, again, avoid the bluey or magenta tones. Some blush colors that have brown blended in them look great on black skin.

## Eye Makeup

Using effective eye contact is one of the most important ingredients in transmitting your message. Your eyes are part of your nonverbal body language. Therefore, your eye makeup should provide a soft, subtle effect around your eyes rather than dominate them. The object here is to have someone who is looking at you see the eyes first, not the eye makeup. The makeup should not intrude or distract from your eyes.

***Eyeshadow, Eyeliner, and Eyebrow Color.*** Select soft, natural colors for your eyeshadow and eyeliner—brown, taupe, or gray rather than "beetle" green, bright blue, or plum, for example. Iridescent color catches the light with a vibrancy that can overpower your eyes.

Your eyeshadow should get lighter as it moves upward. You may wish to apply a darker line in the eye crease, but this can be overdone and could show when you blink your eyes. Always continue the color, subtly, up to the brow itself. Brush the eyeshadow color out slightly at the corners of the eyes.

Avoid applying whitish eyeshadow to the brow bone area.

Apply subtle eyeliner to the upper lids after you have applied your eyeshadow. Use little or no liner under the eyes, with no black smudges. Putting black liner under the eyes can make you look old and ill, especially on TV.

Eyeliner and shadow should be blended so that there are no harsh lines anywhere. Look critically at yourself to be sure that nothing overpowers the eye color, and that the makeup is flattering.

Put your eye makeup on using a magnifying mirror and a bright light so that you can see what you are doing.

Avoid using an eyebrow pencil on the brow, and *never* use a black, harsh line that looks fake. Instead, using a sponge-tipped applicator, try applying gray or brown eyeshadow to your eyebrow hairs. Start at the outer edge, and brush a little powder under the hairs, then smooth them down. This will give you a natural-looking color.

As mentioned above, the choice of eyeshadow and liner color is very important. Your first consideration should be what colors will enhance your eyes without drawing attention to the eye makeup itself. Your second consideration is choosing colors that look well with your eye's natural iris color. Trying to match eyeshadow to the color of your clothes should be your last consideration. If you choose the right daytime eyeshadow colors, you may even be able to wear them most days, no matter what color your clothes are that particular day.

Although every makeup artist and every magazine article or book on the subject seems to have a conflicting opinion on what eye colors go best with what eye makeup colors, you can't go wrong with the following general advice. (Note that the colors recommended are especially attractive on television.) On the chart given below, eye colors are followed by suggested eyeshadow colors:

- Brown eyes, white skin—Most browns, especially gray-browns and medium browns; taupe; slate gray.
- Brown eyes, black skin—Darker browns; charcoal gray (smudged and not too dark, however); grayed purples, if used subtly.
- Blue eyes and blue-gray eyes—Muted blue-grays; slate gray; steel gray; dove gray; taupe; never use bright blue, green, or turquoise.
- Gray eyes—Muted grays one to two shades darker than eye color; grayed taupe; blue-gray; avoid grays that are lighter gray than eye color or the exact gray as eye color; avoid any bright colors.
- Hazel eyes—Medium browns; taupe; medium grays; blue-grays or other muted blues; avoid most greens.
- Green eyes—Any gray, from pale dove gray through a smudged, subtle charcoal gray; smoky taupe; peachy brown; never use bright green.

Eyeliner colors should be chosen after you have selected your eyeshadow colors. Many women do not look good with black eyeliner but look wonderful using a navy blue, chocolate brown, or dark charcoal gray liner, especially if they use a soft eyeliner pencil. Thus, if you have chosen a blue-gray shadow, try experimenting with a subtle application of a navy blue or charcoal-gray liner pencil. Or if you chose a brown or a taupe shadow, try a dark brown liner.

If you are all thumbs, in a hurry, or "blind as a bat," forgo eyeliner completely—it's just not worth it.

One final eyeliner trick that many models use—try drawing a very thin line in navy or royal blue with a soft eyeliner pencil as close to your lower lashes as possible. Many women are able to carefully draw such a line just above the lower lashes, nearly inside the lower lid.

(This is done by gently pulling down on the lower lid with several fingers while applying the liner.) The theory is that this dark-blue line opens up the eyes and makes the whites of the eyes look whiter. Try it yourself and see. (Note that this does not work with a gray or black or lighter blue eyeliner.)

*Mascara.* Mascara comes with two different bases: water and oil. The water-based mascara can be washed off with water and therefore dissolves and flakes when the eye is moist. The other, "waterproof" formula can only be easily removed by using cold cream or a special oil-based remover often called "eye makeup remover." However, no mascara is completely waterproof through a shower or swim. All mascaras eventually flake, and when you use a tissue under the eye after a few hours of wear, you can see how much of the color has moved down onto your skin. This is the biggest argument against the use of mascara; it can settle under your eyes and make you look older.

One way to prevent flaking is to apply the mascara mostly on the tips of the lashes. When the upper eyelids come down to the lower lids, they do not touch so much of the mascara, which thus tends to stay on longer.

Whether or not you use mascara on the lower lashes is a matter of personal choice. However, many women who use it on the lower lashes should not be doing so. These include women who constantly rub their eyes during the day or who tear readily because they wear contact lenses or for another reason. Such women end up with black flakes and smudges under the eyes toward the end of the day.

If you wear contact lenses, you should also avoid using the type of mascara that contains bits of fiber to thicken the formula.

Major cosmetic companies are now developing a clear, no-color mascaras. If you have trouble using mascara or it tends to flake on you, you might try using one of these new formulas.

Most women prefer plain black mascara, but navy blue or charcoal-gray mascara is also very flattering. Violet and other more vivid mascara colors should be avoided.

You might also consider trying false eyelashes. Some people believe that these are more natural looking than large quantities of visible mascara. If you decide to try false lashes, purchase good lashes with a soft look to them, and trim them to fit your own eyelids. Keep them short enough to look like you could have grown them yourself. Applying lots of mascara to false lashes defeats the whole purpose.

False eyelashes are applied with a tiny line of special glue. Actually, they can look very good when you cover the glued edge with a soft dark pencil and blend a little neutral brown or dark gray eyeshadow up over the eyelid.

Other tips: Some women find that applying a small amount of eyelash oil to their eyelashes overnight a couple of times a week keeps their lashes in better condition. (Just make sure you are using a product specially formulated for use around the eyes.) Some women powder their eyelashes between applying coats of mascara, but this is not recommended since eye irritation can result. Finally, if you curl your eyelashes, don't overdo it, or you will get an unattractive baby-doll look.

## Lipstick

Most women wear one or two colors of lipstick regularly—often for years at a time—and are so used to seeing themselves in mirrors and photographs with these shades on that they never change their look by experimenting with other colors. But this is a mistake for the public person. If you have not changed your lipstick colors in years, you may accidentally be wearing colors that are just not the most flattering to your face and your public image.

The main rule of thumb is to avoid fire engine red lipstick. When you wear such a color, people see your lips before they see your eyes or listen to what is being said. If you prefer the darker lipstick colors, there are still many on the market that are not as bright.

The color of your lipstick should more or less match the color of the inside of your mouth, and should not change much with the color of your clothes. Do not select a purplish lipstick to wear with a purple dress, or red with red, or orange with orange. Once you find one or two good, soft, flattering colors, stick to them; they will look good with most clothing colors.

People with white skin should try using lipsticks in any of the following color families: brownish old-rose, neutral brownish pinks, pinks that are not too bright, medium reds mixed with a hint of brown, and any color that closely matches the inside of your mouth.

People with black skin should try using shades that are deeper than those for white skins but do not overemphasize the mouth. Again, your eyes should be what the viewer looks at, not your lips. Try colors such as a muted red (but not too bright), red with a darker brown mixed in, browns in the darker shades, and burgundy or wine red as long as they don't have a lot of purple or blue tones in them.

Everyone, no matter what skin color she has, should avoid bright corals or oranges, magentas, whitish pinks, and deep purplish red.

Many women routinely outline their lips with a lip pencil before applying lipstick. If you do this, make sure that the pencil line does not show after you have applied your lipstick. If it shows to the naked eye, it will show up even more in a photograph or on TV. Using a lip pencil takes skill and should not be attempted if you are not very adept in makeup application.

Using a lip-liner pencil can make the size of your lips more even. To narrow full lips, use a liner inside the lip line. To make thin lips look fuller, use the lip liner just outside the lip line. Similarly, to even up lips of different sizes, outline the thin one outside of its natural line and use lip liner inside the line of the fuller one.

In applying lipstick, many women find that applying base over their lips before applying lipstick looks good. This can help to correct a slightly uneven lip line or any small discolorations in pigment you may have on your lips. Sometimes applying a small amount of powder will also work to set the base before applying lipstick. Powdering your lips lightly before applying lipstick can also help the lipstick last longer.

Lipstick comes in regular screw-up tubes, pots, or in plastic squeeze tubes. Many women find they prefer to use the regular screw-up type directly from the tube; however, if you have always had trouble doing this, buy a stiff lipstick brush and experiment using this to apply the lipstick. If you have never tried using lipstick that comes in a little pot, you may be surprised to find that it is easier to apply than you think. This type of lipstick can be applied with a lip brush or a finger. The type of lipstick that comes in squeeze tubes is often more difficult to apply.

Lip gloss that is too shiny should be avoided, whether it is used alone or over regular lipstick or it is clear, flesh-toned, or colored. Just like a lipstick that is too red, such gloss can draw too much attention to the mouth and away from the eyes. However, there are some glosses on the market that are not high gloss at all; they simply soften the skin of the lips and provide a very low-gloss sheen.

If you are older and have very fine lines around your lips, perhaps in a fan shape around the mouth, your lipstick may bleed or seep out of your lip area onto the skin around your face. If you have this problem, use extra base and powder and avoid darker or brighter lipstick colors. Instead, try a rose pink mixed with a little brown.

Another problem that many women have is lipstick getting on their front teeth. Again, if you have this problem (which is very difficult to correct), you should use less lipstick and avoid the brighter lipstick colors.

Most women should use a bit of moisturizer on their lips at night, summer and winter. This really does help to keep your lips softer. And don't forget to use sunscreen under your lipstick when you go outdoors. This simple habit can make a great difference in the condition of your lips.

## Powder

After applying makeup, nearly every woman should apply at least some translucent finishing powder. If you have very dry skin, you may still need some powder on the tip of your nose and/or your forehead before being photographed or going on TV. If you have medium skin or combination dry and oily skin, apply powder to the "T" zone of your face, where most of the oil production takes place—across the entire forehead and the nose area—plus on the chin. If you have very oily skin, you can fluff lots of powder all over your face.

After you have applied makeup in the morning, try using loose powder, applied with a large, soft puff, brush, or cotton ball. If you use a puff or a brush, keep it very, very clean. Loose powder sets the makeup better than compact powder and can be applied more liberally, with the excess dusted off. Choose a translucent color when buying loose powder; even darker skins can use a loose powder formulated for black skin tones with just a slight tint in it.

Once you have left the house, carry a compact-type of powder with you, preferably a brand labeled "translucent, oil-control." Many regular powders that are colored and come in compacts have the ability to correct color problems on your face but are very poor at cutting down on the shine.

## TELEVISION MAKEUP FOR MEN AND WOMEN

If you are about to go on television for the first time, you are, naturally, very concerned about how you will look. Or maybe you have been on TV before, such as when a reporter unexpectedly stuck a microphone in your face as you were walking out of a building. You may not have been so concerned about how you looked in such a situation, since you had no control over whether your hair was messy or your nose was shiny.

But now you are going to be on camera under more controlled circumstances. Maybe you will be giving a speech that will be televised; maybe you are going on a local or nationally televised talk show; or maybe you are running for public office and the cameras have begun following you around. Perhaps you've been on TV many times before but have finally become concerned about your aging or balding or have noticed that the camera is recording a few extra pounds under the chin.

Not to worry—this section is for you.

The following subsections explain what TV cameras and lights do to your appearance; how to put on your own makeup if there is no make-up artist on-site; and what to expect from a makeup artist if you are fortunate enough to have one.

## Why You Need to Wear Makeup on TV

It is important that you wear makeup whenever you are going to appear on television. This is true for both men and women and whether you apply your own makeup or you are going to be made up by a TV make-up artist.

In the mid-1950s when I was just starting out in the TV industry as the host of several local, live shows, I used to apply makeup to my guests, male and female. Even though TV was in black-and-white in those days, my guests just seemed to look better with makeup than without.

Three or four years after I had been doing this, a producer from CBS asked if I would come and put makeup on one of *his* guests on a show that was a forerunner of "Face the Nation." (His show shared a studio with mine, and he said that he had seen how good my guests looked compared to his.) He told me that the guest was to be Speaker of the House Sam Rayburn and that they would be using four cameras ranging all around him—shooting even from the back—instead of the usual two. The problem was that Mr. Rayburn was bald, and the producer was worried that his head would shine too much, especially when he was shot from behind. So I did Mr. Rayburn's makeup that day. (By the way, it was then that I became a TV makeup artist for CBS—which I still am.)

Mr. Rayburn saw himself on the monitor before and after the makeup was applied, and he and the producers were pleased with the result. The next time he appeared on that show, he couldn't wait to be made up. As he put it, "I want to please all of those old maids and widows out there!"

Those days are long gone, but they were truly the dawn of the use of TV makeup, particularly for men. You, too, should wear makeup when you go on TV. You'll understand the reasons for this even better as you read on in this section.

### What TV Lights and Cameras Do to Your Appearance.
Makeup for television is designed to compensate for two things—bright overhead lights and enhanced cameras. Between them, these can add ten years and ten pounds to your appearance.

The overhead lights found in TV studios are mounted high in the ceiling. One problem with these lights is that they cast shadows on the face, and the sensitive camera lenses take pictures of the shadows. The shadows fall under the eyes and into the natural lines and wrinkles in your face. Television makeup can minimize this process and make you look more as if you were being seen in person.

TV cameras have x-ray eyes. Today's lenses are greatly enhanced, and they see more than the eye can see. As they move into closeup, they do not go out of focus as your eye does. The cameras keep coming, and they maximize details that cannot be seen with the naked eye.

Television cameras emphasize gradations of color, beard whiskers under the skin (even if you just shaved, the whiskers will show up as shadow if they are darkish in color), freckles, wrinkles, dark circles under the eyes, scar tissue, moles, liver spots, or any skin imperfection. An indentation in the skin may come out looking like a black hole. Little beads of sweat are highly visible. The natural skin oils make the forehead, cheeks, and nose look shiny. Bald heads shine like beacons. A little bit of hair spray on the skin can shine like cellophane. The shine makes the face look larger than life and therefore heavier. The lights also flatten the face, tending to drain the color, as does bright sunlight. Pink or red in the skin may look brighter red on camera.

And all of this is just what happens to your face—imagine how odd your clothes can suddenly look.

## Putting on Your Own Makeup for TV: Women

Please read the previous section on basic makeup for women. Since most of the information given in that section applies to TV makeup as well, I will just touch on a few pointers here.

The four basic rules are: (1) Try to look natural, not overdone. Understated is better than exaggerated; (2) Avoid bright colors, which the camera will record as even brighter. This is especially true of bright blue or green eyeshadows and bright red or orangy or purplish lipsticks; (3) Pay particular attention to dark circles or shadows under the eyes; and (4) Use powder to eliminate shine, particularly on the nose and forehead.

Keep your makeup subtle. If you have white skin, choose a base slightly warmer than your skin tone. If you have black skin, choose a base very close to your natural skin color. Indent the cheekbones using rouge as a contour. Contour under the chin; this will also take advantage of the shadow that is cast by the jawbone due to the overhead lights. Eliminate the circles cast by the lights under the eyes by bringing the base up to the lower eyelid. Avoid using bright eyeshadows; instead, use soft browns or grays on the eyelids. Use a translucent, oil-control powder to remove the shine.

Don't apply moisturizer to your face before you make a television appearance; it often shines on camera as if you had very oily skin.

A special word about lipstick. As mentioned above, never use bright red lipstick on TV. Instead, match your lipstick to the inside of your mouth and tongue. It is especially important not to use shiny lip gloss on TV, which catches the light and glistens into the camera. This can make the mouth look abnormally large and attract undue attention to the lip movements.

Never outline the mouth with very dark lip pencil. Such an outline never looks natural and can be plainly seen by the enhanced cameras. When you need to make a thin lip look wider, use a pencil the same color as the lipstick.

Once you have discovered the makeup that looks good on you, do not change it with the fads of commercial, high-fashion makeup. Leave that to runway models and department store cosmetic salespeople.

## Putting on Your Own Makeup for TV: Men

The purpose of television makeup for men is to make them look the same on the home TV set as they look in person—if not a little better.

# YOUR PERSONAL APPEARANCE

As noted previously, you must compensate for the distortions of overhead studio lights and the enhanced camera lenses. The cameras see details of the beard, blemishes, purple veins, red noses, or discolorations you would not normally notice.

Twenty years ago, few men were so concerned about their appearance on TV that they were willing to apply makeup before appearing on camera. Most men who were on TV regularly would allow a TV makeup artist to apply makeup, but they balked at putting it on themselves when no makeup artist was available.

Now all that is changing. Men in many professions are now learning what actors, singers, TV anchors, and others have long known: Even a little makeup can do wonders for your appearance on TV. Politicians particularly are finding that their appearance seems to mysteriously repel or attract votes.

This section is for those men who are willing to improve their appearance on TV by learning how to apply a little makeup to themselves. And remember, often you only need a very little to improve how you look on camera.

TV makeup for men is mainly aimed at doing the following things:

1. Eliminate circles under your eyes. This is done by applying a small amount of base or foundation under the eyes. Use a color one shade lighter than your skin tone. Apply the base with a very light hand and blend well so that it does not show. For this, you can either use a regular foundation or special cover-up for the under-eye area. If you are using the latter, choose one that comes in a pot (which will be soft and creamy) rather than one in a stick like a lipstick shape (which can go on chalky and waxy).

2. Cover up your whisker area (upper lip and beard areas) if you have dark whiskers, *even if you just shaved.* Studio lights penetrate a couple of layers of skin, and the whiskers can show even if you did just shave. The best thing for this is a base formulated for TV, which is easily available in larger cities at theatrical supply stores (the kind that sell costumes and supplies for the stage). You can find such stores listed in the Yellow Pages of the telephone directory. If there is no such store in your area, try a regular creamy base of the kind that comes in a compact and is often called "base and powder." (Important hint: Get a woman to go shopping with you so that

49

you don't accidentally end up with the dry cake type you need to mix with water, which comes in a similar-looking, compact-type container.) Choose a color exactly matching your skin color or one shade darker. Don't attempt to give yourself a fake tan by buying a shade that is too dark. Apply with a dry foam cosmetic sponge, firmly pushing the base into the pores of the skin. Blend well so that it doesn't show.

3. Eliminate shine. Use a translucent, oil-blotting powder on the nose and forehead to eliminate shine. If you are balding, powder your head as well—embarrassing, but it's well worth it. Choose a powder color close to your natural skin color. Translucent powders don't add much color to the skin, so they might appear lighter in the compact than they do on the skin. Such powders are available in any drugstore. If you are black and cannot find the right powder in a drugstore, you may have to go to a department store cosmetic counter that specializes in products for darker skin tones.

4. Absorb perspiration. If you sweat under camera lights, try using a shaving lotion with an alcohol base or apply some witch hazel before you go on camera. You can also blot your face with a tissue just before you go on.

5. Smooth your hair, if necessary. Make sure no errant hairs are sticking straight up at the part. If so, use a touch of hairspray on your fingers or comb to tame them. Never let hairspray get directly onto the skin of your face because it's shiny and will reflect light into the camera lens.

If you have a pet, a two-year-old, or dandruff, brush your lapels and shoulders before going on camera.

Finally, a word about moisturizers for men. While a ruddy, weather-beaten face may seem sexy to some, it won't look very good on camera. The gradations of color, the crow's-feet eye wrinkles, peeling skin, and rough texture are all amplified by the lens of the TV camera. To counteract this, men should use moisturizers and sunscreens or sunblocking lotions regularly. However, do not apply a moisturizer to your face before you go on television, since it will shine too much on camera.

## Being Made Up by a TV Makeup Artist

Most network television bureaus and some local television stations have resident TV makeup artists. If in doubt, ask the producer booking you as a guest if makeup is provided.

A good TV makeup person can't work miracles, but sometimes it seems that he or she does just that. For some people—such as a man who has dark whiskers and jet-lag circles under the eyes and messy hair—even three minutes with a makeup artist can mean the difference between looking like a nervous bandit or a distinguished executive. A woman with dangling earrings, bright blue eyeshadow, bright red lipstick, and a yellow scarf around her neck can turn a come-hither look to a listen-to-me-I-know-what-I'm-talking-about look if the makeup artist just *undoes* her a bit. For most people, the makeup artist can make you look like yourself, but with a professional, pulled-together appearance.

She (I say "she" for simplicity; there are many skilled male TV makeup artists) does this because she knows how to compensate for those TV lights and unblinking cameras. She knows the quirks and limitations and characteristics of that particular studio. She knows how good the studio's lighting person is, if those particular lights do strange things to certain colors (usually whites, yellows, greens, and reds), what colors vibrate on camera, and how the director prefers the guests to look (some are fussy about shiny noses, messy hair, or bright jewelry). She also knows how the background color of the set will work with your face and clothing colors.

She does not use high-fashion makeup techniques. She is probably not a hairdresser. But she will make you look much better than you would without her.

Basically, what the makeup person will do is what you could have done yourself, only she will do it faster and better. She will eliminate the circles under your eyes and apply a base lightly over your face to eliminate the beard, blemishes, or gradations of color; that is, she will even up your skin tone where necessary. Then she will indent the cheekbones (if needed), and possibly contour under the chin to sharpen the jawline. Powder will eliminate the shine. For women, eye makeup, cheek color, and lipstick will complete the procedure. She will also neaten and smooth your hair if necessary.

*At the Studio.* To take advantage of a makeup person's professional skills, arrive early. A rushed makeup job usually looks like a rushed makeup job.

It is important to inform the makeup person if you are wearing contact lenses. It could be a disaster to pop one out just before you go on camera. It is also important not to get any foreign substance in the eye.

Men sometimes feel nervous walking into a makeup room and will often say, "I never use makeup," which may actually mean that they have had a bad experience in the past with an inept makeup person. For example, about a year ago I was about to make up a political analyst who was going on a morning news show. Always a blunt man, he said he "didn't want makeup." When I asked him why, he told me that the last time he'd been made up, the makeup person swathed him in a frilly apron, spent about fifteen minutes working on him, and even got makeup on his shirt collar despite the apron. I told him I wouldn't do any of those things and asked him to please trust me.

He did, and as he was leaving, he told me that he was glad that he had. He thanked me for "restoring his faith in makeup artists."

An inept makeup artist may do what that one did to the political analyst, or she may try to coat the face with heavy makeup, giving an embalmed look. She may even try to apply eye makeup (!) to a man.

In such a case, you are justified in insisting on less makeup or going into the men's room and undoing some of what was done to you. Most makeup artists, however, will make you look great on camera.

Refuse makeup if you have skin lesions or a similar problem. Simply tell the producer in advance. The director may be able to avoid close-ups and will understand the situation. If you have a cold or flu or a contagious condition such as a cold sore or fever blister, tell the makeup artist. If you have had an allergic reaction to makeup in the past, discuss this with her and at least consider letting her apply translucent powder to eliminate the shine.

Both men and women should remove a dark jacket before being made up. Also, take off your glasses as soon as you sit down in the makeup room's chair.

When you are being made up, your first impulse may be to clench your eyes tightly shut. Don't. Instead, open your eyes and look into the mirror or up at the ceiling. The makeup person has to bring the makeup base up to your lower eyelids, which is impossible if you squint and shut your eyes. Looking upward firms the muscle under the eye so that the makeup can be applied to eliminate the circles.

Experienced TV anchors who go on camera daily often rush into the makeup room clutching scripts, seat themselves in the makeup chair with a cheery "hello," and immediately look upward.

While being made up, do not wrinkle up your forehead or frown, because this makes it impossible to eliminate the lines in your face. Smile a little to make the forehead smooth.

Do not drink coffee, read your script or notes, smoke a cigarette or cigar, or try to talk on the telephone while being made up. The makeup person usually has a very limited time in which to apply your makeup. If you are trying to do something else that lowers or turns your head away from her or prevents her from asking you questions, time is being wasted. Give the makeup process your undivided attention.

Similarly, do not turn your head away from the makeup person. She has to look you in the eye to decide what she is going to do. She has to see the way the light hits your bone structure and decide which colors will match your skin. She has to work slightly in front of you. When you turn away, possibly in conversation with the booking producer or your own assistant or someone else, the makeup person must move around in front of you and come between you and the other party. If you must have a conversation with someone, at least keep looking straight ahead into the mirror while you talk.

If you object to something being done to you, query the makeup artist politely. Don't pull your head away suddenly or you may end up with powder on your lap or mascara on your cheek.

After you are done, look at yourself in the mirror. You should look natural. For men, however, the makeup may show in the makeup room a little bit, but it should be invisible on camera. For women, make sure that the color of your lipstick is soft and that everything is well blended. Everyone should give hair and clothes one last check in the makeup room mirror.

If there is time and monitors are available (each studio varies on such factors), the makeup artist may have an opportunity to check your appearance on camera once you are on the set. This is usually called a "camera check" or a "makeup check." Don't be surprised if she comes up to you with more powder or a hairbrush once you are seated and "miked up." One cannot predict the effect of the lights or know in advance what the monitor will reveal. TV correspondents go through this all the time.

Relax. You should feel secure in the knowledge that your appearance is working for you and you are looking your best.

# HAIR

## Women's Hair

Your hairstyle has a significant role to play in creating your total look. It must form a frame around your face that presents you to your audience. Your hair should never dominate your image, obscure your good points, or attract undue attention to itself. (Remember the beehives of the 1960s.)

Your hairstyle should fit your head, creating a soft, natural, flattering aura around your facial features. Consider your assets—your eyes and eye contact, brow bones, cheekbones, jawline, and the length of your neck. The ideal hairstyle should be layered, shaped, and fitted to your individual characteristics. For most women, a face-flattering hairstyle partially covers the ears and comes just to the shoulders.

The hair must not obscure the eyes or keep falling down over them. Eye contact can be preserved by allowing three-quarters of an inch of space above and around the eyes to compensate for the shadows cast by light.

Your hair should curve to fit the cheeks and jawline. A great shock of unruly hair that entirely ignores individual facial contours is unbecoming and makes you appear unable to control it.

Avoid an elaborate, rigid hairdo that has to be fixed with hairspray until it feels like barbed wire. Everyone can name at least one well-known woman, often in her fifties, who hasn't let a hair on her head move in public in a decade. Also avoid a style that is easily disturbed, difficult to manage, or comes apart with the slightest breeze. The hairstyle that takes constant vigilance attracts unfavorable attention. Pushing the hair away from the eyes, fidgeting with the ends, and rearranging strands are distracting gestures.

Adopting a simple, easily cared for style, preferably one that can be washed daily and does not require too much time, is the smart thing to do.

Once you have found an attractive style, stick to it for at least a few years. There is no point in changing your hairstyle with every public appearance. Search until you find a reliable hair stylist, who will do your hair the way you like it.

***Women's Hair Color.*** Avoid artificial hair color if you possibly can, since it is often detectable. The roots eventually become visible, requiring touch-ups. TV cameras enhance the imbalance of color between dark roots and bleached ends.

Also, hair-dye chemicals can damage the hair and split the ends. Cameras often distort the red range, giving the hair an orange cast, and they can turn artificial blond hair tones brassy looking.

Believe it or not, the natural color of your hair is probably the most becoming color you can wear; this is true even if you are turning gray. Nature softens the color of the hair around the face as one grows older by adding gray. Gray at the temples is very distinguished looking. The best possible hair color on camera, in fact, is iron gray. As one ages, dyed black hair looks more and more harsh and unnatural. It looks the same all over the head, while natural hair has many gradations of color to soften the look.

## Men's Hair

Your hair is a highly individual matter, and you, the wearer, must feel that the style is becoming. Keep your hair neat, well trimmed, and layered to fit your individual facial characteristics. Hair looks best when it is long enough in the back to come just above the collar.

Regard your hair as being the picture frame around the face.

Ears are not attractive on TV, and it is usually best to have the top half of them covered by hair. Ears tend to widen the face, turn red when you are tense, and even catch shiny hairspray. A good photographer, for example, may not photograph both ears head on but may have you tilt your head so that one ear is minimized.

If you have always worn the hair short above the ears, look at your face in the mirror and cover the tops of your ears with your fingers. You may see a difference.

In order to avoid having someone cut your hair too short around the ears, don't get a haircut just before a public appearance.

Keep the hair in front of the ears even with the sideburns.

Gray spreading through your hair is very distinguished looking. It is nature's way of softening the look around your face. Dyed dark hair next to older skin is not flattering.

Some beards can be very distinguished looking, but they must be well-cared for. A well-sculpted beard can narrow a wide jawline. The beard determines the expression of your face, so it should not be turned downward.

Scraggly hair that covers the cheeks and upper lip detracts from the facial expression.

A mustache becomes a major part of the impression you make. Use special blunt-ended scissors to trim the hair above the lip line. Your lips should not be covered, since many people unconsciously read lips and need to "see" what is said. A drooping mustache that points downward gives a negative visual image. Confine the mustache within the natural laugh lines, and, if possible, layer the hair up toward the nose in order to avoid blunt edges.

**Being Bald.** If you are bald or balding, it is best to accept it gracefully. You are not alone. Consider it an individual characteristic, and concentrate on making your eyes and face more expressive.

However, there are some things that you can do to minimize that broad expanse of forehead. Realize that your face from chin to eyebrows is five or six inches long, and it is the same distance from your eyebrows to the top of your head. You can habitually tip the head slightly upward, to expose more of the face and less of the forehead. When you lean downward, less of your face shows. You need to keep the jaw level with the floor, and the basic posture of your body turned upward. Notice in your bathroom mirror that you can minimize the amount of visible bare skin by tilting your face up into the light.

Apply a little powder to the light-catching cranial bone as needed to dull the shine. Translucent powder is invisible, but makes a big difference in reducing the glare on top of the head.

Normally the hair would form a flattering frame around the face. With no hair on top, you should maximize the hair you have as much as possible. Keep the sideburns longish, slightly covering the tops of the ears. Bring your hair down to the collar in the back if it is curly, the look suits you, and you feel comfortable with it. Keep the rest of your hair slightly long as well.

*Never* try to bring a long lock of hair across the bald spot in the back of your head, across the top of a bald head, or across a receding hairline in the front. The errant lock rarely stays in place and requires constant and conspicuous attention. This attempted method of covering baldness usually fools no one and makes you look vain and fussy about your appearance.

I recently watched in amazement while a psychiatrist who was about to address a group of his peers carefully wound what must have been an eight-inch-long lock of hair around and over his very bald head and attempt to hold the arrangement together with hairspray. His elaborate effort to look more youthful just ended up looking vain.

Lowering the part does not work well, either, because it throws the symmetry of the face off balance and destroys the harmonious proportions of the hair.

Never use hairspray directly on your skin. It contains lacquer and seals the pores so that makeup or powder will not adhere. It also "reads" very shiny under available natural sunlight or artificial studio lights. To control a few stubborn hairs, spray the hairspray on your fingers and apply lightly to the hair only.

Avoid sunburn on the forehead as much as you can. A sunburned head distracts the eye away from your face. Use a high-numbered PABA sunscreen (fifteen or above) for protection against burning and skin cancer. Wear a hat when out on a boat, riding in a convertible, golfing, or whatever.

Are you tempted to get hair transplants? Unfortunately, they can often be detected. Also, hair transplants are hard to keep secret, especially after you have reached a certain degree of prominence in the public eye. Once they find out about it, the press and public seem to remember for a very long time that you have had hair transplants.

Some hairpieces are fairly successful when done by an expert who blends them carefully with your own hair. One style is woven into your hair, and you never take it off. The whole thing flips up so that you can take a shower. This type has to be redone about every six months as the hair grows.

Many actors and famous people wear hairpieces and everyone knows it. To everyone's delight, NBC News weatherman Willard Scott occasionally takes his hairpiece off on the air. The audience loves him for it.

Full-head wigs, on the other hand, almost always look artificial. Your own hair has gradations of color that wigs often do not imitate successfully. For example, nature gives you a little gray at the temples. The gray gives a salt-and-pepper effect here and there that looks natural. Wigs tend to carry one color combination throughout. It is also difficult to conceal the net base and the hairline.

Being bald is not a disadvantage. All of your other gifts, skills, and personality make you what you are—not what's on or not on your head.

## Dandruff

You should never arrive for a business meeting, a meeting with clients, or a public appearance with dandruff on the shoulders of your jacket or on your lapels. Everyone has the impulse to brush it off for you since you did not.

As I was walking to the subway stop recently, a well-dressed man who was shaking hands with as many people as possible entering the station stopped me by saying: "Hello, I'm Joe So-and-So and I'm running for mayor . . ." As he continued his short spiel, he shook my hand with his right hand and constantly scratched his head with his left hand. He had more dandruff on his new-looking suit than I'd seen on any man's clothes lately. I threw his brochure away as soon as I was out of his sight.

In short, if you know you have a problem with dandruff, there is simply no excuse not to do something about it before your public appearance.

There are many shampoos on the market today that effectively eliminate most cases of dandruff. If commercially available shampoos do not seem to be working on your case of dandruff, consult your doctor. If you have the kind of dandruff that persists most of your life, wash your hair daily with a dandruff shampoo. Also be careful not to use someone else's brush or comb.

On TV, dandruff shows up on your shoulders like grains of sparkling white sand. Usually the studio's floor manager will remove any dandruff with sticky tape, but you cannot count on this. As a public person, it is your responsibility to take steps to eliminate dandruff.

## WOMEN'S HANDS

Your hands will be very much in the picture, and they thus deserve tender, loving care. Use a good hand cream, containing lanolin, to keep them soft. Protect the backs of the hands from dark spots by using a sunblock. Any spots you already have can be covered up by applying a little makeup base.

To make the fingers look longer, taper the nails slightly and use a clear, pink-tinged, or flesh-colored polish. Not only do such colors look professional and good with all clothing colors, but if the nail polish gets chipped or has worn off the tips of your nails, it is not very noticeable.

Long, red fingernails cut off the ends of the fingers and attract too much attention to themselves. Long, red, artificial glue-on nails may seem to express excessive preoccupation with your appearance.

Many busy women think that it is worth the time and expense of going to a professional manicurist a couple of times a month, especially if they travel constantly. If you have never had such a manicure done before, try it once to see if it is for you. Having your nails look good all of the time without much effort on your part may just give you a small boost of confidence every time you look at your hands.

Be sure to ask the manicurist to apply the natural or pearly pink colors suggested earlier, and ask for an extra top-coat layer. Don't let her talk you into a polish that is bicolored, too dark, too bright, or an "evening look."

If you are one of those people who bite your nails or cuticles, now is a good time to break the habit. Getting professional manicures on a regular basis can help because you will be less apt to mess up the manicure that you have paid for and looks so good.

Your hands must look good when you gesture; they must be an effective part of your total look without attracting too much attention away from your face.

## EYEGLASSES

Eyeglasses become a vital part of your general appearance because they control access to your eye contact. It is important that people see your eyes rather than your glasses. Since they are a barrier between the viewer and your eyes, they should be reduced to a minimum and not attract attention on their own.

If you see your glasses first and your eyes second, then do something about them. Find frames that are not too big or too flashy. The design should be simple and should not obscure your brows or alter the expression of your face. Glasses that come down to the tip of your nose are too big for your face and tend to distort your cheekbones. Also avoid frames that come down too low onto the fleshy part of the cheek under the eye. In other words, the glasses should not dominate or obscure your features.

Look for frames that have a thin ribbon of soft, dull-colored metal around the lenses. Avoid gold, silver, or other shiny metal frames, frames that are jet black plastic, or wild colors of any kind. One very flattering idea is to choose a frame color that matches your hair. Or try on rimless glasses that have no metal at all on the lower half of the lenses.

In choosing frames, take into consideration the shape of your face, the size of your cheek and brow bones, the slant of your brows, your hairline, and any facial hair you may have. Glasses can make your face look slimmer and soften sharp angles. They should balance the top and bottom of your features; and they should enhance your own good looks, not overpower your strong points.

Ben Franklin or granny glasses should be avoided in public, because they catch too much light and sit too far out in front of your face.

Glasses should fit snugly enough so that you do not have to constantly push them up into the correct position; such a gesture can be distracting. Have your optician fit your glasses properly to your head and adjust the eye angle for you.

If you wear glasses only for reading, it is fine if you put them on as you refer to your notes, remove them when you have finished, and continue speaking without them.

## Eyeglasses on TV

It is especially important when you are appearing on television that your glasses frames not be shiny, fancy, or flashy, because they obscure your eye contact with the camera. Glasses reflect the studio lights, flashing when you move your face.

If you find that your glasses constantly give you trouble on camera, by all means select a new pair for use on TV. Meanwhile, you can eliminate the shine to some extent by putting cream makeup or a touch of powder on the frames. You can also eliminate some of the glare spots by positioning the glasses so that the bottom is closer to your cheeks than the top. You may feel that this looks slightly strange; but, in fact, it only raises the shafts a little above your ears and does not show on the camera at all.

Another solution is to have your optician send the lenses to a laboratory to have a special clear coating applied. This will eliminate the light flaring off the glasses on camera.

Never wear tinted glasses that shade your eyes on TV, since they change to strange colors under the lights and block your eye contact. They also make you look like a shifty-eyed bandit type. This applies to the combination regular glasses/sunglasses that change with exposure to light, and to permanently tinted glasses, including those that are very faintly or only partially tinted. Yellow, brown, or rose-tinted glasses look especially bad on camera.

Contact lenses are wonderful if you can tolerate them. They now have highly refined characteristics, are relatively inexpensive, and are easier to take care of than ever.

# TWO

# YOUR VOICE

The success of many famous people may be attributed in part to the quality of their speaking voices. To understand this point instantly, think of Richard Burton, who may have had one of the most beautiful voices of this century; Winston Churchill, whose unforgettable voice comforted millions during World War II; and Greta Garbo, who, although we have not heard her speak in many years, has a voice that still haunts our memories.

Just as they do with appearance, people judge the voice of a public person in the first few seconds of listening to it. This is true whether you are famous or not. What would your very first impressions be of the voice of Marilyn Monroe or Mae West if you had been introduced to her? What do you think of the voices of sportscasters John Madden and Howard Cosell? Of the host of the television program "CBS News Sunday Morning," Charles Kuralt? Think of the distinctive voices of Elvis Presley, Diane Sawyer, Jesse Jackson, Jackie Gleason, Cary Grant, Bill Cosby, Burl Ives, Barbara Walters, and George Burns. Despite the very distinctive looks of these individuals, when we think of them we also immediately think of their voices, as well.

# THE IMPORTANCE OF A GOOD VOICE

Your voice is often as important as your appearance, your manner, and your message. It is the tool you use to transmit that message to your audience. The interchange between you and your audience is dependent on your verbal and vocal skills. You can use your voice to get your listeners on your side, convince them of something, sell them something, win their admiration or respect or trust or votes. You can wake them up or put them to sleep, alienate them or woo them, impress them or repel them. The human voice is a very powerful thing.

The important thing to remember, however, is that your audience expects—and deserves—an easy-to-listen-to and pleasant voice.

We live in an age of microwave and satellite communications, with our voices transmitted across the nation and even around the globe. Anyone can be catapulted into the spotlight and be heard around the world. The executive or expert who participates in a video conference that is transmitted via satellite can be heard in a timeless way, in perpetuity.

An unpleasant voice can be a disfiguring element in your public presence; it can cancel out your good traits. Think of a successful athlete who has a small, squeaky voice, or of the respected financier, who is successful but whose voice has a harsh, nasal sound to it. Think of how turned off you are by the telephone or door-to-door salesman who disturbs your dinner and seems to whine at you, his tone almost pleading for a sale. Such people could be more successful if they improved their voices.

Put another way, your voice should be an asset to you in your career, not a handicap.

Also, knowing that you have a good speaking voice can give you the confidence and authority to open the doors of opportunity in your life.

Why do we trust some of our news broadcasters, such as Walter Cronkite, Dan Rather, and Peter Jennings? And why do some of them remain favorites for years? It is partly due to the melodious, low-pitched, totally relaxed quality of their voices, which have no disturbing or attention-diverting qualities. Merely handsome or pretty broadcasters may fade into oblivion. The ones who survive are those with pleasant, elegant voices. Of course, they are also excellent journalists and correspondents. But give that same broadcaster a harsh, nasal voice, and he or she may not survive in the very tough, competitive business of broadcast journalism.

Another group of people who are universally admired for their beautiful voices are the announcers on many classical music radio stations.

Such people often seem to have voices that are a pleasure to listen to. Although some of these announcers were born with such voices, many consciously worked to improve them over the years.

Turning to the business world, why are more and more corporations willing to pay to send their executives to voice-improvement seminars or private voice coaches? Because the corporations want their senior executives, sales personnel, spokespersons, and so on to be effective communicators. This means having accurate pronunciation, clear articulation, pleasant voice placement, and good vocal presentation skills. They want their executives to interact comfortably with other people and to be capable of a variety of speaking skills—from talking at business luncheons, to giving presentations and lectures, to making major addresses.

Also, clients or customers are more apt to listen to—and not tune out—the report or sales pitch of a speaker with a pleasant voice. This competitive edge can make a difference in the financial success of a business as well as in its public image.

No matter what voice you were born with, with practice you can achieve a voice that does justice to your skills and personality. You can lose or modify that regional or foreign accent by observing proper pronunciation. You can get rid of a high nasal placement by using a different part of your vocal apparatus. You can learn to carefully articulate the letters and sounds of our language. You can develop resonance in your chest, and you can learn how to project your voice to the last row in the audience without straining to do so. You can change from a monotonous "Johnny-one-note" to an eloquent, persuasive speaker.

You really *can* do any or all of these things with your voice. This chapter will show you how.

## THE STRUCTURE OF YOUR VOICE

In the early 1960s when I was the director of radio and television for George Washington University in Washington, D.C., I was asked by the chairman of the speech department to help him coach famous individuals on how to appear on television and use the voice properly. His death several years later left me the sole coach of our pupils, and I was then forced to become more of an expert on the subject of the human voice in order to carry on our work.

To supplement what I already knew, I read every textbook I could find and consulted with several outstanding voice teachers about the use of the voice.

Through this research I began to realize that the voice doesn't just come out of the front of the face. There is more to it than that—much more. When you use your voice correctly, you involve your whole body, from the top of your head to your heels. Your entire body is a voice-making box.

Let's start with your brain. It has to have its constant supply of oxygen, and it has to mastermind the whole speaking process.

Moving downward, each of those four little sinus cavities just above and below your eyes hold about a teaspoon of air. They relate to the highest range of your speaking voice and might be compared in size to a high-pitched piccolo in an orchestra. Combined with the nasal cavity, they form a very important part of your speaking process.

Press your fingers over the bridge of your nose, say "ninety-nine," and you will feel a vibration. Nasal sounds made through this "mask" can be unpleasant to the ear. They may come out harsh and strident compared to the deep resonance of the chest tone. The sound made by the top string on a violin has the same characteristic, since only a small amount of air is set in motion.

Next in line are your articulators, which enable you to pronounce your words. Animals can make sounds, but they cannot speak a true language. These articulators make it possible for you to enunciate the elements of speech. Inside your mouth, you will move your tongue along the gum ridges and teeth. You will use the hard palate in the roof of your mouth and the soft palate in the back. You open and close your lips to form the consonants and the vowels.

Then there is that funny little thing called the uvula, which moves when you open the back of your throat. Its other function is to close over the back of your nostrils while you are eating.

You need space between your upper and lower sets of teeth so you can move your articulators freely. You cannot talk with your teeth clenched. Notice how singers in a choir often keep their mouths open, with enough room to place a couple of fingers between their teeth. They articulate all of the words with clarity so that you can easily understand them. Speakers must do the same thing.

The larynx is in the back of your throat. Your vocal cords are actually two pairs of folds of membrane near the larynx. They vibrate when air comes up through your windpipe, producing amplified sound. Put your fingers under your chin as you talk, and you will feel the resonance. These vocal cords open and close when you talk and become tired and inflamed with strain and overuse.

You have to breathe through your lungs in order to power this vocal apparatus. For normal conversation with your friends, you need only a small amount of air in the top of your lungs—so you can use a shallow breath. But to achieve a pleasant chest tone with carrying power, you must breathe with your diaphragmatic muscle. That muscle is very important, since it supplies the air your lungs must send up over the back of your tongue and through your lips.

Think of a bagpipe, which is filled full of air that is used as it is needed. Think of a bellows, which, when squeezed, is capable of focusing a solid stream of air. Consider all that air in your lungs as enough to fill a bassoon. Or think of the resonance in your chest as being similar to the sound of the bottom string of a bass fiddle.

Put your hand on your chest and say "good morning," feeling the resonance. When you control your voice, you can duplicate the range of musical instruments in an orchestra. The high notes are made on thin, taut strings, and the low notes are made on thick, heavy, relaxed strings. The small piccolo goes "eeee," and the big bassoon goes "aaaahhh."

Your diaphragm marks the center of your body and separates the top half from the bottom. It supports and controls your lungs. Breathing from the small of your back helps you understand the function of the diaphragmatic muscle, which forces the air in and out of your lungs. When you run out of air, that muscle makes you breathe. In the first few seconds after birth, the newborn must be induced to use that muscle.

In this chapter, you will read a lot about what proper breathing can do for you, such as sending oxygen to the brain, powering your speech process, relaxing you, and giving you a sense of confidence and well-being that you transmit to your audience.

The backs of your legs are also important in the speech process. They enable you to center your body and support correct erect posture. Those muscles in the backs of the legs help the heart keep the blood flowing through your body with that essential supply of oxygen. This aids the heart action and helps keep the blood from pooling downward with gravity into your feet.

Why does pacing the floor comfort you? Because this activity helps the action of the heart in this way. That's why people often begin pacing the floor almost without realizing it when they are anxious or uncertain or waiting for a decision about something. To understand this point, you have only to think about the stereotype of the father-to-be in one of those old movies—before the days when men were allowed in the delivery room—pacing the floor of the waiting room, smoking anxiously, awaiting the birth of his baby. Or think of how candidates for some kind of award or prize feel when they are backstage waiting for the winner to be announced—several of them would be pacing the floor.

If you were backstage at a live theatrical event, you might notice actors or singers walking up and down a corridor before going on. They are not only going over their lines or thinking about the performance, they are also helping their circulation. Sometimes they will even pump their arms in an exaggerated manner as they walk. This also serves to loosen and warm up the muscles in the upper arms, shoulders, and neck—all of which can contribute indirectly to a better voice.

Your speaking posture depends on the pressure of your heels on the floor. Brace your weight on your feet and center your body by pulling up to your full height, keeping your chin level with the floor and your head high. This gives you the maximum control over your vocal apparatus. From your heels to the top of your head, your whole body is involved in the production of a beautiful voice.

*You* own this wonderful vocal mechanism, and *you* operate it. When you hear your voice on an audio tape, are you happy with it? Or do you say, "That doesn't sound like me!" Do you know in your heart that there is something you could do better, and you just don't know what it is or how to do it? Or is it obvious to you what you would like to change about your voice?

Once you understand the fundamental elements involved, you can devise your own approach to making a beautiful sound. That voice is produced low in your anatomy, rather than low in your voice range. The process is powered by breathing from the abdomen or diaphragm: The larynx carries this air through your vibrators and resonating tissues and cavities; and your articulators pronounce the elements of our language.

Ultimately, you will be at ease with the correct placement and use of your voice, and you won't have to think about it. You will use it naturally every time you speak. You will carry it with you all the time, and it will be a constant pleasure to you, your friends, and your audiences.

# VOICE CHARACTERISTICS

The following is a list of signals that tell you you need to improve the way you speak in public:

- Listeners often ask you to repeat what you just said.
- People notice a speech idiosyncrasy.
- You have a pronounced regional accent.
- You pop the *p* on a microphone, resulting in a dull, unpleasant electronic sound.
- Your throat gets tired when you speak for ten minutes.
- Your listeners' eyes wander or glaze over after you have been speaking for a while because you tend to speak in a monotone.
- You can't control your voice at the end of a long sentence.
- You have to tell people that you are an executive (or whatever position you hold), because they would not know it from listening to your voice.
- You look mature, but your voice sounds too young.
- People often point out that you repeat certain words or phrases (probably unconsciously) over and over again, such as "uh," "well," "so?", "you know," or "hum."
- You tend to sigh, suck your cheek, click your tongue, or have a similar vocal mannerism that bothers others.
- *You* don't like your own voice, and never have liked it.

## Characteristics of a Good Voice

The following list contains some of the characteristics of a pleasant speaking voice. As you read the list, think of how your own voice sounds to your listeners and what voice qualities you might wish you had but do not now have.

A good voice is:

- Pleasant
- Resonant
- Relaxed
- Well modulated
- Low pitched
- Controlled
- Warm

- Melodic
- Concerned
- Eloquent
- Confident
- Authoritative
- Agreeable
- Colorful
- Expressive
- Natural
- Rich
- Full
- Audible
- Positive

## Characteristics of a Bad Voice

This list includes some common characteristics of an unpleasant or bad voice. Again, think of your own voice as you study the list, identifying any unpleasant characteristics that you'd like to change.

A bad voice may be:

- Nasal
- Harsh or strident
- Hoarse or raspy
- Tremulous
- High pitched or shrill
- Whiny
- Breathy
- Timid
- Choppy
- Too loud
- Too soft or inaudible
- Ineffective
- Pompous
- Sarcastic in tone
- Hesitant
- Flat or monotonous
- Tense
- Weak
- Dull

## VOICE QUALITY

### Resonance

A beautiful speaking voice must be both resonant and vibrant. Resonance is the result of the vibration of air in your vocal cavities. These resonating chambers are your sinuses, nasal passages, the back of your throat, and your chest. Resonance requires proper deep breathing for richness and variety.

Visualize your vocal cords as the strings of a musical instrument and the air in your chest as the element that furnishes the desired resonance. By breathing correctly and filling the chest cavity with air, you have given your vocal cords something to vibrate.

A child with a high-pitched voice vibrates a very small amount of air. A barrel-chested baritone with a deep-sounding voice vibrates a large quantity of air. As was mentioned earlier, for normal conversation a shallow breath gives you all the air you need. But when you make a major speech or a lengthy business presentation, you need to power your voice with a large quantity of air.

You can lower the range of your voice by filling your lungs with the help of the diaphragmatic muscle and opening the back of your throat to create more vibration and resonance.

As you completely relax, you avoid any tensions that might interfere with the free movement of your articulators and resonators.

Where do you think the resonance is coming from when you use your vocal apparatus to speak? Do you think it is coming from your nasal cavity—as it does in the high-pitched voice of the telephone operator character made famous by Lily Tomlin? Or do you think it is coming from the bottom of your throat or out of your chest?

To help you find out, put three fingers on the bridge of your nose, and the palm of your other hand on your breastbone. Say something like "Good day! How are you?" Do you feel vibration across your nose, or do you feel it in your chest cavity? Now move your fingers under your throat and up under your jawbone. Say something and see if there is resonance in the back of your throat cavity. Say "awkward" and see if you can feel vibrations coming from your chest.

Only three sounds in our alphabet produce nasal sounds and are allowed to go through your nose. They are *m*, *n*, and *ng*. So if you say, "many have money this morning," you are going to hear nasal resonance. None of the other sounds should go through your nose. When you say, "Good day! How are you?" there are no nasal sounds, and, therefore, you should not feel any vibration in the nose.

Say "chug-a-lug" and open up the back of your throat for the guttural sound. You should feel no resonance in the nose, but you should be aware of it in both the throat and chest cavities.

Now take a deep breath and fill your lungs with air. Hold the air for an instant and then say, "There are buckets in the road." You should be able to feel the chest resonance that is produced by saying such a sentence.

These simple exercises help you to understand your own speech habits as well as the sources of resonance in your own anatomy.

Another good exercise for checking on the resonance coming from your chest is to put the tips of your fingers on your breastbone and say, "mumm mumm mumm mumm." You should be able to feel the vibration.

Resonance gives your voice a pleasant carrying power. When you enter a crowded room, your resonant voice can be heard above the room tone. In a crowded room with a high decibel level, speak lower, rather than higher. You will notice that the people around you easily hear what you are saying.

## Placement

The natural placement of your voice depends on the size of the resonance chambers in your chest, throat, and facial structures. Since amplifying devices distort the upper ranges of the human voice, you should determine the lowest placement that is comfortable and natural for you. This means that the production process is placed as low as possible, but without forcing it artificially low.

Think for a minute about the various placements of the singing voice: The soprano has the highest adult female range, the alto is the lowest, and the mezzosoprano is halfway in between. The tenor has the highest natural adult male voice, while the bass singer has a lower placement, and the basso profundo has a deep, heavy voice with an exceptionally low natural range.

Your natural speaking voice corresponds to one of these placements. Everyone has a low, middle, and upper register. If middle C on the piano is in the middle of your range, then you can go above it and below it—always with the back of the throat open, and the nasal passage closed.

You can lower the placement of your voice by understanding what I mean if I ask you to "talk to me out of your socks." This is an easy-to-remember, seemingly nonsensical sentence that I say to my voice pupils. What I mean is that if you press your heels into the floor, your back straightens, and the diaphragmatic muscle is flexed automatically, causing your voice to come from a placement lower down in the body than if you were talking from out of your nasal cavity.

Likewise, when you memorize the feeling of a chest filled with air, the back of the throat open, then you can safely move up and down in your range without losing that pleasing resonant quality.

A good exercise is to say "he he he," then "ha ha ha," then "ho ho ho," to understand the high, middle, and low placement.

As a voice coach, I have had to help many people improve the placement of their voices. In the early 1960s when I was the voice coach for broadcasters on the "Voice of America" radio network, one of my students had a hard time figuring out exactly where her voice placement was, and how to move the placement lower in her body. In other words, she knew that this change would improve the sound of her voice, but really didn't know how to do it.

I suggested that she listen to some other radio or TV broadcasters and decide for herself about the voice placement—good or bad—of each speaker. She was especially impressed with the voice of Edward R. Murrow, and so she carefully analyzed his voice placement over a period of time and tried to speak in a voice that matched his. She was then able to recall his voice when necessary, to remind herself where to place her own voice.

## Pitch

Pitch relates to the highness and lowness of the sounds you make. The pitch of your voice is governed by the frequency of the vibrations in your larynx. High pitch requires frequent vibrations (think of the voice of Pee Wee Herman); and low pitch requires infrequent vibrations (think of Lauren Bacall's lovely voice).

Compare the sound made by the top string on the violin to that made by the bottom string on a cello. The voice has the same upper and lower registers, and these overlap in the middle of your range.

You should have at least an octave in your voice range to keep from sounding monotonous. This means about four notes above your middle and four notes below. Some eloquent speakers use two and even three octaves in their range of pitch (such as an accomplished Shakespearean actor). High pitches are basically unpleasant to the ear. They are difficult to reproduce or record without distortion. The low pitches are pleasant to the ear, and the lower you pitch your own voice, the less distortion there will be on amplifying devices. (Note, however, that you should never force your voice into unnaturally low ranges.)

You make your spoken material interesting, flexible, and expressive by utilizing changes in pitch. You can consciously lower the pitch of your voice a full octave. You can feel this happening when you move the resonance from the nasal cavity into the chest cavity. With practice, you can do this automatically.

As mentioned in the previous section on placement, pitch is related to the natural singing voices. Think of the woofers and tweeters in your loudspeakers. The tweeters are designed to reproduce the high-pitched sounds such as the soprano voice. The woofers are designed to reproduce the sounds of low frequency such as the baritone voice.

A good exercise for keeping the proper pitch is to say the word "awkward" between the letters of the alphabet. Say "awkward a," "awkward b," "awkward c," etc. Memorize the openness of the back of the throat. When you are able to say the word and the letter with the same pitch, then your pitch is correct. Saying "awkward" forces you to open the back of your throat because the broad *a* is a "back vowel" and can only be pronounced in the back of your throat.

When you are tense, the voice tends to go up in range and pitch. When you are angry, the voice becomes shrill and harsh. When you are tired, the voice becomes husky. When you are sad, the range and pitch go downward.

## Volume

The amount of volume you use determines whether your voice is loud or soft. Volume is measured in decibels. It is closely related to the amount of air in the lungs. By carefully controlling the force and energy, you regulate the loudness and softness of your voice.

With an amplifying device, there is no need to talk loudly since that can drive the needle indicator into the "danger zone." It is the job of the audio operator to regulate the audio levels based on your natural speaking voice; he or she will "ride the gain" to control the final sound.

Remember when speaking to a hard-of-hearing person that loudness alone is not adequate; there must be resonance as well for a slightly hearing-impaired person to hear you.

## Projection

Do you need to project your voice to people in the last row in the balcony, or are you speaking conversationally to a small group of businesspeople? Are you in a gym speaking at graduation exercises, or outdoors at a Fourth of July celebration? Is it a cocktail party with everyone talking at once, or are you speaking in a church where you can hear a pin drop?

Gauge your projection by who will need to hear you and the room tone of the place in which you will speak. A full, rich, resonant voice can be heard in the farthest reaches of just about any room. You do not have to strain to project it. Use the diaphragmatic muscle as the base of your voice and fill your lungs with air to gain control.

Projection is not done with volume. It is not a matter of talking loudly in high decibels. Projection is a matter of using all of the principles of good voice control so that your natural speaking voice is projected properly.

## Timbre

Timbre is how your ear recognizes and identifies one voice from another—how you recognize the voice of one of your children from the others, for example.

Timbre should not be confused with pitch and other voice characteristics. For example, you would recognize Donald Duck's voice whether it was pitched high or low, whether it was whispered or shouted. You recognize Frank Sinatra's singing voice instantly because of its distinctive timbre.

Similarly, your voice has its own distinctive overtones—sounds that make it recognizable to your mother when you call her on the telephone.

## Expression

To become verbally expressive, visualize the words you are saying. Put life into your sounds and pronunciations and feeling and shading into your delivery.

In everyday life, you are most expressive in informal conversation. Transfer this same eloquent expression into your formal speech. If you have trouble doing this and still find yourself speaking with little expression when you are in front of a group, try tape recording a one-on-one conversation at home with your wife or husband or a good friend. Try to forget that the recorder is on. Later, when you are alone, play it back and pinpoint what you liked best about the expressiveness of your conversation . . . keeping an ear cocked for what you didn't like as well.

Imagine the next speech or presentation that you give to your peers or business colleagues being more expressive.

Or if you do not hear much to like about your conversation, record a conversation between you and someone who does use great expression in his or her speech. Pick out someone who is a ham or a "natural-born-actor," a person who is known for telling great jokes or stories or anecdotes, or anyone else who is expressive and uses warmth and color in his or her speech.

Of course, the expression of your voice is controlled by your own interpretation of the material. Individual expression is achieved by intonation, changing rhythms of delivery, effective pauses, phrasing, and variations in pitch and range. Practice reading dramatic material, and train your ear to hear the correct expression.

When working on adding expression to your speech, remember to keep it natural, avoiding artificiality or theatricality in your delivery.

## Tone

The tone of the voice involves pitch, vibration, and modulation. A good voice uses subtle variations of tone. Intonation involves the rise and fall of the voice. The monotone is tedious to the ear because the single tone is uniform and uses one unvarying pitch. Tone-deaf people are insensitive to differences in pitch. You can change the meaning of your words simply by varying the tone of the voice.

In the throaty, husky voice, the lower overtones are prominent. In the thin, harsh voice, the higher overtones are prominent. In all of these extremes, it is important to use sound principles of voice production— open resonators, a relaxed throat, and clear tonal pitch.

To understand what a big difference a change in tone can make, think of the two contrasting voices used by the character Eliza Doolittle in *My Fair Lady,* as Professor Henry Higgins turns the Cockney flower seller into a lady. As he teaches her to speak proper-ly, it is not only her accent and the shrillness of her voice that changes, it is also a change in tone.

## Nasality

Nasality is unpleasant to the ear. The nasal tone quality is harsh, since resonance is limited to a very small area in the mask of the face. When a nasal sound is being made, the muscles of the neck and throat are drawn taut with tension.

To eliminate nasality, relax the back of the throat as though you would say "yaawwnn." This puts the correct distance between the back of the tongue and the soft palate. The uvula rises and closes the nasal passage, so that the sound does not come through the nostrils.

When you hold the back of the throat open, there will be no vibration in the nasal cavity.

## LISTEN TO YOUR VOICE

Become a voice critic. Listen to your own voice and decide how you want it to sound the rest of your life, not just when you are speaking in public, but also in your day-to-day life.

Listen to the voices around you to ascertain if they are pleasant or hard to listen to. Record the voices of actors or broadcasters you admire and figure out what they do with their voices. You will discover how clearly but unobtrusively they pronounce the sounds and syllables. Visualize the way they breathe to produce their vocal tones. Analyze their inflections and emphasis points.

Record a voice you do not like—one that always irritates you, such as a comedian or someone on television. Listen to the placement, the pace, the inflections. What is the obstacle between you and that voice? What unpleasant habit interferes with the message so that you tune out what is being said?

The other day, I heard a lengthy interview on the radio with a singer/songwriter. He expressed himself very well, but *how* he expressed himself was irritating. Every minute or so, in searching for the best words to use in answering a question, he would pause and then say, "I . . . I . . . I," "uh . . . uh . . . uh," "well . . . well . . . well," and similar words. This repeating a word in threes was so obvious that I found myself no longer listening to his answers, but instead anticipating the next triple word and even counting them.

The bottom line is that the voice has only one basic function—to communicate. When a mannerism comes between you and the message, then the speaker has missed the chance to be articulate.

# CHANGING YOUR VOICE

You are not stuck with the voice you were born with. Your voice is the result of many factors: your ethnic background, the part of the country in which you were born or raised, the speech patterns you heard as a child, the schools you attended, how your best friends spoke as you grew up, and often the teachers who influenced your speech.

As an adult, your voice is affected by the people you work with, the person you married, what part of the country you may have moved to, and maybe even your neighbors. If you have lived abroad for some years, particularly in countries such as England or Ireland, you may have unconsciously picked up a bit of the local accent or intonation.

People born in the Midwest may have a nasal placement; those born in New England may say "paak" instead of "park"; those born in the South may use a soft "r"; those born in New York City might have a distinctive twang. An Englishman may inherit the beautiful broad "a" or a Cockney accent. Someone born in Germany, Italy, Australia, or Japan may pronounce certain vowels or consonants with a foreign accent even though that person has lived in the United States for many decades.

Having an interesting accent can be an important part of your persona. For example, early on in my experience as a voice coach in the early 1960s, I worked with Congressman Carl Albert, who was later to become the powerful Speaker of the House of Representatives. He was born in Oklahoma and wanted to improve his speaking voice, but in our sessions together, he admonished me to "only take out half of the Bugtussel."

I never did find out where "Bugtussel" was located (I couldn't find it on a map of Oklahoma), or even understand if it really existed or was just part of a local expression. But I did understand what he was telling me about the importance of retaining part of his normal speech cadence and patterns.

Needless to say, it didn't hurt him with his constituents back home that during his bids for reelection he kept the local hometown flavor in his speech.

Americans do not habitually place a premium on vocal elegance. By the time you enter professional life, your speech pattern is usually set and is a direct result of all of the influences around you.

Very few people in the normal course of life see any reason to change their speech habits. Elocution lessons are considered old-fashioned. A lawyer can go through law school without good speech habits until an appearance before a jury is imminent.

For the political candidate, a regional accent may be charming and fitting on the local scene. But when he proposes to run for national office, he may discover that his speech is suddenly judged by national and even international standards. Newspaper articles describing him may refer to a "charming," "interesting," or "down-home" accent or speaking voice. But the candidate may not *want* to sound like that.

I was the voice coach last year to a businessman who told me during our first session together that he had recently been described in a magazine article as a "business dynamo, with a nonstop, machine-gun voice to match." He said he'd rather sound like a cello than a gun, and we immediately began to work on that "machine-gun" voice of his. He willingly devoted the time and energy necessary to accomplish his goal.

It takes courage and commitment to make vital changes in your speaking voice. People who make the decision to do so should be admired. They are altering inherited, ingrained, and lifetime habits. They may encounter skepticism or even derision at home or among their peers: "What's the matter; are you ashamed of your family?"; or, "I love you the way you are—I thought I married a cute little flirtatious belle"; or, "Sounds like you are becoming affected." Do not worry about such comments; when you accomplish your goal, the doubters will become admirers. They will secretly wish they had the courage to do the same thing.

Most of all, you will have the satisfaction of accomplishing something that will be an asset you will carry with you through your entire life.

I know of one writer at an international radio network who had the opportunity to broadcast her own written material and move to a higher pay bracket. She worked very hard to overcome a harsh nasal placement and develop a pleasant speaking voice, even though her husband was skeptical about her efforts. But she persisted and eventually passed her auditions successfully. One day during a minor argument with her husband, she reverted momentarily to her previous voice. He exclaimed, "Don't talk to me through your nose like that." They both dissolved in laughter.

One broadcaster I coached could not bring himself to put space between his teeth and articulate clearly because as a child he thought he had ugly teeth. (An old-fashioned dentist had done visually unaesthetic work on his teeth that showed when he opened his mouth wide.)

This broadcaster was willing to open his mouth properly for speaking only after another dentist redid his teeth.

A business executive whose job required him to go on an extended speaking tour candidly informed his staff that he was taking speech lessons. They gave him encouragement and understanding, and as a result of his efforts, the tour was very successful.

It pays to enlist the support of your family, friends, and colleagues when you decide to upgrade your speaking skills. Remember, what you are doing is bringing your verbal ability up to the level of your other accomplishments.

Even so, it is difficult to give up the past. Changing your voice takes time and patience—you cannot unlearn those ingrained habits in a few days. It takes several months of daily practice and determination to see results. Your motivation is critical. All of your life, you may have secretly realized that you needed better speech skills and did not know how to go about improving them. This book is a good beginning.

You can do a lot for yourself on your own. Once you start listening to voices you admire and imitating their placement and speech patterns, you are on your way. Choose a good radio voice and repeat the sentences, phrases, and pronunciation. Record that voice on your tape recorder, then record your own voice and play both voices in sequence. Notice the resonance, the pace, the expression, and the emphasis on certain words. Notice the articulation of the consonants and the pronunciation of difficult four-syllable words. Criticize your own voice as though you were listening to a complete stranger.

Practice reading aloud for ten minutes a day. Read your own speeches or newspaper editorials or read to your child before he or she falls asleep at night. Record a piece on the tape recorder and then do it over several times until it sounds right to you. Keep your audio tapes and play them back on a weekly basis to keep track of your progress.

About five years ago, one of my private pupils—a doctor—almost never pronounced a final consonant and resisted every effort to bring about a change. Finally I asked him who was his favorite singer. We bought some of her recordings, and he spent weeks repeating and emphasizing the final consonants just as she did. Now he gets compliments on the clarity of his diction.

You can explore textbooks in the library for helpful techniques. You probably have only a few habits to change, and you can zero in on them. See if you can find some audio tapes from your library or local university of famous speeches or speakers you admire. Listen to some "books on tape" at home or while driving and analyze what you like and dislike about each reader.

If you decide to go to a voice and diction teacher, you can find one to guide you, encourage you, and keep you from getting discouraged or making mistakes. (This is discussed briefly in an upcoming section.)

Or try a speech class at a university or an organized club where you can practice speaking in public. Seek out a speech seminar and ask for a critique by a professional.

Welcome opportunities to make public speeches and treat each appearance as a learning experience. Remember, most successful speakers or broadcasters study speech for years and continue to do voice exercises. In most cases, that lovely speaking voice didn't just happen, it is the result of hard work and practice.

## One Voice or Two?

As a professional, you should speak with only one voice. You cannot have two voices—one that you use for informal conversation and the other one that you trot out just for "on-air" public use. No matter what the situation, use your perfected voice techniques at all times.

You cannot alternate between a chest placement and a nasal placement. It has to be one or the other. You cannot revert to street talk or colloquialisms at will. Once you have changed your voice, you should never go back to the old habits, even momentarily.

I was once introduced to the amateur moderator of a radio show who used a very unprofessional voice in informal conversation. When he sat down in front of the microphone, he put on his moderator voice and did the mike check in what he hoped was a good imitation of a successful broadcaster. To the experienced ear, that voice was phony, obviously forced; even the technical people working with him commented on his two voices.

Once you have achieved a beautiful speaking voice, never deviate from it.

## Speech Therapy

Do not hesitate to seek professional help if you need it. There may be some problems that you simply cannot handle without the help of a specialist.

Once you have identified your problem and perhaps read a book about it from the library, seek a speech teacher or therapist or voice coach. There are many qualified speech experts, and you should not have trouble finding one. Call universities for referrals, look in the Yellow Pages, make inquiries, and check references. Media consultants and drama or broadcasting departments of universities may be helpful.

If necessary, seek competent medical advice for certain speech defects. Avoid anyone with no training, credentials, or depth.

Be sure that what the teacher asks you to do makes sense to you. Find an instructor you can trust; one who has your best interests at heart with whom you can achieve concrete and lasting results.

If after one or two sessions with your speech coach you are dissatisfied with either what you have been told or how things are going, don't get discouraged and give up. Simply find a different voice coach. If one doctor misdiagnoses your illness, you don't give up and remain ill; you get a second opinion from a different doctor.

A good voice coach will have certain characteristics. He or she might:

- Be sensitive to any embarrassment you may have about your problem and put you at ease;
- Listen to what *you* have to say about your accent or high-pitched voice or whatever speech problem you have, and not just didactically inform you of what *he* thinks about it;
- Be patient, so that if your progress is slow, you will not become too impatient with your sessions together;
- Encourage you so that you will continue the sessions as needed;
- Set concrete and attainable goals by which to mark your progress;
- Praise your advances while continuing to point out old faults that you may still be exhibiting;
- Give you simple-to-remember and easy-to-do exercises that you can practice on your own at home;
- Give you homework assignments involving your tape recorder;
- Suggest any books, pamphlets, or other reading material that might effectively supplement your sessions together;
- Tell you frankly if he or she (1) cannot help you in the first place; or (2) can no longer help you to make any more progress.

## Stuttering

Stuttering need not be a deterrent for the public person. I understand from experts in the field of voice therapy that new techniques have been developed which enable the stutterer to become a successful public speaker. These days, the stutterer can be visible and vocal. Stuttering does not need to be a handicap in your private or professional life.

## Practicing with a Tape Recorder

From reading the previous parts of this chapter, you are already aware that the tape recorder can be your best friend and your most brutal critic.

As you work to improve your voice, the tape recorder will faithfully indicate the inevitable distortions common to all amplifying devices. It will show you the progress you are making as you compare your original efforts with small successes. It will save your pride, since you and it are the only witnesses to your efforts. And it will show you true evidence of achievement, as a result of your hard work.

After several takes, you will hear something that pleases you. That progress is encouraging. When you finally achieve a recording with which you find no fault, that faithful companion will exhibit indisputable evidence. You will listen to that tape and wonder if it is really you. You can send the tape to your mother!

The first time your mother calls and says, "May I speak to Mary?" and you say, "This *is* Mary!" you know you are on your way.

You can record an entire speech, your latest presentation during the monthly sales meeting, or your classroom report to your fellow students, and play it back repeatedly—in private, on the plane, or in your car. You can stop and start the recorder anywhere you choose, using it as a learning tool or a memory refresher. You can improve your own techniques, or change the text to make it sound better.

If you wish to record your speeches or informal remarks, you can purchase a very small pocket recorder that runs on batteries. Before your speech, insert the little tape, slip it into an inner pocket, and turn it on just before you approach the podium. Later, at your leisure, you can critique the speech, noting the parts where you did well and the things you want to change or improve.

# CARE OF YOUR VOICE

Your vocal apparatus is fragile and precious. There are a number of ways for you to protect and preserve that delicate instrument.

Avoid fatigue and strain by keeping the throat completely relaxed. Only a relaxed body can house a relaxed voice. A tense body tightens the vocal cords, raising the pitch of the voice and destroying resonance and carrying power.

Using the voice for extended periods under stress requires downtime of total silence. For example, the political candidate who makes five speeches in one day must save the voice in between speeches, lest he or she lose the voice entirely. A harsh and hoarse voice accompanied by a scratchy, sore throat will not help to win any votes.

Similarly, the broadcaster who must stay on the air for hours and hours during an election or national disaster must employ voice-relaxing techniques. The voice of the newscaster is, it often seems, just as much a part of his or her public persona as his or her appearance and journalistic skills.

When you feel that your voice is giving out, do some exercises that relax your whole body. Breathe deeply, take a brisk walk, seek a few moments of privacy, or maintain temporary silence.

You may find that warm tea with lemon is soothing to the throat. Many broadcasters sip room-temperature water containing a few slices of lime to keep the throat comfortable. Singers protect their throats with a warm scarf to avoid extremes of temperature.

Avoid infections and seek expert medical treatment when necessary. If nodules or polyps appear on the vocal cords, have them surgically removed as soon as possible under proper medical advice.

Professionals who have a stuffy nose often irrigate the sinuses with warm salt water. The process nicknamed "sniff and spit" is not very elegant, but it is very effective. Sniff a small amount of warm salt water up the nose, and spit it out, until the nasal passages are clear of phlegm and you can breathe easily. This allows the sinuses above the eyes to drain and will help to eliminate nasal drip and the accompanying irritated throat. Do this twice a day to keep the nasal passages free and clear.

In short, protecting and preserving your voice is a part of being a successful public person.

# BREATHING

Breathing is the most natural and important thing you do. The newborn baby has to breathe to live. The athlete has to synchronize breathing with muscular effort. Opera singers and flute players depend on making use of a large quantity of air. For normal conversation you can get along by drawing a shallow breath, which fills only the upper part of the lungs. But when you are the person up there on the platform, you need to fill your lungs with air and control your breathing.

When you breathe correctly, you center your body and are firmly balanced and relaxed. You automatically place your vocal apparatus in the correct position for use of the diaphragmatic muscle. That muscle is the source of the power you need to speak with resonance.

Remember that breathing supplies the essential oxygen to your bloodstream, which in turn transmits it to your brain and throughout your body. Remember that the human body cannot store oxygen; it needs to receive a constant supply of it. To fill your lungs completely, raise the chest with the support of your diaphragm.

Fill your lungs with air from the bottom to the top—breathe in so that your abdomen bulges outward. Fill the rib section next, then the chest up to the armpits. Keep the breath coming until you feel that the area under your front collarbones is full of air. Fill all of your resonating chambers, including the back of your throat and nose. You want to have the sensation that air is filling the chest cavity from the abdominal muscle up to your throat.

Think of your chest as a basket, a barrel, or a bagpipe that you fill to bursting. That lung full of air is ready to be used for effective speaking. You control it. It also relaxes you and gives you a sense of well-being because of that oxygen it pumps into your bloodstream. It relieves the tension in your body yet keeps you alert.

It all goes back to the basic principles of practicing yoga for relaxation and power. Lamaze breathing, as taught to the expectant mother, uses some of the same principles to relax the muscles and lessen pain. It has even been said that singers often outlive nonsingers because their hearts and lungs get essential exercise from strong muscle control. An athlete's confidence is partly based on good breathing habits, ample lung capacity, and strong heart muscles.

Always take a deep breath before you utter the first word of what you are about to say. Whenever you feel yourself running out of breath, pause at the end of your sentence or paragraph to fill your lungs again.

Wear comfortable clothes with plenty of room around the neck and waist. This gives you a chance to breathe freely, without constraint.

As was mentioned above, oxygen must be constantly replenished. You need it for physical stamina to sustain you to the end of your presentation or speech and to keep your brain energized.

## The Good Morning Breath

Since your vocal apparatus dominates the top half of your body, you will find it interesting to operate your voice-making instrument in a new way. The following exercise establishes the powerful support of the diaphragmatic muscle.

When you wake in the morning, lie flat on your back with no pillow. Stretch your body to its full length by pushing the heels as far down as possible and your head as far up as possible. Make your stomach fall into the small of your back, and raise your rib cage. Place the palm of one hand on the diaphragmatic muscle, just below the ribs, and the other palm on your breastbone. Notice how the muscle controls and supports the air that goes into your lungs as you breathe deeply. Now, pull in a deep breath that fills your lungs from the bottom to the top. Fill the rib cage completely. Say "yawn, awe, awe, yawn," and feel that resonance in your chest. Say "hah hah hah" to exhale all of the air out of your lungs. Experience the power the muscle has to replenish the air.

When the lungs are filled to capacity, say "gooood mmmmor-rrnnning." Put your hand on your chest and feel the vibration and resonance there.

Now, sit on the side of the bed with heels dug into the floor, the body erect. Resist the pull of gravity to achieve that same resonance in the chest. Stand up, heels down with head up, and walk across the room, murmuring "good morning, good morning." Walk proudly, knowing that you know how to breathe with your diaphragmatic muscle.

## The Audible Breath

The audible breath is a soft gasp for air, which can be heard on today's sensitive microphones. Speakers are frequently unaware of it until they hear it reproduced on an audio tape. It is distracting to hear a speaker pull in a breath between sentences. This is so noticeable—and to me irritating—in the speaking habits of a certain local radio weather reporter in my hometown of Washington, D.C., that I have to turn down the volume when she gives her reports.

The audible breath is shallow, taken from the top of the lungs and from the front of the face. When you breathe from deep in the lungs, and from the back of the throat, the breath cannot be heard. Therefore, to make the breath inaudible, move the process backward and downward toward the abdomen. Practice this technique with your tape recorder until it works well for you.

## THE SPACE BETWEEN YOUR TEETH

You cannot speak clearly with your teeth clenched together. You have to put space between your upper and lower teeth in order to go through the gymnastics of correctly pronouncing all of the sounds in our language. Your articulators have to have space in which to move. When the teeth are too close together, it is almost impossible to open up the back of the throat for resonance. A lifetime habit of keeping the teeth close together results in indistinct articulation.

When you watch members of a choir as they are singing certain words, you can see what they are saying as well as hear what they are saying.

There are several ways to get the feeling of space between the teeth. Try dropping the jaw, and notice how much easier it is to say your words naturally. Some find it helpful to practice with a wine cork placed between the teeth. You need not be self-conscious about opening your mouth; do it naturally, just enough to be clearly understood.

## PHONETICS

Our language is made up of about forty phonetic sounds. These are divided into consonants, vowels, and diphthongs. Some of these sounds are voiced (vibrated by the vocal cords) and some are unvoiced (not vibrated by the vocal cords).

The consonants are divided into groups called plosives, nasals, fricatives, glides, affricates, and semivowels. The plosives have to be "exploded"; the nasals are vibrated through the nasal cavity; the fricatives are made by the friction of air being forced through the articulators; glide sounds move on to the vowel that follows them; affricates are a combination of plosives and fricatives; and semivowels, which are both voiced and vibrated, sound similar to vowels.

Vowels require exaggerated movements of the lips and the tongue. Some are pronounced in the front of the articulators, some in the middle of the throat, and some in the back of the throat.

Diphthongs are two sounds pronounced together.

Correct articulation of the sounds requires free movement of the lips and tongue on the gum ridges, teeth, hard palate, and soft palate.

If you are interested in phonetics, many good books on the subject are available, which will include exercises for practicing the various sounds. Such books will also discuss the International Phonetic Alphabet (IPA), which is the universally accepted norm for pronunciation worldwide.

## ARTICULATION AND PRONUNCIATION

The correct, confident articulation of all of the sounds in our language is imperative for the public person. Your pronunciation of the letters of the alphabet must be clearly heard by your listeners.

Without thinking about it, try saying aloud, "That is a mighty hardy horse, full of strength." Did you say "midy" instead of "mighty"? "Hah dy" instead of "hardy," or "harty" instead of "hardy"? "Hahs" instead of "horse"? "Strankth" instead of "strength"?

These differences could be attributed to regional accents. Think of how differently people with marked local accents from London, Brooklyn, Texas, or Vermont might pronounce the phrase "of course, I am" or a sentence such as "I refuse to leave the land of my fathers." A friend of mine from South Carolina pronounces "beer" as something akin to "bay-r"—sort of like she's saying "bear" with two syllables. Also, I once heard about a comedian from Texas who gives a spiel about how Texans speak. It included the comment that some Texans would pronounce the words "war," "where," "wire," and even "why are" all the same, close to something like "wah-r."

However, if you mispronounce words, it may not be regional in origin. You could have what has been called "lazy lips"; that is, you just don't bother to enunciate particularly clearly in your daily speech. (An example from the sentence given above would be your saying "midy" instead of "mighty.") Or you may "swallow" certain letters or sounds, such as when a Cockney-speaking person drops the letter "h" and says

" 'ardly" instead of "hardly." Or you may slur certain sounds, such as the southerner or midwesterner who says "fishin' " instead of "fishing."

Finally, you may just consistently mispronounce certain words because most other Americans seem to mispronounce them. For example, say "athlete" aloud. Did you say it with three syllables ("ath-e-lete") or two ("ath-lete")? It has two syllables, yet many Americans seem to say it with three. Other commonly mispronounced words—and there are dozens of them—include "adem" for "atom," "partically" for "particularly," "pin" when they mean "pen," and "phodagraph" for "photograph."

Another common mispronunciation is adding a letter to a word where it doesn't belong. For example, some people who grew up in Pennsylvania may say, "I am going to 'warsh' my clothes" and "Warshington, D.C."

Whatever problems you may be having with improper pronunciation or articulation (which means making distinct pronunciations), it is very true that when your speech is difficult to understand, the ear strains to hear what is being said. When you "swallow" the consonants or leave certain letters out, the mind tries to fill in the missing sounds.

During normal conversation, your friends can easily understand you. But when you are contending with room noise, coughing, broadcast static, and amplifying-device distortions, your articulation must be correct.

Also, when you talk too fast, you take shortcuts across the pronunciation of the consonants and vowels. The ear cannot grasp what you are saying, and the meaning you wish to impart is not clear. The way to slow down the rate of your speech is simply to take the time to articulate all of the sounds and syllables in your words.

The key to learning how to speak clearly is to enunciate clearly, without exaggeration. Speak conversationally, but at the same time pronounce all of the sounds, letters, and syllables in your words. In this way, you will sound perfectly natural to your listeners.

Avoid stylized elocution. Overly precise pronunciations are irritating, as they come out sounding pompous, cold, and boring. Such pronunciations are fine in the exaggerated speech of the imperious butler in one of those classic British plays, but not in day-to-day speech.

Don't risk mispronouncing words. Use your dictionary as a friend. When you face difficult words with many syllables, turn your dictionary into a textbook and develop the habit of constantly referring to it.

People in my voice improvement seminars tell me that they have benefited greatly from my advice to carry a pocket dictionary around and, whenever convenient, to go down any column practicing the pronunciation of three- and four-syllable words such as "gutta-percha," "guttersnipe," and "gymnasium." Strangely enough, this really does help them to improve their pronunciation.

I also tell my trainees that they don't have to be a TV news anchor or a radio announcer or an actress to take advantage of this. The insurance salesman, gift shop owner, personnel director, graduate student, or docent at the local museum can benefit just as well.

In the front of most dictionaries, you will find a pronunciation guide that is used by cultivated speakers. Take a moment to look at the notes and then begin to learn the exact meaning of the marks that indicate a hard and soft vowel, the slant lines, stress, and accent marks, hyphens, dots, and abbreviations. These guides will help you pronounce any word with confidence. Pick a word you never could say properly and practice it five times. Select four- and five-syllable words at random and enjoy the process of mastering them and making them a part of your normal speech.

Enunciate words that begin with each letter of the alphabet. Ask yourself such questions as, "Do I say 'wite,' instead of 'white'?" Then turn to "wh" in the dictionary and huff your way through words that begin with those letters. Is it hard for you to say "lullaby" with all of those "l" sounds? Turn to "l" and go down the pages. Do your speech writers leave out certain words because they know you cannot say them properly? Tackle those words—and similar ones—until they are easy for you to use.

Read into a tape recorder and listen for the sounds that need to be improved. Buy a good speech book that concentrates on pronunciations. Continue to read aloud and become more of a verbal person. Train your ear to hear your own pronunciations, and you will eventually enjoy knowing that you articulate your words clearly and correctly.

# THREE

## PUBLIC
## SPEAKING

I remember watching President John F. Kennedy give his inaugural address of 1961 as I sat in the CBS News press booth along with Walter Cronkite and others. It was a very cold January day with snow underfoot. Along with thousands of Americans present or watching on television, I was spellbound by his remarks, which have since become known as one of the greatest speeches of our time.

It was in this speech that he made this stirring comment: "In the long history of the world, only a few generations have been granted the role of defending freedom in its hour of maximum danger. I do not shrink from this responsibility—I welcome it. . . . The energy, the faith, the devotion which we bring to this endeavor will light our country and all who serve it—and the glow from that fire can truly light the world. And so, my fellow Americans: Ask not what your country can do for you—ask what you can do for your country."

Why was this such a great speech? Why was Kennedy such a great speaker? Of course, many people also regarded him as a great president. But it was this speech that started it all for many of his admirers.

You may never make a speech that people will come to refer to in history books. However, with experience and a little luck, one day you may make a speech that your listeners call great, one that may be quoted or otherwise remembered. All it takes is some work and some know-how.

Some people find it easy to be "verbal." They seem to speak effectively at any time, and both they and their listeners enjoy the experience.

But among the many aspects of this business of appearing in public, the one that many of my clients have told me over the years that they dread the most is getting up there and giving a speech. Years ago, one of my business clients said to me that he'd "rather have surgery than give a speech."

I have found that this is often true even for those who are otherwise self-confident. Many of my clients worry about their performance and want to have their speaking skills equal their professional achievements. They *want* to get up on that platform and appear at their public best, but they find this difficult to do.

That's why it's always a great joy to me when I am able to see one of my clients become a better speaker. One of them, who was an expert in real estate investing whom I coached about six years ago, says that her career actually got stalled because she avoided all opportunities to speak and delegated them to subordinates. I worked with her for several months until she got over her fears and began to accept speaking engagements. It was only when she learned to give speeches that her career took off—she later landed an important job because her reputation as a dynamic speaker came to the attention of a prospective employer.

This chapter will help you to prepare and deliver a speech you can be proud of. It doesn't matter whether you are one of those naturally verbal people or one who needs encouragement or some practice in order to become an effective speaker.

## MAKING A COMMITMENT TO GIVE A SPEECH

When you are approached to make a speech, consider the depth of your commitment before you accept. Agree to the obligation only if you intend to honor it. People who cancel their speech dates frequently or on little notice soon get an unfavorable reputation.

Once you have accepted, reserve the date in your schedule and give it the time, consideration, and preparation that the engagement deserves. Each and every performance should be of major importance to you and to your audience.

In your mind, don't call any speaking engagement that you have agreed to do "just a minor speech," or you will end up giving it scant attention and your lack of preparation or your delivery style might reflect this and be sensed by your audience.

In order to arrive at the right place, at the right time, on the right day, get the important facts in writing—location, date, time of day, physical and financial arrangements, travel arrangements (including such details as airport-to-hotel transportation, if any), and the identity of your hosts. Ask for detailed directions in order to avoid last-minute confusion.

Write down the name and telephone number of the person who is making the preliminary arrangements and/or the person who is expecting you, and a number where those persons can be reached on the morning of your speech (even if it is on-site).

Also if you have any special needs such as a lowered podium, a box to stand on, hot tea with honey before you speak, a snack, or whatever, request these in advance and preferably in writing.

Ask in advance who will be introducing you, and make sure you know the correct way to spell and pronounce the name. Be sure that the sponsors know the correct spelling and pronunciation of your name. Also make sure they know what form of address you prefer to use ("doctor" or "professor," for example), how you want your formal title or profession worded ("an expert on nuclear disarmament and the author of ten books on the subject"), and, finally, the correct name of the organization with which you are affiliated.

If the information about your speech is to be included in a printed program, leaflets, ads, posters, or whatever, confirm the details in writing beforehand.

If you are asked for your picture, don't send a color snapshot or a fifteen-year-old photo of you before your hairline receded or you put on those extra thirty pounds. Send a fairly recent, black-and-white print, either 5"x7" or 8"x10".

It amazes me how many public figures do not bother to get a good, recent photograph taken of themselves for publicity purposes. If you have not yet had such a picture made, you will find out that it is well worth the effort and that there will be multiple uses for the prints.

Confirm the details the day before, and recheck directions just to be sure about them. Allow yourself at least thirty minutes leeway—time to get lost or delayed in traffic. An hour is even better. Arrive on time for your own peace of mind and in consideration of your hosts' blood pressure. Keeping people waiting for even a few minutes makes for a very awkward situation, and it can create a negative impression before you even step up to the platform.

When you are traveling out of town, keep a running record of the travel arrangements, who made the reservations in what name, and how the tickets are to be paid for. Stick receipts, as you go, in an envelope that you brought along for just that purpose; keep it handy in your briefcase or purse.

Large or unfamiliar airports are often confusing, so if you are to be met, specify which entrance, what airline, or a certain location out in front. Work out a system of recognition—a description of your appearance, perhaps, or have the person greeting you hold up a small sign with your name on it.

Always know what hotel you are staying in, in case no one meets you. Linger at the agreed-upon meeting place if your flight comes in early. Allow time for your host to get through a traffic jam, then place a page to him or her on the airport's public-address system.

If you are going to go directly to the site of the speech without checking into your hotel first, call the hotel to reconfirm your reservation from the airport or from the site. I once had to take my luggage to the speaking site and ended up not finishing up there until the wee hours of the morning. When I finally got to my hotel, they had canceled my reservation and given my room to someone else because they thought I wasn't coming. Fortunately, they were able to find me a room in another hotel close by, but had it been a time of peak hotel bookings, I might not have been so lucky.

Be sure to have an alternate plan, in case everything goes wrong. Before you leave the airport, call the telephone number you have been given and say you're on your way in a taxi. If you're going directly from the airport to the speaking site, make sure you get full directions about room number or banquet hall name, so as not to waste time when you get to the site asking where you are supposed to be.

You will know in advance the nature of the function at which you are speaking—a reception, a formal dinner, a rubber-chicken lunch, or a barbecue. You will know whether you are going to be at a podium, at a speaker's table, or mingling with the public. This information will enable you to have the right clothes with you, plus one alternate outfit.

Finally, check out the room in which you will be speaking in advance. Note such details as the background you will be standing in front of (you may want to change the colors of your clothes, for example), the height of the podium, how the mike adjusts up and down, the lights (if possible), where the head table is (if any), where the restroom is, and so on.

# PREPARING YOUR SPEECH

Preparing your speech is hard work. First, determine the subject and the central purpose of your presentation. Find out exactly how long you will be expected to talk. Find out if there will be a question-and-answer session following your speech and if the time allotted to your speech includes the Q-and-A. Plan to keep strictly to the time given to you. Know what is expected of you, and anticipate what the audience expects to learn from you.

Set goals regarding the main points you want your listeners to remember. You will refer to these points again and again. Once these key points have been identified and written down, the rest of the speech will fall into place quickly.

Will you be given a warning if your speech is running overtime? What if you are *not* willing to take questions from the audience? Find out the answers to these questions in advance.

Find out who will be in your audience and their degree of familiarity with your subject. Decide just how technical you should get. Remember: *Nothing is worse than a speech that talks down to the audience or is completely over its head.*

Collect the material for your speech, research it, and check the accuracy of your information, particularly of figures, quotations, dates, and proper names and their pronunciations. Consult other experts and sources as necessary. Put your thoughts together in logical sequence, and organize your material around the necessary points you intend to make. Once you have all of the facts, put them into the proper order. Put these notes aside, and later review the order of your main points to see if you need to change them.

Stick to the subject matter and keep the presentation as brief as possible. Express your ideas in simple words and short phrases so that your writing is lucid, concise, and relevant. Remember, much of our daily conversation is composed of one-syllable words. Make your speech personal, using the pronouns "I," "we," "you," and "us."

Remember, too, that when writing for speaking, your sentences cannot be too long and convoluted. Since your material is meant to be said aloud, it must be simplified—brief and to the point. Material that is to be read with the eye (such as newspaper copy, press releases, or editorials) can go into greater detail with more qualifying phrases. Writing for speaking is more like writing a telegram, with just the bare-bones information given.

As you write your speech, try out phrases and sentences by saying them aloud to hear how they sound. Take out anything that sounds too stilted or contrived.

You should pay careful attention to your use of correct grammar and pronunciation of proper names, foreign words, and otherwise difficult words.

After you have polished several speeches, perfect one or two of the ones that you feel good about. Such speeches can later be used if you are asked to give a speech on short notice. Subsequent speeches can always be adapted to different audiences and/or lengths.

## Organizing Your Speech

Get to the point of your speech as quickly as possible. Assemble everything on the same subject in one place. Do not move from one idea to another until you have exhausted all of the relevant material. If you discover you have omitted a necessary item or thought or illustration, move it to the category in which it belongs.

Organize your ideas into a logical sequence with each point leading to the next and giving emphasis to the whole. Let the ideas flow logically from one to another. Clarify your material to simplify it into easily understood terms. Keep your listeners' interest in mind. Throw out material that does not relate to this particular audience. Always try to say something meaningful and individualized to your listeners.

Once you have achieved momentum, keep it going with positive ideas. Use specific information—facts, statistics, research, anecdotes, or quotes—to support your statements.

Divide your speech into three parts: the *opening*, the *body*, and the *close*. In order of importance, the opening ranks first, the close ranks second, and the body of your speech ranks third.

## The Opening

As the most important part of your speech, the opening sets the tone for the entire presentation and gives the audience a preview of what they are about to experience. Your opening must immediately establish a positive bond between you and your audience.

State the central idea of your entire presentation. Emphasize your main premise in such a way that the audience (1) immediately recognizes it as your main premise, and (2) quickly comprehends what you mean. With luck its members will also agree with you and be eager to hear what you have to say in the rest of your speech.

Polish the opening and revise it several times so that it is concise and will grab the audience's attention. *Make the audience look forward to the rest of your speech.* At the very beginning, establish a momentum that carries your main idea through the body of your presentation.

In order to immediately create a mutual sense of trust and respect with your audience, try to deliver your opening from memory, rather than reading it from your written notes. This also allows you to establish good eye contact early on with your listeners.

## The Body

The body of your speech should be nothing more than an orderly and logical presentation of the important points you wish to make. Develop each point as you move your central idea along. Present stimulating ideas that are worth thinking about and debating. Stick to each individual subject, treat it as a whole, and, when it is completed, move on to the next idea. Plan to alert your listeners to the fact that you are moving on to a new section of your speech through pauses and a change in your tone of voice.

You will find that you can present five or six clear-cut ideas in a fifteen- or twenty-minute speech. Your audience cannot grasp and will not remember much more than that. By confining yourself to a few, well-chosen points, you indicate your grasp of the subject and your ability to transmit the material so that it can be understood.

***Jokes and the Use of Humor.*** Jokes are optional for use in your speech. If you are a good storyteller and you think that particular audience will enjoy your jokes, go ahead and use them. But if you think that it is going to be difficult for you to make the audience laugh, don't attempt to tell any jokes. There is nothing worse than a joke that falls flat.

Some speakers employ joke writers or collect stories from many sources, including joke books or books containing quotations or anecdotes. At certain functions, such as a "roast," jokes are a necessity.

Even speakers who generally don't use humor in their speeches keep a classic, sure-fire joke or two in their heads in case it is needed in an unusual situation, such as to defuse a hostile question or silence a heckler or wake up a crowd.

In any case, rehearse your funny stories or try them out on friends, throwing out those that bomb. Be sensitive to the occasion, gauge your audience, and always be sure your jokes are appropriate.

Bad jokes and cheap shots will not go over with most audiences. It should not even have to be stated that you should avoid any joke that could be construed to be racist, sexist, or an ethnic slur. Jokes about religion or sex are often told, but that doesn't mean you should tell such jokes. A good litmus test for deciding whether to use such a joke is to think how it would seem printed word for word with your name attached to it in your hometown newspaper the next morning.

But gentle, kind humor is always welcome, be it witty, topical humor or the down-home kind. Jokes about the town you are speaking in always go over well, if they are carefully chosen and tasteful. Humor releases your audience and creates a bonding of openness and trust between you and your listeners.

TV and radio talk-show host and writer Larry King is famous as one of the funniest speakers on the lecture circuit. He can tell one humorous story after another about himself and others on a wide variety of topics. He even tells humorous stories about past speeches he's given, the unusual groups who have invited him to speak, and their reactions to his sometimes tall tales.

Mr. King's use of humor is a classic example of the bonding that can occur between a good speaker and the audience. Members of his audiences leave his speeches smiling and with a warm feeling.

*Quotations and Anecdotes.* Quotations can be very effective when used to substantiate the premise of your presentation. Use impeccable sources that the audience will respect as authorities in the field or of historical interest. Check your quotations for accuracy before repeating them in public. When used judiciously, a few well-chosen and relevant quotes can add to the effectiveness of your speech.

Sometimes a true story or anecdote will make your speech more interesting. Lawyers and doctors often successfully refer to specific cases that are unusual, interesting, or historical. U.S. congressmen and congresswomen and other politicians are also known for using stories in an interesting way. For example, during the 1988 presidential campaign, in his public addresses Governor Michael Dukakis frequently told his listeners stories about his immigrant Greek parents. These stories were often reprinted in the press to a much wider audience than his immediate circle of listeners.

You can easily read or listen to a speech by someone you admire in your field and see how that person uses anecdotes effectively.

If you have trouble finding good speeches to listen to, you might try listening to some of the tapes of Garrison Keillor (the former host of "A Prairie Home Companion" radio show) or humorist Will Rogers. Study how these and similar Mark Twain-type humorists tell anecdotes and "spin out a tale." Even though many of their stories are fiction, you can learn quite a bit from their style of storytelling.

***Saying Something Memorable.*** The Reverend Martin Luther King, Jr., clergyman and civil rights leader, was one of the most riveting speakers of his time. His speeches were punctuated by alternating shouts of agreement and rapt attention on the part of his listeners. His speech delivered during the 1963 March on Washington has been called one of the best speeches ever given anywhere. This was certainly due in part to the simple, inspirational, and often-repeated phrase, "I have a dream."

Other memorable sentences that tend to stick in our minds include: "Give me your huddled masses, yearning to breathe free"; "Let them eat cake"; "Give me liberty or give me death!"; and "United we stand, divided we fall."

You don't have to be a famous orator such as Patrick Henry, Daniel Webster, Winston Churchill, or Oscar Wilde to say something memorable. Some very famous phrases and sayings have passed down to us through history as anonymous quotations or were said or written by people who were not very well known.

Learn to turn a phrase your audience will remember long after your speech is over. Strive for the "quotable quote," the "zinger," or a memorable way to phrase the heart of your message that your listener cannot forget.

Memorable phrases should be worded like a telegram—simple, direct, and brief—but catching the attention of the listener. You should use such a phrase several times in the body of your speech, but also consider using it in your opening and close, as appropriate.

We tend to think in terms of code words, rather than long sentences. It is one way to take a complex issue and reduce it to a simple expression.

Often that one memorable phrase or short sentence can describe a complicated situation, which might otherwise take an entire paragraph to explain.

## The Close

The close of your speech is its second most important part. Decide in advance what the ending should be. You should regard your close as the climax to your remarks. It should bring you and your audience to a logical conclusion. Make the ending powerful.

An effective close might summarize your speech in words you expect your audience to remember. Spend time and thought on the wording to make it effective and memorable. Or you might close your speech with an upbeat look at the future. Whatever you decide, bring your speech to a definite conclusion that clearly signals the end to your audience. A good speaker knows when to stop and doesn't ramble on. *A speech should end before the audience wants it to end instead of ending long after the audience wishes it had ended.*

At the conclusion of your presentation, plan to look your audience in the eye, smile, and say something pleasant. Expect your audience to enjoy your speech, and it will enjoy it. Anticipate applause and acknowledge it. Plan to let your audience know that you, too, enjoyed the whole process. You will want to let your body language as well as your facial expression reflect that fact—look relaxed, content with having given a good speech, and self-confident all at the same time.

## Visuals

Visuals are useful only to the extent that they enhance the content of your speech. Carefully chosen slides, pictures, flip charts, graphs, illustrations, or props may give added clarity and interest to your presentation, but they should be used only if they do add visual interest to the speech. You may also wish to prepare a relevant handout.

If you decide to use a slide projector, synchronize the audio and video in advance in an annotated script. In such a script, make a left-hand column with the numbers and titles of your slides and the right-hand column with the text you will be reading.

When using visuals to be projected, a cardinal rule is don't flash up complex, typed charts or tables with lots of words or numbers on them that can't be read or understood easily. Nothing puts an audience to sleep faster than boring visuals, and nothing wakes it up faster than exciting ones.

Double-check charts and slides for proper spellings and typographic errors. Don't let yourself join the ranks of speech-givers who have said, "Oops—that's not right" as a slide or other visual was flashed onto a screen.

Rehearse the visual presentation in advance, to familiarize yourself with the technical equipment you require. Check out the room in which you will appear for electric outlets, and learn how to dim the lights.

## Your Manuscript

Now that your speech is in its final draft, have it typed in large letters so that it can be easily read. Use either a special, large-type machine, or have it done in capital letters, triple-spaced. (If you are having it typed in capital letters, have a sample page typed for you; some people are uncomfortable reading capitals.)

Leave wide margins for notes and leave the bottom fourth of each page blank, so that you will not have to look downward to read your manuscript.

Number each page with a colored pen so there will never be any doubt about page order. Clearly mark the opening and the close. Put numbers in the margins to indicate the individual points in the body of your speech. Underline the "buzz words," which telegraph the meaning of each point. If you do all of these things, you will be able to maintain better eye contact with your listeners.

Underline and mark up your manuscript for easy interpretation. Use a single line to connect phrases or titles that are spoken as one word. Use a double line or a different color marking pen to emphasize important words, phrases, and ideas. Indicate a pause with a single slash and a longer pause with a double slash. Enclose qualifying phrases in parentheses. Enhance the punctuation marks with a bold pen so they can be followed easily. Mark paragraphs with a horizontal slash that extends into the margin. Put asterisks to indicate the points at which you should breathe. Emphasize quotation marks with your pen to remind you to enclose them in a little frame of silence that sets them apart from the rest of the sentence.

You may find it helpful to annotate the margins of your manuscript into major headings. Also you might want to indicate pauses as broadcasters do with three ellipsis dots (" . . . ") written into the script.

Devise your own system of marking your manuscript that lets you see at a glance the interpretation of the meaning you wish to transmit. Using such a system helps you get off the page as much as possible and speak directly to your audience. Consider your manuscript as a guide, and try not to read it verbatim.

Never have a secretary or aide prepare your speech for you without reviewing it thoroughly and marking up the manuscript yourself.

Mount the finished manuscript into a plain black, loose-leaf folder, and it is ready to be carried to the podium, safe from wind, coffee stains, or other encounters en route.

Remember, your delivery technique will depend on how well your original manuscript was prepared.

## Speaking from Notes

If you possibly can, do not read directly from your typed manuscript, but instead speak from notes written on 5"x7" cards. Keep the manuscript for ready reference, but tuck the cards into the side pocket of your loose-leaf binder.

Transfer your outline to the cards, using large type. Label the first card "open" and the last card "close." In between, have a card for each important point you wish to make. Number the cards with a bold pen, and mark up the cards using the same technique you used on your original manuscript. Your cards and manuscript will be interchangeable.

When you use the manuscript only as a guideline, you establish contact with your audience and speak to it directly. There is no need to memorize the material, just to familiarize yourself with it. Know what you are going to say and go ahead and say it, but know when to stop.

If you are able to ignore the manuscript and speak from your notes, your presentation will be greatly enhanced. However, there may be exceptions—such as a need to refer to technical data. In that case, put the number of the appropriate page of your manuscript on the card for easy reference.

## Practice

It is important to practice and rehearse your speech in advance until you feel confident that you have mastered its contents. Go through the performance experience in your mind.

Visualize the room in which you will speak, the podium or table, and the clothes you will wear. Think about the members of your audience, how pleased they are to have you speak to them, and how pleased you are to have the opportunity to speak to them. Such "visualization" techniques actually work. If you have never tried them before, now is a good time to experiment with them.

Think about how you will sit as you wait to be called to the microphone, concentrating on presenting a picture with your facial expression and body language that is not stiff or awkward but pleasant, relaxed, confident, and in control. This is important because before you are introduced (or as you are being introduced), many members of the audience will be staring at you, judging you before you rise to speak.

Think through the subject matter in your speech and how it will all fit together—your opening, the points you will make, and your close. Think of the positive reaction of the audience.

Stage a dress rehearsal in front of a mirror to see how your gestures can enhance your meaning. Watch your posture and body language. Eliminate distracting mannerisms. If possible, practice your speech before one or two real people—your spouse or a coworker, perhaps.

Record your speech on a tape recorder to see how your voice will sound. Polish the phrases, sentences, and paragraphs for emphasis. Evaluate your performance and critique the replay. Write down your comments, both positive and negative.

Leave nothing to chance. If video tape is available to you, you will find it a revealing experience to watch a video tape of your performance.

You will find all of this advance preparation most rewarding when you walk up on that platform to make your speech.

**Pauses within Your Speech.** Silence can be powerful. Pauses can be used effectively in your speech. Use them as you would use punctuation marks, to emphasize phrases, sentences, or even paragraphs. You can give a statement added significance by using short pauses before and after it. A frame of silence around a parenthetical phrase or a quotation makes it stand out from the rest of the sentence.

Pauses can alert your audience to pay special attention to a certain thought, as if you'd said, "Listen to this!"

Use pauses to separate your thoughts into logical units that your audience can easily grasp. Once you have made an important point, pause before you move on to the next one.

Pauses slow your delivery when you talk too fast. They give you a chance to breathe. When you feel that your voice is getting strained and tense and the pitch is rising into the nasal cavity, use a pause to move the production of vocal sound downward. You can also use pauses to avoid monotony or to indicate a change in volume.

Both you and your audience benefit from the use of pauses. They enable your listeners to follow the logical progression of your units of thought. Significant ideas need breathing space and should not be crowded too closely together.

Strategically placed pauses cause the audience to wait expectantly for your next statement. They help you to hold the attention of your audience.

If you get applause to a certain remark in your speech, be sure to pause long enough for it to die down before beginning your next sentence. Otherwise the audience may miss the beginning of the sentence, which can be very irritating. All of us have experienced this during a movie or play punctuated by laughter from the audience.

Mark pauses on your manuscript by using single, double, and triple slashes to indicate the length of the pause. A triple slash at the end of a paragraph clearly gives you time to take a breath.

**Brevity.** The Gettysburg Address is one of the best-known and often-quoted speeches in the English language. Delivered by President Abraham Lincoln on the site of a battlefield on November 19, 1863, its purpose was to dedicate a portion of the site to a cemetery. Lincoln wrote two similar versions of the speech before giving it that day, and he wrote down three other versions—all very similar—after the speech.

What many people forget, however, is that despite its impact, the Gettysburg Address is actually a very *short* speech—only ten sentences long. The following version of the speech is the fifth, and last, version that Lincoln hand wrote of the speech. It is said to be the closest to the one that he actually delivered that day on the battlefield:

Fourscore and seven years ago our fathers brought forth on this continent, a new nation, conceived in Liberty, and dedicated to the proposition that all men are created equal.

Now we are engaged in a great civil war, testing whether that nation, or any nation so conceived and so dedicated, can long endure. We are met on a great battlefield of that war. We have come to dedicate a portion of that field, as a final resting place for those who here gave their lives that that nation might live. It is altogether fitting and proper that we should do this.

But, in a larger sense, we can not dedicate—we can not consecrate—we can not hallow—this ground. The brave men, living and dead, who struggled here, have consecrated it, far above our poor power to add or detract. The world will little note, nor long remember what we say here, but it can never forget what they did here. It is for us the living, rather, to be dedicated here to the unfinished work which they who fought here have thus far so nobly advanced. It is rather for us to be here dedicated to the great task remaining before us—that from these honored dead we take increased devotion to that cause for which they gave the last full measure of devotion—that we here highly resolve that these dead shall not have died in vain—that this nation, under God, shall have a new birth of freedom—and that government of the people, by the people, for the people, shall not perish from the earth.

In the address, Lincoln said that "the world will little note, nor long remember what we say here," but that has obviously not been the case. History tells us that the main speaker at the dedication ceremonies, Edward Everett, wrote a letter to President Lincoln afterward saying: "I should be glad if I could flatter myself that I came as near to the central idea of the occasion in two hours as you did in two minutes."

It is obvious, then, that brevity is a major key to a good speech. Nowadays we are conditioned by the media to receive our messages in a short span of time. We sometimes think we can learn all we want to know about the world in the first two minutes of a network news broadcast.

During a long evening, a nine-minute keynote speech is greatly appreciated. The speaker who drones on endlessly and relentlessly through a written text loses the audience. With today's audiences' short attention spans, listeners get tired of sitting and may squirm in discomfort.

And remember, you can say quite a bit in nine or ten minutes.

You can estimate that about 130 to 170 words take a minute to deliver. Time your speech with a stopwatch to make sure that it fits within the time frame that you have been given. If you find that it is too long, cut out sentences and paragraphs rather than increase the rate of your delivery.

***Talking Too Fast.*** You may have been told that you talk too fast but do not know how to slow down your rate of speech. There is more than meets the eye to being understood by your audience than just slowing down your rate of speech.

The untrained speedy talker must learn to keep the speech pattern under control. When you whiz by important words and phrases, your listener has to strain to understand what is being said and will soon lose interest in trying to follow you.

The proper way to slow your rate of speaking is to carefully pronounce all of the letters, sounds, and syllables in your words. Don't leave anything out: Clearly and correctly articulate all of the consonants and vowels.

When you take the time to clearly pronounce each word and sentence, you automatically slow the rate of your speech and you will comply with the "listening rate" of your audience. Then, by adding meaningful pauses and emphasis, you will become an eloquent speaker.

As mentioned earlier, an audience has a listening rate of between 130 to 170 words per minute. To be clearly understood, you should not exceed that rate. Again, using a tape recorder, time yourself with a stopwatch or the sweep hand of your wristwatch to find out what your speaking rate currently is.

Aside from your audiences' "listening rate" is what I call in my seminars their "comprehension speed." This refers to your listeners' ability to *readily* understand what you are saying at the speed that you are saying it.

In other words, it is important that you develop the ability to gauge your listeners' ability to understand clearly and comprehend the meaning of your material when you give a speech. For example, I find that many highly intelligent people think faster than they talk. Their minds are speeding far ahead to the next thought or sentence.

They may also know the material they are talking about so well from constant study and/or repetition that they find themselves racing through it at a great rate—faster than the comprehension speed of their listeners.

For some members of your audience, English may be a second language, and they may be doing a mental translation of what you are saying into their own language. Or the younger members of your audience may appreciate a speaker who does not rush through the material.

Sometimes audience comprehension can be affected by room tone, extraneous noise (are waiters clearing dessert dishes or serving coffee as you begin your speech?), or microphone distortion. The trick is for you to adapt the rate and speed of your delivery to the ability of your listeners to follow what you say. It is important to observe the listening limitations of your listeners.

***Eliminating the "Uh."*** Almost everyone says "uh." It is a common but irritating speech habit.

The first step in breaking this lifelong and often firmly entrenched habit is to become acutely aware of it. Listen critically to the people around you and count the "uh's" in their speech. Listen to radio and TV announcers, public speakers, and friends. Make a mental note of how often that "uh" is used.

A famous speech teacher is known for carrying around a pocket full of dry beans, and every time a pupil said "uh" in his presence, he threw a bean out on the floor.

Listen to the tape recording you made of your speech, and mark down the number of times you said "uh." (Or use beans, if you wish.) Envision your thought process when you say "uh." Usually, you say it when you hesitate and are not quite sure what you are going to say next. You use it as a device to gain a little time, to get your thoughts in order.

One technique that you can try is to eliminate the "uh" by stringing your words more closely together ever so slightly. Know in advance exactly what you are going to say.

Practice this: When you pause and would normally say "uh," substitute silence for the sound. Open the back of the throat and breathe silently during the pause. Then firmly launch into your next thought. Keep quiet during the pause.

By being conscious of this speech blemish and with diligent practice, you can completely eliminate that troublesome "uh." If you try to carry on your normal, everyday conversations without ever using "uh" and practice substituting silence for it in your public speaking, with time and effort you will be able to overcome this mannerism.

If instead of "uh," your problem is often repeating another meaningless phrase such as "well" or "you know," the same tips given above should work.

## Stage Fright

Many public people—including famous actors and singers—experience varying degrees of stage fright throughout their successful careers. They are not alone; this phenomenon is perfectly normal. In fact, some talented and learned people simply refuse to appear in public, and their stage fright can become a tangible factor in blocking the development of a promising career. Others find that they suffer from stage fright every single time they appear in public. For such people, it becomes a lifelong agony.

Stage fright goes back to the primitive instinct we all have that tells us to run from danger. We learn to use logic and reason to conquer this instinctive reaction.

Do you suffer from any of these symptoms of stage fright? Do your palms sweat, your knees weaken, or you feel that you cannot get your breath? Does your mouth go dry, perspiration break out on your forehead or upper lip, your voice quaver, your stomach feel queasy, or your heart beat so fast you think you will suffocate? These symptoms can disrupt your mental processes and physical coordination and cause your speech to be less than it could be.

For many people, the fear of making a speech in public is very real. They may find private conversational speech easy and natural, but they cannot sleep the night before giving a public speech due to nervous tension. They feel they are not in control and that they will probably be completely speechless or even "die up there" on the stage in front of everyone. But, somehow, they are still alive when it is all over, and they have gotten through the ordeal one way or another. They may even have learned something from the experience.

Even people who have acute stage fright may feel a rush of euphoria (based on a feeling of "I *did* it!") or an intense mix of a feeling of accomplishment and relief that it's over after a successful speech.

Then there is the type of person who feels nervous symptoms of stage fright *after* it is all over. For example, one actress I knew claimed that she never felt stage fright before she went on, but that as soon as the performance was over, her knees began to shake uncontrollably, and she had to run to the restroom to recover her composure.

Stage fright can have a variety of vexing causes. You may shrink from the prospect of being evaluated in public. You may fear the thought of failing in front of a group of your peers. You may experience anxiety at the thought of that big audience out there looking at you.

There may be a significant person in the audience who has been critical of you in the past but whose approval seems crucial to your career or whose approval you secretly covet.

It may be that being verbal is a new experience for you and has to be a learned skill. You may be a naturally shy and quiet person. You may be haunted by the memory of one bad experience in public. You may have avoided public appearances all your life and are therefore simply lacking experience.

Or tension may have been caused by an unforeseen technical dilemma, such as a microphone that will not work or an inept prompter operator.

You may have made quite a few public appearances before with no hint of stage fright, only to experience it for the first time because you have recently had a debilitating experience, such as illness, bereavement, divorce, loss of a job, or a tragedy in your family.

Finally, your stage fright may be triggered because your plane was late and you arrived out of breath; you were caught in a sudden downpour that nearly ruined your hair or clothes; you looked down and saw that you were wearing one black and one brown shoe; or someone said something uncomplimentary to you and you have not yet had time to recover from it.

Whatever the cause of your stage fright, you should immerse yourself in the task at hand and face each element of your performance one by one. You can break the cycle of terror or anxiety by setting up a series of steps that will give you confidence and authority and put *you* in control. Your goal is to master the situation, keep your composure, do what you came to do, enjoy the whole procedure, and transmit that cordiality to your audience. If you succeed in doing that, your public appearance will have been a success.

Conquering stage fright involves meticulous advance preparation, even more so than the usual amount of preparation described earlier. Plan the details of your physical appearance, wear the right clothes, and then forget about them since you know you look wonderful (review the chapter called "Your Personal Appearance").

Work on and reword your speech until you know it is right and you are thoroughly familiar with it. Rehearse it again and again. Have your notes in easy-to-follow order, knowing they are correctly annotated and numbered. Clearly and consistently focus on the heart of your message so that your audience will easily follow along with you.

Familiarize yourself with the details of the room, stage, or platform from which you will speak. Go through in your mind and rehearse at home every move, gesture, and action you will take before you start talking. Leave nothing to chance. Eliminate all of the uncertainties.

Rehearse your walk to the stage in advance of your appearance. In private, you can develop a reassuring familiarity with the situation you will face. Slowly begin to move, maintaining the feeling of being in control. Do not rush or hurry. Take a few seconds to adjust your posture upward, then breathe deeply, filling your lungs with air. Look in the direction of the podium, and advance confidently toward it.

When you arrive at the imaginary podium, turn toward the microphone and adjust it to your correct height. Survey your listeners and make eye contact with them. One of the worst mistakes you can make is to go to the podium, fiddle with your notes and adjust your microphone, and begin speaking with your head looking down at your notes without having looked straight at your audience.

Use that vital pause mentioned above to breathe and open the back of your throat. Pleasantly light up your face and part your lips slightly to begin your opening sentence (with which you should be completely familiar). Think for a second or two before you speak.

After rehearsing your speech, practice leaving the podium and walking from the room or to your designated seat.

Practicing these things can help you develop the self-assurance you will need to face your audience with confidence.

Rehearse other situations that you will face in the same way. Visualize the room and the circumstances of your appearance. Anticipate surprises by going through the motions in private until you feel confident and in control.

One of my clients who suffered from acute stage fright was a vice-president of a major banking association in Washington, D.C. She had been asked to give one particularly important address to a very distinguished audience. She told me that she was afraid that she would experience the symptoms of stage fright that she had had in the past—for her, these were an inability to swallow, a mouth that felt "as dry as cotton," and a throat that tightened up. When I asked her why she was afraid she would experience these symptoms during this particular speech, she said that this would be the most important speech of her career to date.

The key to calming her fears turned out to be my convincing her to rehearse and rehearse and rehearse her speech again, ticking off the tips I describe in this section to help calm her down. She also learned how to open the back of her throat, relax the muscles in the neck, and to memorize the first words of the speech.

I also coached her to keep saying to herself that "this was only one more speech," in an attempt to convince her subconscious that she could do it.

Using these guidelines, we were able to calm most of her fears, and she gave quite a good speech. She was subsequently able to accept other major speaking invitations with much more confidence. Now she is one of the association's designated spokespersons.

If you suffer from stage fright—of any degree ranging from a mild case on up to the paralyzing type that my client suffered from (i.e., your throat goes so tight and dry that you have difficulty talking)—you can conquer it by going through these same rehearsal techniques outlined here.

Know in advance what relaxation techniques work for you. Adopt a relaxing exercise that reduces tension.

Many famous athletes have a little ritual that they go through before athletic competitions involving their clothing, warming up, giving themselves a pep talk, visualizing winning, etc. With some, this involves the superstition that the ritual will bring them luck. But the point is that you can do the same thing by developing a relaxation technique that works for you to reduce stage fright.

However, keep in mind that *minor* symptoms of stage fright can be helpful to your presentation: The rapid heartbeat is nature's way of supplying extra oxygen to your brain; breathing deeply aids the circulation of your blood; and extra adrenaline gives you the energy to keep alert. A little bit of stage fright has a positive aspect because it rivets your attention on what you are doing. It can sharpen and improve your performance skills.

Radiate a sense of warmth, caring, sincerity, and credibility. If you project a sense of liking yourself, your audience will like you, too.

All of this requires patience and practice, but it is well worth the effort, and it will conquer stage fright for you.

Just before your appearance, you may find that a personal check-off list is helpful, just as the airline pilot checks off the essential items before a flight. Your private list might include saying some of the following to yourself:

- My appearance is good: My hair, makeup (if applicable), and clothes are right.

- I am using good eye contact.
- My posture is good, and I am relaxed up here in front.
- My body language is friendly.
- This is really one of the best speeches that I've ever written. I can't wait to give it to the audience.
- I am familiar with this speech; I know what I am going to say.
- My notes are well organized and easy for me to follow.
- This is a great audience.
- This audience likes me. I *want* to be up here. In fact, I *enjoy* being up here, and the audience knows it.
- I know how to relax throughout this speech.
- I am transmitting confidence and authority.
- My speaking skills are effective.
- I know that when this speech is over, I will be happy with my performance.
- They are going to wish that I will keep on talking, but I'm going to end my speech before that.
- I look forward to making future speeches. I get a lot of satisfaction out of the applause and well-wishers' comments at the end of my speech.

**Being Shy.** Being naturally shy is related to but different from stage fright. You may feel that you are simply too shy to speak in public. You blush, sweat, stammer, and/or feel ashamed of your performance. If so, you are not alone.

You can overcome your shyness when you recognize it for what it is and list the skills you need to make a performance you can be proud of. Work on these skills in private, one at a time. Start with small, informal appearances among friends and gradually build confidence in yourself. It will be a great personal satisfaction to you to learn that you can become an effective public speaker.

## Your Audience

There is more to knowing your audience than you might expect. For example:

- If you have been asked to speak before a group of Veterans of Foreign Wars, did you bother to ask the organizers if it will be a mixed-sex or nearly all male audience?

- You have been told you will be speaking in a hall that you know holds 500 people. But did you ask before you wrote the final version of your speech how many people are actually expected to attend? A speech can be effectively adapted to a smaller audience, if you know you will have a smaller audience.
- Will you be expected to include a sprinkling of comments in your speech on local subjects? Many audiences warm up well to remarks or humorous references to the community where the speech is being given.
- Have you found out if there will be any VIPs in the audience you should mention?
- Are there any special, possibly disruptive, circumstances having to do with the audience that you should know about in advance? For example, might there be hecklers in the audience or will people be milling around in the back of the hall buying alcoholic beverages during your speech?

In short, you should identify your audience and adapt your performance to its expectations. Learn as much as you can about your audience before you come face to face.

Inquire about the age level, degree of education and experience, and any social, religious, or political affiliations that members of the audience may have in common. Is this a hostile or friendly group? What do you have in common with your audience?

Your listeners have come to hear you for a specific purpose: possibly to increase their own knowledge, to become more professional on their jobs, to decide how to vote, to celebrate an occasion, or for their annual convention or meeting. You owe your audience careful consideration, and as you prepare your speech, make sure to present something meaningful for everyone.

Keep in mind that some of your listeners may have traveled a great distance or rearranged a busy schedule just to hear your speech. Some may be people in your field who admire you greatly and will be listening with keen interest. If you remind yourself of these facts, you will become enthusiastic about your speech, and this enthusiasm will be transmitted to your audience.

Know what you want to accomplish with this group. Put yourself in your audience's place. Understand its expectations of you, and let it know where you are coming from. Early in your speech, you'll need to convince your listeners that you are an expert in your field, that you speak with authority, that you are pleased to have the opportunity to address them, and that you won't be "boring them to death."

When you go before an audience, it will be aware of your intellectual prowess, your face, your appearance, your manner, your voice, and your message. These are all-powerful tools for you to use effectively. Blend them all together into one smooth performance.

Your audience wants you to look the part. It wants to have confidence in you. It wants to trust and believe in you. Things happen between you and your audience when you communicate self-confidence and composure, and when you have a single, overriding objective.

Be prepared to be sensitive to the reactions to your speech. Will you engender rapt attention, or will your listeners tune you out because they cannot understand you? Plan to maintain eye contact throughout the room as you communicate your message. Strive not to speak up to them or down to them—strive to speak *with* them. You should let your listeners know that you know who they are, where they are coming from, and that you will not waste their time.

Even though you are a spellbinding speaker, there will always be a few people in your audience you cannot reach. Plan to ignore them, and concentrate on the ones who are listening to you attentively.

You should strive to keep your listeners alert and aware of your train of thought. Never keep talking just because you haven't finished your text. When you realize you are losing your audience's attention, plan to shift your gears, shorten your remarks to the bare essentials, and move on to your close.

If your forte is question and answer—and you feel that this format shows you in your best light—you may on occasion want to shorten your speech and allow more time for questions. Capitalize on situations in which you are the most comfortable and capable.

After your speech, if the audience crowds around you and asks you meaningful questions, you will know that you were a real success and that all of that preparation was well worth the effort.

## A Word about Professional Speech Writers

Busy professional people frequently do not have time to write all of their own speeches and are dependent on others to do the writing for them, or at least the first draft. You may assign the task to a member of your staff, or you may consider hiring a professional speech writer.

As you are going about the process of choosing a speech writer, keep in mind that there are quite a few bad or inexperienced speech writers out there. Don't be afraid to ask to see several sample speeches from those you are considering.

Look for a good writer with whom you can feel compatible. You need a person who knows your field, something about you and your past accomplishments, and is capable of conducting accurate research. Your speech writer should also be someone who can keep your confidences.

As you work with your writer, he or she will learn to adapt the construction of the speech to your style of delivery—even to leaving out words you do not like to pronounce.

Once the first draft of the speech is completed, you can both go over it, making suggestions for possible changes and improvements. The speech must not carry the mark of the writer, but, rather, of you, the speaker. You must eventually make the speech your own, getting away from the written text as much as possible. The open and close, particularly, must be in your own words.

The speech writer should hear you deliver the finished speech, and, from that, find ways to improve subsequent efforts. The speech writer can thus adapt to your own individual speaking style and manner.

## GIVING YOUR SPEECH

### Being Introduced

Listen carefully to what is said about you as you are being introduced so that you can make an appropriate response.

You have already double-checked to be sure that your host has your correct name and title, knows how to pronounce your name, and knows the subject or title of your speech.

Acknowledge the introduction graciously, and know in advance what your introductory remarks will be. Say something personal in your response, using the name of your host and recognizing the identity of your audience. Let your introduction establish a bond with your audience that you will maintain throughout your presentation.

## Pause before You Speak

In a previous section under practicing your speech, we discussed pauses *within* your speech. This section concerns another important type of pause—pausing *before* you speak.

Before you say your first word, always pause for a second of silence. You can simply say to yourself "one" silently. The word "one," which contains a vowel pronounced in the back of the mouth, requires you to naturally open the back of your throat.

By ending the pause with this silent "one," you are assured that your first sentence won't come out of a tense nasal passage, high in your vocal range. The glide-sound "w," when combined with the open throat, becomes "wuh." Saying this sound silently puts space between your upper and lower teeth for easy articulation. Your first words come out correctly placed, low in your vocal range.

Practice this silent pause and make it your own. That beginning pause noticeably quiets the audience with expectation. It makes you look authoritative and confident, like you are in control and know what you are doing.

The pause also allows you a few seconds of silence during which you can gain the attention of people rattling coffee cups or chatting with their table companions.

After the pause, even if your first words are simply "Good evening, ladies and gentlemen," you have made a positive start, which is sometimes the hardest part of making a speech. From then on, concentrate on your message.

## Oral Emphasis

You can place emphasis on any of the many elements in your speech, such as the most interesting point, the apex of your thinking, your major conclusions, or your new ideas for the future. What you decide to emphasize should be the main points that you want your audience to remember.

Once you have decided what should be emphasized, bring all of your speechmaking skills into play. Use resonance, pauses, candor, intonation, pitch, or volume to highlight your text.

Sentences, too, each have a point of emphasis. You stress the important word or words and throw away or subordinate the unimportant ones. Typical throw-away words are articles, conjunctions, or prepositions. This emphasis adds variety to your delivery. Monotony results when all the words in a sentence are given equal emphasis.

You can change the meaning of any sentence simply by choosing which words you want to emphasize. For example, the following is a nonsense sentence, with each word in turn emphasized to change the meaning. The sentence is given first, followed by the meaning of that particular emphasis:

- "I will go to the well," means what it says.
- "*I* will go to the well," means I will go, not you.
- "I *will* go to the well," means I will go in the future.
- "I will *go* to the well," means I will go, not stay here.
- "I will go to *the* well," means I will go to that one particular well.
- "I will go to the *well*," means I will go the well, not the pump.

By putting a short pause before and after the emphasized word and by using resonance from the chest, the meaning of each word in the sentence is changed. You use the same technique in emphasizing a thought, a sentence, or a significant point in your speech.

You sort out the meaning of your message for your listeners. You decide what you want them to hear, to remember, and to understand. *You* decide where the emphasis will be.

## Your Posture

Be aware of your posture at all times, whether you are walking, sitting, or standing. Basic good posture involves centering your body and holding yourself erect with your head up.

Walk to the podium or the front of the stage with authority, pressing your heels into the floor and stretching your body to its full height. Keep your neck long, your head high, and your jaw level with the floor. Breathe deeply to keep the oxygen supply high. But don't walk in a stiff, artificial, or awkward manner; concentrate on presenting a relaxed picture.

Adjust the podium mike to your height.

If you are short, you should stand slightly to one side of a podium that is too tall for you. Or to raise your height while standing, carry a sturdy, small, metal suitcase, and place it unobtrusively behind the podium. It is important for your audience to see you at all times.

Place your notepad on the podium but do not touch it, put your hands on it, or lean on it. When you lean on a podium, it breaks the body line and wrinkles the sleeves of your jacket. It also diminishes your ability to breathe from the diaphragmatic muscle. Remember, you need to be free to breathe out of the small of your back and to gain resonance in your chest by "talking out of your heels," so to speak. This flattens the tummy and lifts the rib cage.

If you sit at a desk or table during your presentation, put your notes on the table but, again, do not lean on it with your hands placed forward. Even seated, you should support and center your body by pressing your heels into the floor. Keep your hands off the table so that they are not seen in the foreground of the picture you are presenting with your body: Your face is more important than your hands. Even if everyone else who is on a panel with you leans on the table with their hands placed forward, you should be the one to use erect and correct (but relaxed) posture.

If you are sitting in a chair—with or without a table or desk in front of you—do not cross your legs with your hands forward on your knees. This makes the hands too conspicuous and eliminates your ability to breathe and speak freely. Sit slightly forward in the chair, ignoring the back and the arms, set your legs backward, and press your heels into the floor.

Occasionally you may have to sit in an upholstered chair that tends to swallow you completely. In such a case, sit on the edge of the seat and lean slightly forward. Try crossing your legs at the ankles, balancing the weight of your body with one foot. See how this looks in front of a mirror.

If you are a short person, you can raise your height while sitting by using a cushion that you carry around with you inside a soft briefcase. If needed, you can sit unobtrusively on the briefcase.

The lifelong habit of crossing your legs while seated is very strong. Even though many successful public persons unconsciously do it, it is not good posture.

## Your Own Space

When you are at the podium, there is a certain amount of space that you will occupy during your public appearance. Take a mental reading of the parameters of that space. Think of it as a platform upon which you firmly stand. Think of it as a little haven, a secure place in which you can relax and from which you will deliver your message.

Keep your body movements and gestures within that visual space. Regard that space as protective, and feel at home as you occupy it.

## Body Language

Your body language is very revealing. It says things about you that you can't tell consciously. Your body has an unspoken language of its own, quite independent of what you say.

When you are relaxed and in control, you transmit that feeling of well-being to your audience. When you are under visible stress and ill at ease, the audience wonders why you are up there on the platform.

Your body language can make you appear receptive toward your audience, or it can make you appear hostile. Observe the body language of the people at the speakers' table. Decide how each one of them is reacting to the current speaker. Watch the body language of the group when it does not agree with the speaker. Notice the enthusiasm when an audience genuinely likes the speaker and his or her message. Let your body language indicate that you are sensitive to your own audience.

When you cross your arms, jut out your jaw, and sit rigid and straight-backed, your body is saying "stay away." When you sit relaxed yet erect, arms and legs at ease and leaning slightly forward, your body is communicating openness. When you appear anxious and distant, your body is putting space between you and another individual. You tend to stand close to your friends and increase the space between you and a formal acquaintance or a stranger.

As you make your speech, study the body language of the members of your audience. Are they tuning you out, just waiting for you to be through—or are they listening with rapt attention? Establish yourself as a caring person. Make your attitude say, "I care about you; I am sensitive to your feelings." As mentioned previously, good eye contact will also help you to send out this message.

When you are standing, learn to stand still. It is one of the most difficult lessons to learn. When you are self-conscious about every movement—when you worry about what your arms and legs are doing—you transmit uneasiness and lack of control. Pare your physical movements down to the minimum.

### *Upward-Turning Versus Downward-Turning Body Language.*
Everything about your body language should be angled upward, not downward.

Imagine two football coaches after an important game. The loser has his head bowed, his eyes downcast, and his body slumped over—frustration, disappointment, and anger etched in every line. Beside him stands the winning coach, with face turned upward, a big smile, arms outstretched, body erect—joy, self-confidence, and exuberance written in every line.

This may be an extreme case, but you need to adapt your platform stance to the same principle of being positive instead of negative, of being pleasant instead of grim.

Performers are constantly being reminded to look upward into the light, to smile instead of frown, and to look like they are enjoying themselves. One reason for this is that all lights cast downward shadows, especially under the eyes and around any wrinkles near the mouth. Thus, when you see your picture, you may think that you looked "old and mean." These distortions must be taken into consideration, whether the light is outdoor available light, or high-mounted studio or platform lights.

Practice looking pleasant in front of the bathroom mirror. Raise the eyebrows slightly, part the lips, keep the chin up level with the floor—generally, everything upward-turning.

**Summary of Good and Bad Body Language.** Good body language includes the following advice:

- Look like a winner with head erect, a slight smile, eyes upward
- Extend your body fully
- Keep your hands at rest, loosely folded and relaxed
- Lean slightly forward when someone speaks to you
- Light up your facial expression
- Turn everything upward
- Be always "at the ready" and alert
- Maintain a high energy level
- "Embrace" your audience

To avoid bad body language, don't do any of the following:

- Look like a loser, slouching, frowning, head and eyes downcast
- Slump backward with your legs crossed
- Wring your hands nervously
- Ignore the people around you
- Look indifferent or grim

- Look downward
- Fidget with a pencil, pen, or your glasses
- Tap your foot or swing a leg rhythmically
- Look into space, look bored, or squirm
- Toss your hair, brush it back, or constantly move it out of your eyes
- Yawn, chew gum, or chew on your lower lip
- Scratch anything
- Repel and reject your audience

## Gestures

Gestures serve to emphasize the meaning that you wish to transmit to your audience. Your gestures should be natural and effective. They should enhance your message, clarify your meaning, or emphasize an important point. You can use gestures to express a mood or an emotion—anger, for example, or impatience, or indifference. A gesture made during a silent pause in your speech can be more powerful than words.

You must feel at ease with your gestures and trust your natural instincts. To improve your effective use of gestures, start by studying your own spontaneous hand movements. You can then work to refine them into more professional expressions of your meaning. But always keep your gestures simple and restrained.

The closed fist expresses hostility, while the open palm expresses welcoming openness. Arms folded across the chest close out the observer, while outstretched arms invite the observer in.

Eliminate unnecessary and distracting nongesture mannerisms, since they tend to be magnified in public. (Examples include flicking a finger against a fingernail, drumming fingers, combing your beard with your fingers, playing with your hair, rubbing your forehead, and cracking your knuckles.) A small, often unnoticed habit may become distracting or irritating.

In public, gestures are confined to a fairly clearly defined framework. At the podium, you should concentrate on confining your gestures to the space between your chin and chest. When you bring the hands too high, they obscure your face and denote tension. Low gestures are lost to view and tend to be "downers" instead of "uppers." Chest-high gestures are best because they transmit strength, quiet authority, and assurance. To touch your face, your hair, or your body looks self-conscious and uncertain.

Try to keep the elbows close to the body. When not using your hands, keep them out of sight—at your sides or quietly folded. Do not become self-conscious about what to do with your hands. Let your gestures come naturally, growing logically from the meaning of your presentation.

Practice before a mirror or a friend. If possible, look at video tapes of your performance to discover what you really do with your gestures and body language. You may see something that you don't like, since the camera is very revealing, but this will help you in the end. By striving for good taste, simplicity, and restraint in your use of gestures, you will find that they will become a natural part of your public presence.

## Eye Contact

When you establish eye contact with your listener, you create a bond of communication. You can establish eye contact in many different ways and in many different circumstances. When you are introduced to a person, you do not look him in the necktie, you look him straight in the eye. It is even possible to establish eye contact with the people surrounding you in a crowded room. As a public person, you can scan the room, decide that these people are your friends, and that you personally communicate with each one using eye contact.

During a prolonged conversation, you should vary the technique by occasionally looking away to break eye contact or by looking in first the right eye, then the left. You can tell when you are communicating with a person by the look in the eyes, and you can also tell when he or she has tuned you out and is no longer listening to you. The person who never looks you in the eye appears to have something to hide.

When speaking to a large audience, slowly move your eyes from person to person, moving from the left side of the room to the right. Then, look from the front to the back. During the course of your speech, everyone in the audience will feel that she or he has been included. Those in the last row in the balcony will not be able to see your eyes, but they will know that you have included them in your glance by your head movements.

## Taking Questions

Finish your speech before you take questions. You break the thought pattern and momentum of your speech if you have to pause to take questions from the audience. If someone raises his hand or asks a question before your speech is done, acknowledge the interruption with a nod and simply say, "I'll be happy to take your questions at the end of my speech."

When you do take questions, listen carefully to them, and give thoughtful answers. Good questions give you an opportunity to reemphasize your basic premise and to gauge the receptivity of your listeners.

Do not hesitate to say that you do not know the answer to a difficult or irrelevant question. Gently disagree with a false premise. Answer obviously hostile questions calmly or with mild humor.

At the appropriate time, terminate the questioning in a polite yet decisive manner, thanking your audience with a smile.

## Coping with the Unexpected

The more speeches you give, the more you realize that something can always go wrong. You will frequently be faced with an unexpected situation. Your audience will judge you by and react to the manner in which you handle the emergency.

At all times, keep your composure and stay in control of the situation as you decisively solve the problem. It is useless to show anger, resentment, or blame someone. Philosophically accept the unexpected, even as you are devising a solution.

Among the things that can happen are: Film or tapes can be erased or lost, microphones can develop odd noises, a baby can cry loudly, or, if you are outdoors, an airplane can fly overhead and drown out your words, or a motorcycle can roar down the street just at a critical moment. Be prepared to accept such happenings with good grace and patience.

Several typical situations you may have to cope with are discussed below, along with suggestions on what to do about them:

***The microphone goes dead just before you start your speech.*** After the audio person has made his or her last panic-stricken but futile efforts to get the mike working, simply indicate that you can get along without it. Move off the platform, down closer to the front of your audience, and ask everyone to move up close around you to fill up the seats in front. Smile. Keep in control of the situation. Deliver your remarks in a more personal, conversational way, perhaps even taking off your jacket or sitting down. Project your voice so that the people in the back rows can hear you clearly. (Actors can do it; so can you.) Keep steady eye contact with your listeners, talk to them one-on-one, and you may just have turned a potential disaster into a personal triumph.

***Your mouth becomes dry and you feel like you cannot say a word.*** This condition is caused by tension that constricts and tightens up the throat. To alleviate it, drop your jaw and rub the underside of the tongue against the inside of the lower and upper front teeth. This activates the lubricating saliva glands, relaxing the back of the throat and giving you the moisture you need in your mouth. Sipping water will also help.

***Your plane is grounded by weather and you may arrive late. Or you have just been bumped from your flight.*** Go to the nearest phone and call every relevant phone number you have. Keep calm, reminding yourself that none of this is your fault and you are doing everything you can to alleviate the situation. When you do arrive, there is no need to apologize, since your audience will have been informed about your delay. Thank the audience for its patience and proceed to deliver your speech as though nothing had happened. If you deem it appropriate, make a joke about airline delays (leaving out the name of the airline in question, of course).

***Your host mispronounces your name or the name of your company or gives your title incorrectly.*** Set the record straight with gentle good humor (if possible) and obvious good will in a way that will not offend your host. But don't let it pass uncorrected.

***When you arrive at the site, you learn that you have five minutes instead of the twenty that you were promised for your remarks.*** Quickly shuffle your notes. Include the opening and close that you intended to use. Select your most important points, streamlining your remarks about each one. Betray no visible discomfort. A short speech is good, and you may not only surprise yourself, but find that you have a new shorter version of your standard speech that can stand you in good stead later.

***The air conditioning has gone off in a hot, crowded room.*** Take off your jacket and invite your listeners to do the same. If there are windows in the room, ask someone to open them.

*The audience turns hostile, or pickets disrupt your speech.*
Remain calm and authoritative. Answer all questions in a straightforward manner. Wait patiently while the police or security handle the disruption. Judiciously shorten your presentation if necessary.

*You are the last speaker at the end of a long, tedious evening.*
Gauge the mood and level of fatigue of your listeners. They may be exhausted by four previous, long-winded speakers. When your turn comes, say or do something to wake them up (such as inviting them to stand up and stretch for thirty seconds, or pacing around on the stage to get some energy into your remarks, or telling one very good joke, or informing them that "they can wake up now—it's *almost* time to go home"). Then, be mercifully brief. They will probably remember your remarks better than those of the other speakers.

*You have been shaking hands all day and now, after your speech, you are faced with another roomful of people.* Shaking hands can be strenuous. Learn how to wear no rings on the inside fingers to avoid becoming hurt by people who want to give your hand an enthusiastic squeeze. Political candidates have been known to suffer tendonitis, tennis elbow, and slight sprains from nonstop handshaking. You can avoid handshaking by keeping your right hand behind your back, or lightly touching the well-wisher's elbow or arm before the hand is offered to shake.

## Other Types of Problems

If a different sort of problem occurs that is the fault of the sponsors of the event or their support staff (such as there is no slide projector; too many tickets were given out and standees are noisily milling around in the back of the room; you weren't told that you were expected to debate your arch enemy on the platform; or the press has been banned from your speech when you were told that it would be admitted), be gracious about the situation both during the time you are on the platform and in private afterward when speaking to your hosts.

Once you have established yourself as a "difficult" person, it is hard to shake such a reputation. It is best to simply state what displeased you (privately, after your speech) to those involved, but in a calm, noncritical way, ending with a statement such as, "I can well understand how such a thing can happen. I hope you'll invite me to speak again, and next time I'm sure everything will be just great."

## A PRE-SPEECH CHECKLIST
## FOR OUT-OF-TOWN SPEECHES

A typical speech these days for many public people is a one-time, out-of-town speech where you arrive at the city the night before you will be delivering your speech. Such a speech may be for you to accept or present an award, to address a college graduation, to give a keynote address at the annual meeting of an association or other group, or to address a political or charitable group.

If this sounds like you, you may find the following checklist to be useful.

Unless you are exhausted from late-night travel from the day before, get up early the morning of your speech. Before you shower or eat breakfast, put on athletic shoes and comfortable exercise clothes that you brought with you, and do one of the following types of exercises, each constituting a different level of exertion:

1. *Light:* Put your hotel room key and wallet in your pocket and walk around the corridors of the hotel for at least ten minutes at a moderate-to-brisk pace. (Never mind the stares of others you may meet in the corridors.) This minimal amount of exercise will serve, at least, to wake you up; warm up and loosen up your muscles; and get your circulation going, your heart pumping, and extra oxygen to the brain.

2. *Moderate:* Do some simple stretching and breathing exercises in your room to warm up, then walk, jog, or walk-and-run around at least two or three blocks near the hotel. (Don't forget to cool down properly afterward.) This will give you all the benefits of light exercise with the additional benefits of getting some fresh air, invigorating you more, and giving you a sense of accomplishment when you are done.

3. *Vigorous:* If your normal schedule at home includes vigorous and/or regular exercise, inquire at the concierge desk of your hotel the night before if there is a health club in or near the hotel that you may use. If there is, spend twenty to thirty minutes in the club or pool doing whatever you would normally do. As an alternative, go for a good jog or run outside, again including your normal warm-up and cool-down routine. This activity will give you the feeling of well-being that you

usually get as a result of your exercise—a good thing to have on the morning of an important speech.

At this point, do not think about the *contents* of your speech. Instead, smile and enjoy the exercise period. Say to yourself, "I'm looking forward to giving this speech. It's going to go very well. I can't wait to get up there on the platform."

It goes without saying that you should check with your doctor before attempting any new exercise. But often, the doctors of even people who are overweight, elderly, or out of shape will allow them to do moderate walking exercise if they warm up and cool down properly.

If you smoke, try to cut way down on your normal morning smoking; better yet, try not to smoke until after your speech is over.

After your exercise, review—briefly—your speech's opening and close. Then, take a warm (not hot) shower or bath in the winter, or a tepid or cool one in the summer. While you are at it, wash your hair, scrub under your fingernails, and massage your feet.

Practice your opening and close aloud while you bathe or shower and get ready in front of the mirror. Smile. Try out different emphases of key phrases. Practice thanking your audience as you look in the mirror.

You should emerge from the bathroom feeling relaxed yet invigorated and in the best of moods, with little signs of tiredness or nervousness or stress lingering about you.

After dressing, make sure your personal appearance is at its best.

Eat a light but leisurely breakfast. To aid in your concentration, you may prefer to order in room service rather than going to the public restaurant. Breakfast tips:

- Try having milk or herbal tea instead of coffee.
- Avoid fatty meats or fried foods (no sausages).
- Include some whole-grain bread product, passing up the doughnut, Danish, or pastry.
- Eat a piece of raw fruit rather than drinking orange juice, which can get stomach acid churning.
- If the hotel food ends up tasting unsatisfactory, as is often the case, at least try to settle for some herbal tea, whole-wheat toast, and fruit.

Instead of reading the morning newspaper or talking with colleagues as you eat breakfast, go over the body of your speech in your mind and review our notes. At a minimum, memorize a key word or phrase for each major section of the speech, so that at least you have reviewed the order of the subjects it contains. This way, even though you may be mostly reading a typed speech or speaking off the cuff (with your cards only holding the opening, a list of subjects in their proper order, and the close), then you will still be able to change subjects with authority and without breaking the rhythm of your speech by fumbling around with what comes next.

One memory aid that you can use to help you to memorize the important points of your speech is to assign one point per finger. Then, once you are on the podium, you can use your fingers (unobtrusively, of course) to help you recall the order of points.

After you have finished breakfast, you will be all ready to go ahead and give a wonderful speech.

## BEING A SUBSTITUTE SPEAKER

It happens occasionally that the scheduled speaker for an event will be unable to give his or her speech. The speaker may have been called away on urgent business—to the White House on political business, to Moscow on diplomatic business, to Tokyo on economic business—or he may have suddenly taken ill, had a death in the family, been involved in a transportation accident, become stranded somewhere due to a hurricane, or whatever.

One has the impression that some people, from a variety of professions, could give an excellent speech to nearly any audience on a surprisingly wide variety of topics at the proverbial drop-of-a-hat's notice. A list of such people might include car manufacturing executive Lee Iacocca, politician and minister Reverend Jesse Jackson, former United Nations Ambassador Jeane Kirkpatrick, journalist/writer/TV news-show host William F. Buckley, Jr., singer Pearl Bailey, corporate genius Donald Trump, and publisher/businessman Malcolm Forbes.

Your name may not appear on such a list of luminaries, but, nevertheless, you may one day find yourself asked to be a last-minute substitute speaker. If you feel comfortable speaking before that particular audience, you should go ahead and accept such an invitation. It will be a good test of your speechmaking skills, and you may learn from the experience and even enjoy yourself.

Furthermore, like the understudy "whose star broke her leg and she got to go on and the rest is history," you may even step up one more rung on your professional ladder because you did so well. This may prove to be a valuable opportunity to enhance your reputation in your field.

## Preparation

The first thing to do under such circumstances is, of course, to find out as much as you can about the audience, your hosts, the site, transportation to and from the site, etc., exactly as you would for a regular speech.

After that, you should find out about the scheduled speaker: his or her name, title, and organization; the subject he or she was to speak on; if it would be possible to obtain a copy of his or her prepared speech for your reference; and a little about why he or she cannot make the speech.

The latter is a good thing to know since you might refer to the reason in an opening joke, if the circumstances of the cancelation are not unhappy. For example, transportation jokes and weather-related delay jokes can be shared by all and insult no one.

Next, you will prepare your speech. This preparation will, of course, involve several factors, such as how much preparation time you have (there is a huge difference between one evening and one week), how many previous speeches you have given on a similar or the same subject, how long you have to speak, and how experienced a speechmaker you are.

For example, if you are an expert on real estate investment or stock investments, and you have given similar speeches often on the subject, your job of preparing for this speech will be a simple one.

You may even be the kind of speaker who talks without notes or just with one small card tucked into your pocket or purse. If you always speak from notes, you may be able to do a quick edit or rewrite of a good speech that you have given recently elsewhere, and all you might need to do is add some updated statistics or refer to some recent happenings in your sphere of expertise, and—*voilà*—a new speech is born.

But what if you have been asked to speak on a subject closer to the one that was canceled, and it is somewhat more specialized or detailed or serious than the speeches you are used to delivering? Assuming you are knowledgeable enough about the subject to give the new speech, you might begin by making a list of all of the main points that should be covered; writing down a dynamic opening and close, and practicing them until you have them down pat; doing any additional research necessary for the body of the speech; and writing out the speech as much as there is time for.

A slight variation of this might be that you call back your hosts and explain that there simply will not be enough time for you to prepare thoroughly on the subject as they have suggested, but that you would like to select one aspect of the suggested subject and expand on it in detail in the speech. (Obviously, you would select an aspect with which you are well acquainted and one that will appeal to your particular audience.)

One other type of popular substitute speech is the quasi-humorous/quasi-serious speech given so well by such marvelous speakers as political analyst, writer, and *Washington Post* reporter Mark Shields, political humorist and pianist Mark Russell, and others.

Of course, this type of speech is not necessarily given just as a substitute speech—on the contrary, it is among the best kinds of speeches being given today—but it can also make an excellent last-minute, substitution speech. This is true because during this kind of speech you can use anecdotes and stories and jokes that have been included in other speeches (i.e., material that you are already familiar with and that you know will receive a good response from your audience). At the same time the tone of such a speech is by nature informal—you can take your coat off, walk around the platform, interact with the people in the front row, laugh at your own stories, and otherwise entertain the members of the audience instead of worrying about boring them or living up to the expectations of the speaker who canceled. The other speaker may be more famous than you and may, after all, have attracted the crowd in the first place.

In giving such a speech, the subject matter becomes less important in that more of your time will be spent telling stories or jokes than in giving statistics, and you would be able to spend less time preparing the speech.

## Giving Your Speech

Once you have decided on what type of speech you are going to give and have prepared it as well as possible in the time allotted, you are ready to go to the speech site. If you have stage fright or are nervous for any reason—you may be substituting for a very famous person or will shortly be addressing the largest or most important crowd of your life—then give yourself extra time to arrive so that you will have time to relax at the site.

Before the ceremonies begin, ask to speak with the person who will be introducing you to find out: (1) if your name and the subject of your speech got printed in the program that was handed out, or if the name and the subject of the first canceled speaker appears in it; (2) what percentage of the audience, if any, knows that you are to speak instead of the other speaker; and (3) if that person introducing you will mention the name of the canceled speaker or if you should refer to the canceled speaker.

In this way, there will be no confusion, surprise, or seeming disorganization up there on the platform when references to the canceled speaker are made. It is important that any such references be made smoothly and with taste so that the audience does not sense anything is amiss.

Probably the toughest situations to handle are: No one in the audience knows that you will be speaking instead of the scheduled speaker; all printed materials such as posters and programs mention the canceled speaker and not you; the other speaker was well known and many people in the audience came just to hear him or her and would not otherwise have attended the function; the scheduled speaker canceled because of some personal tragedy.

If you have to face such a situation, get past the introductions as gracefully and with as much dignity as possible. Use humor in your opening remarks (if appropriate) to get the audience members to laugh, loosen up, and be on your side so that they will pay attention to you and forget that you are a substitute. Once past your first couple of sentences, launch into your speech with energy and a pleasant, relaxed demeanor. Your audience will soon forget all about the other speaker.

When an opening joke about the absence of the other speaker is appropriate, don't hesitate to think up something clever in advance and practice it over and over before your speech so that you can say it on the platform without awkwardness.

About five years ago, I attended a meeting of businessmen where the scheduled speaker was one of those jet set, international financiers. The substitute speaker began by saying, "Mr. _____ will not be speaking today—he was called suddenly to Zurich . . . seems that he got a telegram that said something about there being a mix-up between a winning lottery number and the numbers of one of his Swiss bank accounts." This was an off-the-wall joke, but it relaxed the members of the audience, some of whom were still chuckling about it when the speaker was well into the more serious body of his speech.

Once you have completed your speech, take an extra few minutes to linger near the platform, allowing members of the audience to come up and congratulate you or ask questions. That way, you will feel even better about your speech and will gain even more confidence for the next time that you are asked to be a substitute speaker.

## A Sample Opening

Let's close this section by quoting the opening remarks of another substitute speaker that I heard last year at a medium-size meeting of a local businessperson's group.

The original speaker was a fairly well-known investment counselor and CPA; the substitute speaker was a man well-known for his humor who had been asked to give the speech with only a couple of days' notice. I'm quoting him at length because he did such a good job, and it might give you some ideas for your own speeches given under similar circumstances.

After being introduced, this is (very roughly) how it went:

"Well, well, well," he began, grinning and surveying the audience slowly from left to right. "So here we all are. Except that *you* are down there and *I* am up here, and believe me, I'd rather that it was vice versa. . . . When they asked me to speak here on a couple of hours' notice, I asked them if they minded if I gave a speech that I had given before, and they said, 'No, of course not,' so I brought along this speech that I gave to the Auxiliary of the Ladies' Garden Club of Hackensack, New Jersey. . . ." He paused for a laugh and pulled out a small stack of 3"X5" cards. "Or was it the Auxiliary of the Men's Garden Club? . . . . I forget.

"Anyway, I'm sure you'll give a collective sigh of relief. . . ." He paused and motioned with the cards for the audience to give their impromptu version of a collective sigh of relief, then tossed the cards behind him as he said, ". . . When I tell you that I have decided against giving that speech today.

"Instead, I'm going to give you *this* speech . . ." He pulled out a neatly folded packet of accordion-pleated computer printer paper, which he slowly and carefully unfolded, then held it by the top edge, letting the rest of the paper drop several feet to the ground. He paused for a short laugh, looked pointedly at the audience, and tossed that paper behind him. Finally, he said, "Actually, instead of that one, I'm going to read you the last thirty years of baseball scores . . . without the team names, so that you can guess them. . . .

"But seriously, I think I will speak to you today about _____. Okay?" At this point he launched into his real speech, which was actually a serious one. But long before he began his real speech, he had the audience attentive, relaxed, and in his pocket, having long since forgotten about the originally scheduled speaker.

## A SPEECH TO REMEMBER

I was a young woman during the dark days just before and during World War II. Americans, along with millions of other Allies, huddled close to their radios, listening half with dread and half with hope to the news as the storm clouds gathered in Europe and then broke over the world.

Many famous speeches were given before, during, and immediately after the war, and many famous phrases came out of those speeches.

For example, we remember what Franklin Delano Roosevelt said during his first inaugural address in 1933: "The only thing we have to fear is fear itself."

Later this beloved president would become famous for his radio broadcasts that came to be called "fireside chats."

He used simple, honest sentences in his speeches that everyone could relate to. They were simple, but memorable. Also he delivered his speeches in his own unique way, effectively using a slow pace and pauses.

But another voice from another continent also remains vivid in my memory. It happened in the late 1930s and the early 1940s at a time when Hitler's power had been growing rapidly and the entire world was watching to see what he would say and do next.

England declared war on Germany on September 3, 1939. Winston Churchill was appointed to his old post in charge of the Navy. When the Germans invaded the Low Countries on May 10, 1940, the English prime minister Neville Chamberlain resigned, and Churchill became prime minister.

Churchill knew the magnitude of what he was facing as a leader of a fearful yet brave people. And his speeches in those early days in office were eagerly listened to not only by the English, but by millions living in many countries. He spoke before the House of Commons for the first time as prime minister on May 13, 1940. Afterward, his words were rebroadcast again and again around the world. Why? Because it was in that speech that he said, "I have nothing to offer but blood, toil, tears, and sweat"—words that rang out proudly and to many became a symbol of hope.

It was through such words as these that Churchill helped to rally the British people, to help them resist giving up hope despite the bad years that were to follow. The positive effect on the Allies from that single, seemingly simple speech was incalculable. Englishmen claim that that speech helped to stiffen the backbone of a threatened nation.

You may never know what effect something that you say in public will have on your listeners. Probably Churchill himself, at the time that he uttered those words, did not know the effect that they would have on the Allies.

But when you write and then give your speeches, you should strive to have an effect on your listeners. Some of them may just remember your speech long after you have forgotten it.

# FOUR

# HANDLING
# THE MEDIA

E ver since the first newspaper sent out its first reporter to get a story, members of the press have followed and observed and tried to get news from public figures. And since that time, public figures have had to learn to deal with the media one way or another—by learning to hide well, run fast, evade questions, lie convincingly, tell too much, or, if they're real pros, tell just enough to satisfy that press person so he or she will *go away*.

Some reporters are better at this game than others. And some public figures are better at it than others, too.

The best illustration of this I can think of involves two men—one on either side of the fence—both of whom are very good at fulfilling their respective roles.

On one side is longtime ABC White House correspondent Sam Donaldson, who is famous for his incredibly pointed and usually unwelcome questions to several U.S. presidents. Mr. Donaldson recently left the White House beat, but during his years there he loved to shout his questions out anytime, anywhere, such as after a photo opportunity in the Rose Garden. On the other side is former President Ronald Reagan, a man who, above all, is a master at handling reporters.

A rumor once floated around Washington regarding Mr. Donaldson's habit of shouting questions at the president across a certain stretch of White House lawn as he got off the helicopter after a weekend trip to Camp David. It was said that Mr. Reagan would often ask his pilot to rev up the engine when he saw Mr. Donaldson to drown out his shouted questions, most of which began, "Mr. President! Mr. President! Is it true that you . . . ?"

Maybe Mr. Reagan never exactly ordered the motor to be revved up. Or maybe he did—to drown out not only Mr. Donaldson, but all the reporters who stood there in a hungry pack at the end of most weekends.

Whatever the truth is, there was Mr. Donaldson doing what he did so well, trying to get a story or a quote; and there was Mr. Reagan doing what he did so well, handling the press on his own terms.

## A TWO-WAY STREET

You and the media need each other. You need them for those times when you want to disseminate accurate information. The press media need you as a news source. As a result, in your public life, you should always strive to have the best possible relations with the members of the press as well as the news-gathering organizations they represent.

You may have a love-hate relationship with the press. Members of the press may infiltrate your staff, misquote you, publish inaccuracies about you, or even damage your reputation. In turn, you may deliberately withhold vital information that reporters covet.

The press may follow you around and pry into your personal life both past and present or ask you questions that you may feel are insulting or none of its business.

Roughly since the time of Richard Nixon's presidency and the Watergate affair, members of the press have indeed been prying more and more into the personal lives and past behaviors of political candidates and incumbents.

The press seems to have become much more powerful in recent years and, as a consequence, more feared by public figures. Some members of the public seem to feel that every detail of the private life of a well-known person, particularly a candidate, is fair game for investigation and should be known to the public or the voter, no matter what is revealed or by what means it was investigated. Others feel that, these days, the press is going too far—a prime example of which might be the newspaper reporters who staked out presidential-hopeful Gary Hart at his townhouse one fateful night.

Don't think that just because you are not a political candidate you are safe from the scrutiny of the press. Increasingly, other types of public figures—from computer hackers to socialites, athletes to nominees for the Supreme Court, Wall Street wizards to several televangelists—have become the subjects of intense press investigations.

For that reason, you must always strive for a positive relationship with the media. You and your public relations people must have a media policy that works for both of you. For example, you should try to respond promptly to inquiries (since all members of the press have deadlines) and seek opportunities to give the media material they need. Above all, you have to be truthful, and yet carefully disclose only the information deemed necessary. Cooperate in every way possible without doing damage to yourself. If the press publishes a story concerning you that is dead wrong, you should release accurate information to counter the story as soon as possible so that a correction can be made without delay and while the incident is fresh in the public's mind.

Effective use of the media enables you to potentially reach millions of people who otherwise might not hear what you have to say. When you are being interviewed or quoted or a sound bite of something you said is used on the evening news, you are, in a sense, using the media. This is true whether your goal is to win votes, sell your new book, raise money for charity, defend your reputation or point of view, widen your reputation among your business or professional peers, get new clients, become better known as an expert or analyst on a specialized subject, or simply to tell the world about a new product, event, or artistic or scientific accomplishment. In other words, every time you deal with the media, you are being provided with a golden opportunity to say what you want to say.

As a "mediagenic" person, you will find yourself entering an array of media situations, not all of which directly involve reporters or members of the press. You will use your communication skills to cope with both the expected and the unexpected.

Here are some of the situations in which you may find yourself:

- Making a speech
- Participating in a press conference
- Presiding at a club or other kind of group meeting

- Teaching a course
- Moderating or serving as a member of a panel
- Being interviewed by a reporter—for newspaper, newsletter, magazine, TV, or radio
- Conducting a seminar
- Debating a current vital issue
- Conducting a tour
- Making a face-to-face confrontation
- Announcing your candidacy for public office
- Acting as a spokesperson for a VIP client as his or her attorney, physician, etc.
- Having a very important telephone conversation, such as making a business deal or talking an important person into doing something (giving you a job, donating money, or endorsing your new book)
- Participating in a video teleconference; participating in a two-way audio conference
- Canvassing for charity
- Doing a thirty-second sound bite
- Appearing on a radio or TV program as a guest
- Being the keynote speaker at an important affair or introducing the keynote speaker at an important affair
- Testifying before a congressional subcommittee
- Answering hostile questions
- Being "ambushed" by a reporter with a hand mike
- Reading a formal statement, even in the middle of a crisis or a natural disaster
- Gracefully thanking employees or supporters

Thus, in many of the above situations, while you may not be dealing directly with the media, what you are doing is often being observed by members of the public and can therefore end up the business of a reporter as well.

This chapter will help you to feel comfortable in a wide variety of media-related situations. Most types of media situations are included in this chapter, with the exception of TV studio appearances, which are covered separately in the following chapter, "Appearing on Television." (Note, however, that a few TV-related situations such as teleconferences are included in this chapter.)

# THE PRESS CONFERENCE

As a public person, you may be called upon to participate in press conferences, of which there are many different types in these days of instant news. You may be announcing your candidacy for public office, explaining a medical breakthrough, or speaking to the press in the aftermath of a national disaster.

Nearly every entity that exists today gives press conferences—from museums and zoos to NASA. Businesses now hold press conferences for a variety of reasons, including to announce: a new product or service; a merger; a sale or acquisition of a subsidiary enterprise; a patent on a new drug or chemical or manufacturing process; or the opening of a new plant or closing of an old one.

A company may call a press conference to defend or explain something—often a negative situation—such as pollution, an explosion, a product named "unsafe" by a consumer group, nonpayment of taxes, a legal suit, a strike by workers, or a group picketing headquarters for whatever reason.

Governments, too, routinely give press conferences. City governments, for example, may schedule them to allow the mayor to: field questions from the press; explain why the police chief is quitting after one year on the job or why the students' test scores are so high this year; announce a new employee policy; invite the press to tour a new library or hospital; or discuss crime statistics.

Celebrities such as actors, athletes, and authors hold their own press conferences to explain their divorces, scrapes with the law, libel suits, fights with press photographers, or anything else that they want to give their side of to the press.

When dealing with reporters, remember that they have been assigned by their editors to bring back some solid information. Television reporters need to tape a brief sound bite that can be used, perhaps, on that evening's news. Radio reporters may be attending your press conference only for background information or a quote; or they may ask you afterward to do an interview or come to the studio to appear on a talk show. Print journalists may need background information from which to do a story or a column.

All reporters are after terrific, newsmaking, to-the-point quotations.

Prepare carefully for your press conference. Have a prepared statement that you can distribute and read over a microphone to the assembled press. In your statement, always present your most important points first. (Think of tomorrow's headlines.) After you have read or distributed your statement or press release, you can take questions from the reporters.

Anticipate the questions you will be asked, and rehearse your answers. Decide in advance the pertinent information you wish to impart or see in the next day's newspaper. Assume a leadership role, answering questions with authority and confidence. Also decide in advance what you are not going to say, and stick to your decision.

Gauge your audience and dress to fit the situation, using the style best suited to your message, whether it be formal or conversational. Whatever your style, keep your answers to questions smooth, credible, and brief.

Regard the press conference as an opportunity to inform the public of the truth. Honesty is sometimes painful, but the truth will inevitably emerge, so it is better to level with reporters from the very beginning. Remember you are seeking credibility, which is hard to earn and even harder to keep. Stubborn silence destroys public confidence and ends up having reporters seek other sources and delve deeply for hidden or potentially embarrassing revelations. Do not try to lie or misrepresent the facts.

Lying to the public or media simply doesn't work. When you stretch or distort the truth, it takes multiple statements to cover the falsehood. You just can't remember how to keep all of those false statements straight.

The public must trust you and believe in you. That trust cannot be abused or betrayed. The highly prized balance of faith and trust is fragile and must be nurtured and defended. Once that trust is lost, it is difficult to regain it.

Do not treat the reporters themselves with contempt—as though you think you can tell them anything you want and they will believe it. Do not attempt to put a "spin" on the truth for the sake of public relations. Do not assume that the public will buy double-talk because you think it is gullible; the public deserves and wants correct information.

Before your press conference begins, you should have decided what you want the press and the public to hear. Think in advance about a concise statement. Get your point across with few words. You might rehearse with a stopwatch and a tape recorder to determine how much you can say in ten, twenty, thirty, sixty, and ninety seconds. Literally write a telegram-type quotation in advance, so that the prepared statement will come to you when you need to remember it. Answer the questions directly and without hesitation. Define your strategy and avoid surprises.

If you are releasing a statement slated for the evening news, time your press conference so that reporters have time to attend, then get back to their stations in time to edit their material for the newscast. Timing is important.

It is customary after the formal part of a press conference for reporters to gather around the speaker or speakers. They want to ask their own questions and are seeking material for special articles or an individual sound bite for the evening news.

Presidential press conferences are very, very carefully prepared and rehearsed in advance. The staff maintains an up-to-date briefing book on all questions it anticipates the press might ask. The president has a seating chart for the regular, senior members of the press corps and may scan the room in advance on a closed-circuit television screen in order to become familiar with the press seating arrangements.


## THE PRESS KIT

Putting together a professional press kit is a real art. The kit is designed to accomplish a definite purpose, such as obtaining news coverage of a public event, generating interest in a project or a new product, or releasing pertinent information.

The overall look of your press kit is important, and the artwork and design have to be chosen carefully. Even the quality and color of the paper can make a difference.

The press kit might contain several of the following:

- A well-written press release on your official letterhead or printed on specially designed press release paper containing all pertinent information—who, what, when, where, why, and the "gee whiz" factor explaining why the reader should cover your event (or whatever else is revealed in the press release) and not throw it in the trash. Be sure to include a contact name (as in, "For more information, contact Fred Howe"), complete address (including suite number and zip code), and a daytime telephone number where that person can be reached. Also include a phrase at the top stating, "For release on _____" (the date you want your news released to the public).

- Biographical material.
- A list of photo opportunities for radio, TV, and other media.
- Black-and-white glossy photographs (not color photos—except for special subjects where color is deemed necessary) with captions (usually 5"X7" or 8"X10").
- Supplementary lists of key or specialized contact persons with names, addresses, and phone numbers.
- Press invitations or one-event press passes with instructions on parking, how to enter secured buildings, etc.
- Pamphlets stating your organization's goal, activities, and history.

All of this should be enclosed in an attractive cover. The type with two pockets inside is often used.

Some press kits are very serious and almost "stodgy" in appearance. Some are very forward looking, with zippy graphics, lots of color used in brochures and on the press releases, and modernistic logos, etc.

Other press kits that I have seen are original to the point of being clever, such as those that use objects—not just printed materials—to get your attention and make sure you will not throw the kit away unopened.

For example, I once saw a press kit from the Philippines when Imelda Marcos was the first lady during the 1970s. She was about to make an official visit to the United States, and the Philippine government sent out press kits enclosed in handmade baskets.

Another unusual press kit that I saw was sent out during the 1988 presidential campaign. It consisted of a colorful press release tucked into a shoebox sent out by a manufacturer of athletic gear and other types of clothing. The shoebox contained a pair of limited edition sneakers "dedicated to campaign '88," according to the press release. The shoes were red, white, and blue, of course, and on the tongue was printed "Exercise Your Right to Vote." On the anklebone-area of each shoe was space to put your choice of stickers (which came loose inside the shoebox) saying either "Vote for Bush" or "Vote for Dukakis."

Did the shoe company really have much to do with the campaign? Probably not. Usually a public relations firm comes up with such wild ideas, and the materials are sent out following approval of the client-manufacturer. Was it a clever press kit, a good promotion? Let's just say it was quite an attention-getter.

Of course, most businesses and nonprofit organizations send out more traditional, professional-looking press kits containing materials printed on high quality paper, using graphics and designs that are more conservative in appearance. Yet they, too, can be very eye-catching and successful.

Whatever style of press kit you or your organization sends out, it is a good idea to call your press contacts ahead, explaining what they will be receiving and verifying the correct name and address of the recipient. If the press kit is promoting a particular event, make a follow-up call about five days before to find out if it is listed in the media "day book" for coverage.

It goes without saying that your list of people to receive your press releases or complete press kit should be complete, up-to-date, and accurate. It never hurts to double-check that people's names are spelled correctly.

## YOUR RELATIONS WITH MEMBERS OF THE PRESS

Carefully develop a reputation with the press for being an authority in your field. Always have some accurate and dependable facts or figures at hand to give to the press on demand. Faithfully return press phone calls. Always have something ready to say in the fewest possible words.

Also, cultivate your relations with members of the press. For example, if you have a specialized area of expertise, seek out reporters with the same specialty or beat and get to know them. Once they know you and have your name in their "books"—and learn to trust what you have to say—they will come to regard you as a worthy news source and will turn to you when they need information.

### The Nature of Reporters

Reporters are required to make news. The nature of their business is that the bare facts alone may be dull. When the assignment editor sends a reporter out to cover you as a news source, that reporter must come back to the newsroom with something unique and interesting that will compete for space with other hard news items.

Reporters have to work extremely hard to get their byline printed or telecast. As a result, they ask tough and carefully crafted questions. Reporters are extremely persistent in their efforts; many will never take "no" for an answer. Some reporters work hard to establish a tough reputation and then strive to uphold that image.

I mentioned Sam Donaldson earlier as someone who has long been accused of being too abrasive, willing to do nearly anything to get his questions answered. Yet, if you met Mr. Donaldson at a party or other informal gathering, you would probably find him to be a warm and friendly guest, telling jokes with a keen sense of humor. You might very well ask yourself if this charming, relaxed, funny guy is the same man who seems to be pushy or disrespectful to the president of our country. Of course it is the same man. But when he's a reporter, he is the hardnosed reporter he was trained to be. Behind the scenes, he's quite different. Actually, Mr. Donaldson probably thoroughly enjoys his "bad boy" reputation and would tell you all about it with great relish.

Reporters normally have access to background material about you or the issue at hand. As a result, you have to be prepared as well, visualizing what you want that reporter to write about you or what the short sound bite will look and sound like on the TV news. You have to anticipate the meanest and most embarrassing questions the reporter could ask you. You cannot afford to get ruffled or angry.

Everyone has seen incidences where political candidates, actors, and other public figures have lost their composure when being asked pointed questions about members of their families, their sex lives, cheating in college, financial scandals, or other events from their pasts. Whether or not you think that such questions are an obvious invasion of privacy, reporters will continue to ask such questions, and those being questioned must do their best to prepare themselves to answer or fend off the questions without showing too much anger, surprise, or hurt.

When you are asked a loaded or skewed question, pause slightly before you answer to give yourself a chance to pick your words carefully. If need be, stall for a few seconds of time by repeating the reporter's question and commenting that "it is a significant problem," or something similar. Then give a carefully worded answer that you would like to see as tomorrow's headline.

Try to turn the media encounter to your advantage, and walk away feeling that they never laid a hand on you. You have to give an answer, you have to respond, you have to look the reporter in the eye and say something. Just try to say the right thing, even if it is only that you are sorry you won't be responding to that particular question at that particular time.

When you have perfected your media skills beforehand, when you know who you are and what is right for you, you can benefit from publicity. Do what you can to minimize exploitation and overexposure.

As I suggested, it pays to become acquainted with individual reporters and to get to know the ones who are most important to you. Lobbyists, public relations people, press secretaries, and the like make an effort to understand the backgrounds, style of reporting, and any possible prejudices of key reporters. Underneath, reporters have their own opinions, attitudes, likes, and dislikes. Professionally, they must try to sublimate these feelings and be impartial. However, there is evidence that they treat some public figures more kindly than others.

Some public persons have reporters as personal friends, invite them to their homes, and obviously enjoy a friendly press. Not only was President John F. Kennedy known for obtaining favorable reactions from the press, he was a man who enjoyed personal friendships with several reporters. Members of the press were often invited to participate in the Kennedy clan's famous touch-football games on Cape Cod.

Other public figures are habitually hostile and distrustful of the press, and their discomfort is obvious.

You don't have to cultivate a reporter to the extent that you become friends, but there is nothing wrong with having a pleasant "hallway acquaintanceship" with a number of reporters when you run into each other accidentally or at professional or social events.

## Answering Difficult Questions

Consider buying yourself a black looseleaf notebook in which to keep a record of the questions you are asked most frequently and to record some excellent, to-the-point answers that are thought out in advance. In the book, you can also record pertinent facts, figures, and dates concerning the topic you are addressing.

On the front page of the book, fill in the most critical questions a reporter could ask you. List the difficult, mean, hard questions first, the ones you dread, the ones that could have dire consequences if answered incorrectly. Also include questions that require technical data or complicated factual material. If necessary, write an index for the book in the front.

After each question, write a complete and careful answer. You may be an expert in your field, thoroughly familiar with your subject, but in the chaotic demands of the moment, you may not have a chance to think clearly and formulate careful answers. You can review your responses quickly—even in a taxi or an elevator—before an important confrontation with a reporter. Without such a notebook, you may make a misstatement or act hesitant, and on TV this can be disastrous.

Remember, the answers you write down in your briefing book should be formulated for the listener or the public viewer, rather than for the reporter. You are assembling key points that state your position, and you will find various ways to repeatedly include those key points in your message. Depending on the situation, you can make the same points in different ways, but they should remain in the finished article or broadcast.

CEOs, politicians, and other public figures are often asked the same questions in every city in which they speak. They need to give the same answers but couched in a different language.

Keep the material in your notebook up-to-date, including information from relevant clippings and current press articles. Your staff can be most helpful in spotting good additions to your book. Include useful statistics, quotes, and results of relevant studies or polls that support your position.

The material in your notebook can be reduced to fit into a book which you can carry in your pocket. You can refer to such a book en route to refresh your memory. You will be able to say unhesitatingly just what you want to say, and no more. You will radiate confidence and control because you know your subject thoroughly, and you will feel comfortable and relaxed with your responses.

## Showing Hostility to Others in Public

Be careful when you are criticizing an individual or a group in public or during a press conference. If your comments are later perceived by the press and public as too vitriolic or self-serving, your words could backfire on you. Later they may not remember what you said, but they may remember how "nasty" you were to that person or group.

I heard a man tell the following story on the radio recently. He was running for the U.S. Senate a few years ago and was way behind in the polls. Several weeks before the election, in a desperate attempt to lessen the gap, he began to criticize his opponent severely, even running very negative campaign ads. The attack on his opponent didn't work, however—he still lost by a sizable margin. On the radio, he noted that the attempt to discredit his opponent had not been worth it and had backfired on him. Years later, he is still trying to live down the reputation he gained as a nasty person, while his former opponent is enjoying himself in the Senate.

When you criticize or embarrass a colleague in public, you are sending a message about your own motives.

Likewise, a colleague who purposefully embarrasses you may be grandstanding, jealous, or in a status contest with you. Airing dirty linen or making false accusations should be avoided because of the adverse consequences for both parties. If it happens to you, try to remain calm and use humor in order to avoid showing your anger in public.

At times you can gracefully avoid public hostility by asking your adversary to discuss the matter with you in private or by issuing a public statement that gives the truth of the matter without criticizing your colleague back.

## THE NEWS MEDIA STAKEOUT

What if members of the press are camped outside your house, waiting for you to emerge? They may have come equipped with an amazing assortment of gear—lights, cameras, and amplifying devices. They may wait hours for you, the hapless newsmaker, to bolt through their ranks to the safety of your car.

It may seem as if they are living there day after day, exchanging food and newspapers, swapping stories, interviewing your neighbors, and snapping to attention whenever you open the door to let the dog out.

There are even stories about the subject of a stakeout bringing coffee and snacks outside to the reporters and film crews on cold winter nights, answering no questions, but helping to keep them warm and fed. This sort of thing is likely to happen on nights such as Christmas Eve and New Year's Eve. Reporters cringe when they are assigned to spend such holidays away from their families, out in the cold and the dark, but they often have to do just that to get the story in the morning edition of the paper or to get a video clip for the next morning's TV news.

Fairly recent examples of public figures undergoing the close scrutiny of a stakeout outside their personal residences include Colonel Oliver North, of the Iran-Contra Affair, and then-vice-presidential candidate Senator Dan Quayle.

When the media was staking out Colonel North's home during the Iran-Contra Affair, he was mobbed by reporters and camera crews as he drove up his driveway on the way to work each morning. His response was usually to look straight forward, car windows up, and drive right past. Occasionally, he would smile and wave. But he rarely *said* a word.

Soon after he was named a vice-presidential candidate, Dan Quayle became the subject of a stakeout outside his home. One morning, he found himself having to deal with shouted questions from reporters about his military record as he tried to take out the garbage. He gave a couple of joking replies before going back in his house.

The "clips" from these stakeout activities were seen on the nightly newscasts. How well these two men handled themselves in this situation was studied as closely as what they said.

If they aren't camped outside your home, reporters may have assembled their paraphernalia at a key exit near your office or a place you are visiting, or have gathered near your car or limousine. The press has been known to thunder in full cry in pursuit of a witness or celebrity. Or you may be surprised by a reporter who rounds a corner, pokes a microphone in your face, and demands a statement or asks the very question that you had hoped you could get through the day without being asked.

Determine in advance what the reporters want to know, why they are there, and the questions they will ask you—especially the very tough or unfair questions. Anticipate your response based on the advice of your legal advisers, consultants, or staff.

When you are the object of a stakeout or are being pursued by the press wherever you go, it is important, once again, that you keep in control of the situation. Once you have planned in advance what you intend to say, do just that and nothing more. Never say anything you did not intend to say.

Don't waste your breath complaining to the reporters about their following you. Don't be rude if you have nothing to say to them. Simply nod and say "hello" as you pass and keep on walking; or stop and politely say "I'm sorry, but I have no comment to make on that." In short, even though you may feel irritated or even angry inside about the situation, always strive to appear to be calm and in charge.

On the other hand, if you have information you wish the media to have, take advantage of the opportunity to give it to them.

# BECOMING A POLITICAL CANDIDATE

When you become a candidate for public office, you walk into the full glare of media publicity. The public wants to know everything about you. Reporters will interview your high school and college professors, your first girl friend, and your mother. They will look you up in the old yearbooks, find out that you had a big Adam's apple, that your ears stick out, and that you were voted "most likely to party to the grave." They will find out if you were showing abnormal signs of ambition or ego at age five, if you ever cheated on a test, or if your first husband did all of the cooking.

They will be interested if you grew up too rich or too poor, if you ever got arrested for punching somebody out or driving your car recklessly, if you have declared all of your income on your income tax forms, if you have thirty unpaid parking tickets, or if you are under the thumb of too many special-interest groups.

As a viable candidate, you have now moved from the background to center stage. It is important that you keep in mind that everything you do is fair game for the press. Your political opponents may try to destroy your political advantage using any possible means. Assume that everything you say and do (or have said and done in the past) could be a headline in tomorrow's paper.

If you have something major to hide, it is best not to enter the political arena at all, because you cannot count on anything remaining a secret. Anticipate that a long-past scandal will be dug up to force your withdrawal from the campaign. If a difficult situation does develop, be frank and honest up front and immediately try to defuse the dangerous situation as much as possible. Keep your private life very private, but be prepared for invasions of that privacy.

As a candidate, you will be facing a variety of media-oriented functions from the time you announce your candidacy until after the election-night celebration.

You may find yourself in some very interesting situations—speaking from atop a flatbed truck, climbing in and out of awkward vehicles, standing in front of a symbolic backdrop, or wearing a silly-looking gift hat or sweatshirt.

You will participate in small, medium, and large press conferences. You will speak at innumerable dinners, luncheons, and banquets, and possibly at barbecues, state fairs, local parades, and the like. You will eat the same awful dinner dozens of times and wonder if a certain caterer who is voting for your chief rival is following you around.

You may find yourself giving the same speech four times a day, each time to a slightly different audience. You will learn to tailor your remarks to the interests of each group without changing your basic position on the issues. In one place, you may be cheered; in the next, booed. Your emotional state will range from depression to elation.

During the campaign, you will be surrounded by a welter of advisers, consultants, pollsters, supporters, and fund raisers. You may wonder if you really need all of these people, and why you ever hired so-and-so. You may feel like you'll never have another minute of peace and privacy again.

Today's political candidate must spend an inordinate amount of time in fund-raising activities in order to mount a media blitz. Time on television and radio may increase as personal appearances and "press-the-flesh" encounters decrease. Indeed, the power of the media is such that a successful candidate may now appear less and less in public. The phrase "media permutation" means that an obscure challenger who uses the media effectively can become as well known as the incumbent he or she seeks to defeat.

As state governors, both Jimmy Carter and Michael Dukakis were relatively unknown when they became candidates for the presidency. Many voters heard about them for the first time through media reports. Certainly it can be said that the way the media works today—as an integral part of the American political process—contributed greatly to both of their candidacies.

Your media skills are a major key to a successful campaign. You must wear, say, and do the right thing. A pleasant, well-modulated, resonant speaking voice is a great asset. Debating experience, voice lessons, and practicing speaking in public may all help you to acquire vocal excellence. (See chapters two and three.) You will need a versatile, coordinated wardrobe. Your position on major issues, your campaign speeches, and your press releases must be well thought out and carefully crafted in advance.

Before you declare your candidacy, make any necessary changes in your appearance, speech habits, or body language. Once the campaign is under way, it is difficult to explain to the public and the press a change in hair style or color, a new beard, or sudden weight loss, speech lessons, or a facelift. Do such things early on, long before you become a visible part of the media.

As a rule, I'd say that any major changes in your appearance or other aspects of your public persona should be made about two years in advance for a Congressional seat, and four to six years for a Senate or gubernatorial seat. Other campaigns vary with the term of office.

I know a man who plans to run for the U.S. House of Representatives in a couple of years. He has *already* been advised to consider having his teeth fixed, shaving off his rather bushy mustache, and having the ubiquitous "uhs" in his speech eliminated. By the time the press takes a good look at him as a candidate, the public will only know this new version of him.

Similarly, the time to make a name change is not when you are about to announce your candidacy for public office. If your last name is long, difficult to pronounce, or seems to have more consonants and fewer vowels than most other names, try to make any change you feel will simplify it long before you hit the campaign trail.

Likewise, if you have always been called "Bobby" or "Beth" by everyone, the year before you run is no time to ask reporters and supporters to start referring to you in public as "Robert" or "Margaret." And if everyone calls you "Mortimer," including your mother, this is no time to try to act like "one of the boys" by urging everyone to start calling you "Mort."

If, on the other hand, the press and members of the public and strangers have always referred to you as "William" or "Patricia" but all along your family and friends have called you "Billy" or "Patty," then you have no problem; people can continue to call you whatever they called you before your candidacy.

It is also important that you adopt the stance and body language befitting the office for which you are running. Let us assume that you are running for governor of your state. During your campaign, you obviously should not run around acting like the dog catcher; instead, you want to act like the governor. Your posture, statements, body language, clothes—all contribute to the image of a person who will make an excellent governor.

In your speeches, assume you *are* the future governor. Say such things as:

"As your governor, I will support . . ."

"When I am elected governor, I will listen to . . ."

"We can work together to achieve sound government policies for . . ."

As mentioned above, you should remember that everything you say goes on the record and can be brought back to haunt you. This is especially important for the political candidate to realize. If you don't say it, you will never have to deny or explain it. Remember: *You can never truly retrieve a misstatement.* Your correction or qualifying statement may never catch up with the original news story.

As a candidate, you should seek to exude the confidence, authority, control, and ability to handle the office that you seek.

## Your Campaign Wardrobe

The previous sections on clothing in the chapter "Your Personal Appearance" give thorough advice on clothing choices for the political candidate. A few more tips are included here.

During an active campaign, you are constantly on the go. For both men and women, a few good basic suits will serve you well and emerge from the dry cleaner's in good shape. Well-chosen accessories will enable you to travel light and at the same time be ready for any occasion.

Let us assume you will travel in one day to five different locations in your state or district, attending a variety of functions and rallies. You may travel by private plane on a tight schedule, with crowds at each airport. A car should be waiting to whisk you to the next function.

For men, the basic good-quality navy or gray suit described in the clothing chapter will carry you through the day. If you want to appear more informal, you can wear a navy blazer, gray pants, gray shirt, and a quiet tie from breakfast through dinner. If one of the stops is a barbecue in a rural setting, carry along a gray tweed jacket and perhaps an extra pair of shined shoes if it's raining or muddy. If there is an opportunity to change clothes before the evening function, wear the navy blazer with matching navy pants, a fresh gray shirt, and a dressier silk, foulard tie. Be sure to wear long, black socks to cover the shins when sitting on a platform.

One candidate for public office whom I had coached for several months on his appearance and voice was about to give one of the most important public appearances of his life. I had helped him learn how to feel comfortable giving a speech. I had helped him purchase a new campaign wardrobe. I had forgotten to tell him that he should always wear long, black socks when sitting on a platform.

I will never forget that night, sitting in the first row of the auditorium, staring at six inches of bare white shins as he crossed and recrossed his legs for several hours.

Carefully consider your audience at each stop, and, as mentioned in the chapter on clothing, adapt your wardrobe accordingly. If you are speaking to factory workers, don't wear your three-piece suit with your Phi Beta Kappa key hanging from a chain on your vest. Wear the same suit but take the vest off. If it is hot and everyone is wearing no jacket and has their shirt-sleeves rolled up, you can do the same, knowing that the gray shirt will not "bloom" into any cameras.

Remember that each group will see you only once and that you do not need to wear something different to each event. Carry an extra shirt, a disposable razor, deodorant, and extra socks in your emergency kit.

For women, the same basic, good-quality suit, with a few extra blouses and appropriate jewelry, can be adapted to each occasion. A synthetic suede suit with a solid-colored, matching blouse is a perfect choice. It will look elegant all day, will not wrinkle, and can be washed overnight. Assemble your emergency kit with deodorant and makeup for quick touch-ups in the ladies' room.

Remember that in all cases, you are not dressing like the audience, you are appearing as the future governor or senator or whomever; you are dressing as the occupant of the office to which you seek to be elected.

## Using Gestures in Public

If you are riding in a motorcade or appearing at a political rally, you need to practice in advance the gestures you will make. Think of fitting gestures you have seen made by famous people you admire, such as waves to the crowd and gestures of greeting or farewell. Victory gestures made by heads of state, presidents, and political leaders become a vital part of their images, forever reappearing in photographs and video clips and even popping up in political cartoons. (Think of the two-fingered "V" sign used by Winston Churchill and Richard Nixon.)

Whatever gestures will be required of you should be rehearsed in advance until they become completely natural and right for you. Do not let your gestures block your face, which is your most important feature.

## Television Debates

The stakes are extremely high for political candidates in television debates. The very outcome of an election is sometimes determined by what is said at a key debate. The press and public's verdict of "who won" can influence votes.

Many hours of preparation are involved in TV debates. Participants anticipate every possible area of discussion and questions that may be asked. Many candidates rehearse with their advisers as if they were really debating. The candidates know that the panelists, too, are preparing tough and revealing questions to bring out the issues.

At the actual debate, it is a dramatic moment when the antagonists walk out onto the stage, knowing that so much is at stake.

In the great debates by presidential candidates, it sometimes seems like history could hinge on one chance remark. A major error in clothes, makeup, body language, or timing takes on abnormal significance in the public mind. One little unfavorable episode during these debates is repeated over and over again on video tape.

Cameras limit what the public sees, and at the same time, they enhance the happenings they choose to transmit. Many dramatic political moments that have been captured during debates have become classics.

## Making a Political "Spot"

Political television commercials, or "spots," are a phenomenon of the media age. They carry the message directly to the television viewer in his or her own living room. Commercials can be very effective, depending on their production quality, and they account for a large chunk of many a campaign budget.

Spots employ various techniques, including the negative attack on the opponent and/or his record; the candidate shown in informal settings surrounded by family and friends; the biographical sketch that traces the record of public service; or the issues identified by pollsters feeling the pulse of the voting public.

An entire coterie of producers, consultants, and advisers has sprung up in recent decades whose sole purpose is to bring these ads into being. When you are making your spots, hire the best talent that you can find. Among others, you will be working with your own media consultant(s), one or more producers, a director, and technical people.

After the producer and others have done their advance work, you will have a concept and a script. Often a billboard "cartoon" is prepared that shows how the finished sequences of the production will look—the opening, the various components that portray the message, and the close. Slogans will be fine-tuned. The sound track will indicate music and the announcer's copy or spoken narrative.

If you are to speak in the spot, you will have an advance script from which you can memorize your lines or at least familiarize yourself with prompter copy. Proper clothing will be selected in advance. You will be informed ahead of time of your role during the production.

On the day of the shooting, ample time must be allowed to set up the technical gear. Technical people always seem to be readjusting their equipment up to the last minute. You may be surprised at how much gear is required for even a simple shoot.

When all is ready, there will be several rehearsals. Positions and action will be blocked out and synchronized with the sound. Each take will be timed to the second. After a take, if you are informed that it ran too long, it is usually best to edit out some of the copy for the next take rather than speed up your delivery.

Each take will be numbered and evaluated for final editing. When you finally achieve a "keeper," the producer will probably ask for "just one more" for safety or because hope springs eternal that the next take will be even better.

Some politicians pride themselves on the fact that they can do a spot in one take. They may be the type of person who becomes fatigued and exasperated when there are too many repeats. They may also find it difficult to keep each take fresh and spontaneous.

Whatever your personal preference may be about doing one or many takes, pace yourself for a long haul that may include technical difficulties, frustrating interruptions in an otherwise perfect take, and possibly time-consuming script rewrites.

In the hands of people who know what they are doing and know what the finished spot must look like, the results are most rewarding—and they can help you win an election.

## Making a Speech at a Political Convention

When you are chosen to be one of the platform speakers at a political convention, keep in mind that elections can be influenced by "barn-burner" speeches, and that reputations can be made by a superb performance on a podium in the middle of the hurly-burly of the political arena.

Remember New York Governor Mario Cuomo's speech at the 1984 Democratic National Convention? Not only was it called an electrifying speech, but it catapulted him into the national spotlight. And people are still talking about Texas State Treasurer Ann Richard's keynoter at the 1988 Democratic Convention.

If you are asked to speak at a political convention, don't be surprised if you are given an outline of various points that the party is suggesting you include in your speech.

Live with the finished speech day and night, so to speak, to familiarize yourself with its basic purpose and the key points. Practice the speech on your tape recorder, decide how you will deliver it, and work on emphasizing the "buzz words."

Anticipate the places where the audience is likely to applaud, and mark them on your copy of the speech. During the actual presentation, plan to wait until the applause subsides before going on to your next line.

During the speech, expect distracting, constant movement and noise from the floor. This is inevitable, due to wandering technical crews and floor reporters and restless waves of long-suffering delegates.

Also know that you will be televised from a number of angles and that the various images will be projected to the audience in various closeup and long shots.

It is likely that a practice podium identical to the one on stage will be set up backstage at the convention hall. You will probably be given an opportunity to familiarize yourself in advance with the actual stage and podium.

Technicians will point out the positions of the lights, cameras, and double prompters. They will show you where to look and stand and will make adjustments to the height of the podium itself.

Stay within the time allotted to you. Keep your voice lowered when you deliver your speech, knowing that you cannot outshout the commotion on the convention floor. By keeping your voice resonant, you allow the audio person to control the volume, and as a result, everyone will be able to hear you clearly.

Smile and enjoy yourself up there. Try to give the speech of your life, and you may just relish the feeling of being up there for the rest of your life.

## GOING ON RADIO

Radio is a personal medium enabling you to talk conversationally to just one listener. On the other hand, the nature of radio is such that it can reach instantly into distant parts of the world.

On radio, time constraints are relaxed. Instead of being confined to a thirty-second sound bite, you will usually be allotted much more time.

The radio studio is designed to produce nearly perfect sound. The walls, ceiling, and floors are specially soundproofed to be as acoustically perfect as possible. The microphones are either fixed to the table or mounted on flexible, adjustable arms.

Once you are in the radio studio, you should be aware of several things. For starters, some tables can act like a drum that resounds to the tap of your fingers. Use the table to hold your notes, which you will usually slide noiselessly across the surface. Otherwise, ignore the table and do not touch it.

Establish a comfortable distance of several inches between your mouth and the mike, maintaining that space throughout the broadcast. In other words, don't lean into the mike every time you start to speak. If you are in doubt about how far away is optimal, either ask before you go on or copy what your interviewer does.

When you are asked for an audio check, use the same voice you will be employing throughout the show. Speak actual words into the mike during the audio check rather than saying "one, two, three."

Remember, too, that during an audio check, even though you may not be on the air yet, the mike is live and more people than you realize—including reporters—may be listening in on what you are saying. An audio check is no time to make ethnic jokes, say negative things about someone, or make any other comments that you may regret later.

Also, don't forget that "your voice is all you have" on radio. The image the listener has of you comes across solely from the way you use your voice. The listener depends on the clarity of your pronunciation and the emphasis you place on the meaning of your material. A well-modulated, resonant voice is wonderful to listen to; a harsh nasal voice is offensive to the ear. And as I said before, too many "uhs," "you knows," or similar useless expressions are especially irritating on radio.

Keep your voice in the lower ranges to avoid the distortion of the amplifying device. Clearly articulate the consonants and vowels of the phonetic alphabet; this slows the fast talker and conforms more closely to the listening rate of your audience. You can practice with a tape recorder to determine the sound of your own voice.

Read the chapter entitled "Your Voice" for more detail on how to develop a pleasant speaking voice.

Other tips on speaking on the radio:

- *Listen* to the sound of your own voice as you speak. If you think you have been speaking in a monotone, add some warmth to your voice and vary your tone.
- If you laugh in response to something said to you, don't laugh too loudly or in the high ranges.
- Don't interrupt your host or interviewer. Wait until he or she finishes speaking before you respond. The same is true if you are one of at least three people speaking. Nothing is worse to the radio listener than hearing several people constantly talking over each other. Since the audience lacks the visual clues that TV pictures provide indicating who is speaking, the result on radio is merely babble.
- If there are three or more people on the radio at once, and your voice sounds at all like one of the other's voices, it doesn't hurt to use their names, as in "Yes, Bob, that's what I've always thought," to give the listener verbal clues as to who's speaking.
- If the other people you are on the air with are saying much more than you, you can get the attention of the interviewer more often by silently signaling with your hand to him or her that you want to speak.
- Don't be afraid to relax during a radio interview. You'll come across over the airwaves as a sincere and likable person if you do. If you have to cough during a broadcast, turn away from the mike and muffle the sound in the crook of your elbow. Or ask in advance if there is a "cough button" on your mike that you can press to deaden the sound.

## ATTENDING A MEDIA TRAINING SEMINAR

To further enhance your media skills, you might decide to attend a training seminar or workshop. If you do, be sure to select one that is suited to your individual needs.

Determine how the workshop will relate to your own individual goals. Study the methods used by the training staff, and find out about activities in which you will participate. Attend with an open mind, and consider the learning experience an opportunity to add skills to those you already have.

A good media training seminar that includes dealing with television reporters should have you appear on a real video camera in a variety of simulated situations. For example, you might give a short statement from a podium, participate in an interview, take part in a panel discussion, or answer hostile questions from colleagues posing as members of the press.

An "ambush interview" might be staged in which the hapless trainee is surprised outside the door by a gaggle of lights, cameras, microphones, and tape recorders, with "reporters" shouting questions that are intentionally unfair or embarrassing.

Looking at yourself on video tape reveals the often brutal truth and gives you an opportunity to really see and hear yourself as you appear to others on tape. If what you see and hear comes as a bit of a shock, remember the distortions inherent in microphones, lights, and lenses. With the instruction you receive covering basic techniques, you should be able to critique your appearance and performance dispassionately.

Ask yourself questions about your own impressions of how you looked and came across on tape. This will provide valuable insights about your public persona.

For example, was your hair sticking up in the back or coming down over your eyes, and was that all you noticed on the first viewing of the tape? Did your plaid or red tie distract you from looking at your face? Was some other detail of your appearance distracting or overpowering? Did you notice a double chin that you've been ignoring, and now you know it's time to lose a few pounds? Did your facial expression look closed up, defensive, arrogant, or impatient? Did your body language or gestures express a negative message about finding yourself in that particular press situation?

Or, on the other hand, did you appear to be friendly yet in command of the situation? Did you come across as calm, fending off rude questions with a smile and a sense of humor?

What did you see that you want to improve on?

I know a spokesperson for a major business magazine who tells me that he appears frequently on TV and radio, gives quite a few lectures, and talks often to reporters. He says that he had worked to improve his public self, but that the single most important thing he had done to improve himself for the public eye was to get video-taped by a media consultant. He had thought, up until that experience, that he "looked okay" and "talked okay," but that the tape "horrified" him because he saw all sorts of things that were wrong—his tone of voice, his fake-looking gestures, his sloppy posture, etc.

In a good seminar, you will be given an opportunity to make a second appearance on camera so that you can benefit from suggestions that have been made by your trainers and colleagues as well as what you have learned in class. You, too, will become a critic of other performers, able to understand the obstacles they have overcome.

All of your questions should be answered. Anything that you have always wanted to know the answer to should be clarified.

Specialized seminars can also be very useful—for candidates for political office, for example. In such seminars, you can receive valuable information on how to conduct and organize your campaign, funding and finances, polltaking, defining the issues, campaign rhetoric, and direct-mail solicitations. All this is in addition to improving your media appearance skills. Experts from diversified fields are brought in as instructors and lecturers.

Other worthwhile workshops deal with professional or management skills, becoming upwardly mobile, leadership, assertiveness, and public speaking.

Another option is to seek individualized and personal consultation. You may find—often to your surprise—that you need only an hour or two with a capable consultant. Such consultants can be hired for voice and diction training, personal appearance and clothes analysis, and applying makeup for television appearances. You can find such a consultant through recommendations or public relations firms.

Just remember to choose your consultant carefully. Make sure that she or he is fully qualified to help you. There are many money-hungry, unqualified people out there these days billing themselves as "media consultants." Just because a person once had a job for a year writing press releases or speeches for an association or congressman doesn't qualify him or her as a media consultant. Ask for references or a brief, oral outline of his or her experience (not just his or her opinions) over the phone. In this way, you can quickly judge the consultant's qualifications.

I once knew a young woman who had landed her first job as an anchor on a local TV news program at a station where makeup services were not provided to the anchors. Before she went to her first day on the job, she decided to get some advice about makeup and clothes colors from a consultant. Unfortunately, she chose the wrong type of consultant. Instead of going to someone in the television industry, she went to a friend of hers who sold makeup at a cosmetic counter in an upscale local department store, whose advice in a nutshell was to "look dramatic."

When she showed up for her first broadcast, the fledgling anchor was wearing eyeshadow in three colors, too much black eyeliner, ruby-red lipstick, and blush that nearly outshone the lipstick. She was also wearing a bright red jacket over a white blouse with a shiny gold necklace. Needless to say, she got noticed that night—not only by the viewers, but by the executives who had hired her, one of whom was at the door of the studio as she exited. He complimented her on her job of giving the news and gently told her that they were going to send her to an expert consultant on TV makeup and wardrobe.

As she told me this story later, she said she didn't have the nerve to tell the executive that she had *already* received makeup and clothes advice. All she could think about was the $100 she had spent buying makeup from her friend and the cost of the new red jacket.

You may be given questionable advice from a trainer or consultant, which does not relate to your own personal needs or circumstances. As an intelligent person, you should evaluate the worth and application of the suggestions given.

For example, when a prominent scientist was appointed president of his national scientific association, he knew that his main weakness would be as a public spokesperson for the association. Whenever he was interviewed or addressed the public, he tended to come across as stiff and formal. He ended up going to a well-known consultant on public speaking, who advised him to "force himself" to use gestures, at first exaggerating them, and later refining them until they became a part of his speaking style.

This seemed like good advice, except that the scientist ended up using wide, wooden gestures, that never became refined and a part of his natural speaking style. After a couple of speaking engagements, his staff talked him out of following the advice of that consultant.

In the end, the counsel of a second consultant helped. This consisted of having him concentrate on relaxing by doing deep breathing exercises before his speech or interview, look directly at his interviewer or a couple of people he chose out of the audience, smile, and consciously relax his body when he felt himself stiffening up. He's now a much sought-after speaker.

In the end, after considering all of the advice, it is important for you to think of your own public image and do what is right for you. Set your own goals, and be yourself—albeit a bit more polished, professional, self-assured, and finely tuned.

# THE PANEL DISCUSSION

## Moderating a Panel Discussion

As you spend more time in the public eye, you will probably be called upon to moderate a panel discussion at a seminar or conference or on radio or television. When this happens, do your homework in advance. For example, talk to each participant and be sure each knows the ground rules. The panel members must understand the time constraints and the basic format of the discussion. They need to know the order in which they will speak, the subject matter, and the points you expect each to cover.

If possible, have a rehearsal before you go in front of the audience, the microphones, or the cameras. Make yourself a little seating chart, which readily gives you the correct name, title, and affiliation of each panelist. Note on your chart the correct pronunciation of any difficult words or names.

As the moderator, it is your responsibility to keep things moving according to the time schedule and to moderate the content of the material to be covered. You may have to referee panelists with differing opinions, when both want to talk at the same time or an argument ensues. You, on the other hand, have to be fair, objective, and impartial.

During the discussion, pay attention to the speaker, and make notes in case you need to make changes in the general presentation. It goes without saying that you have to be well-informed on the subject so that if the discussion goes astray, you can bring it back on track.

Try not to interrupt or talk over a speaker. Don't criticize, speak harshly to, or talk down to a panel member. It is also your job to be sure that the person who is crowded out of an exchange of ideas has an opportunity to be heard.

Know what your opening statement will be, the major points that should be covered before the time is up, and how you intend to bring the panel discussion to a logical conclusion.

If you want to see some real pros at panel moderation, tune in to the "MacNeil, Lehrer Newshour" on PBS stations most weeknights and watch these talented hosts in action.

## Being a Panel Member

When you are participating in a panel discussion, it is important that you understand what the producer or moderator expects to accomplish.

Ascertain the contribution he or she expects you to make, the subject you are to discuss, and how technical you should get so that you can do your homework. Chat with the moderator in advance to learn how and when you will be called upon. Understand the format, whether it is to be a telephone call-in, a teaching situation, a video-taped conference, or a confrontation-style debate.

A typical panel discussion might consist of your being one of five people who share a half-hour, fast-paced discussion program. Your portion may only be four minutes maximum that might be broken into five or six short statements. There will not be time to pontificate—no time to tell everything you know. A professor may be able to take nearly unlimited time in his or her classroom, but as a guest on a panel discussion program with time constraints, he or she will be lucky to have thirty uninterrupted seconds. In such a situation, it is obvious that you must prepare and formulate your key phrases in advance. Select phrases that are brief, to the point, and effective.

Know the names and correct titles of all of the other participants, and ask in advance whether you will be using first or last names or formal titles. Note them on a little card, in the order in which they are seated.

Observe time restrictions, such as station breaks, time signals from the floor, or a fifteen-second opening answer to a vital "teaser" question.

Find out if you will have an opportunity for rebuttal. When two people talk at the same time, no one can understand what they are saying. If a participant interrupts you, you may have to yield the floor temporarily, but return when he or she is finished and politely but firmly continue making your point.

Do not monopolize time allotted to another participant. Pay attention to everything that is said, and respond respectfully but firmly.

If you are well prepared and have kept your points short but very informative and interesting, you will develop a reputation as a sought-after panel member. You will be invited back.

## THE TELECONFERENCE

Teleconferences have become a very efficient way of transmitting information to audiences anywhere in the world. By satellite transmission, video-conference networks can be set up, using uplinks, downlinks, and microwave.

The originating site may be connected to viewers or other participants meeting in any number of hotel or public meeting rooms, universities, hospitals, libraries, or television stations. It is possible to connect a hundred or more nationwide locations to an expert located in a central studio. It is possible for experts to exchange information with their counterparts in various locations around the world, with two-way communication and even interpreters, if necessary. Associations, corporations, or other entities can conduct teleconferences with various locations, using courses of study, manuals, workbooks, and a variety of teaching techniques and visuals.

## CONDUCTING AN INTERVIEW

At some point in your career as a public person, you may be called upon to conduct an interview. You may be questioning a famous guest, talking to an author about a recently published book, or even interviewing a news source.

Your first step might be to watch several TV interviews by excellent interviewers such as Ted Koppel of ABC News "Nightline" and Charlie Rose of CBS News "Nightwatch."

Mr. Koppel is admired for his astute questions, his unflappable demeanor, and the fact that he is invariably well prepared. Mr. Rose is known for his warmth, his intelligence, and his uncanny ability to bring out the very best in his guests due to his attentive listening style. His questions are based on what the guest has said and not necessarily on written notes.

People who are interviewed frequently have told me many times after being interviewed by either Mr. Koppel or Mr. Rose that "that was the best interview I've ever been through." Also, when famous persons are asked to name the best interviewers in the news business, those are two names that are inevitably included on "the short list."

To prepare for your interview, obtain background information both about the person you will be interviewing and the subject of the interview. After reading through this research material, write questions out in advance. You should not depend on these questions entirely, since what the interviewee says will trigger new questions. But it helps you to organize your thoughts to write them out in advance. And, if the interview stalls in the middle or your mind goes blank, you'll have your prepared questions to turn to.

During the actual interview, listen carefully to the answers, framing your next question to advance the central theme of the interview. Have your questions at the tip of your tongue, while the interviewee is responding, and make a verbal bridge into the next idea, such as by saying, "If what you say is true, then it follows that. . . ." *Never* ask a convoluted three- or four-part question; such questions are impossible to answer and are extremely irritating to the interviewee and listener alike.

Too many interviewers are so anxious to include their own points of view that they state their own position in the question. Needless to say, this does not add to the development of the interview.

Build the interview up to a logical conclusion, give the interviewee a hint that the time is almost up by the way you pose your last question ("We're almost out of time, but tell me . . ." or "We only have a minute left, but what is . . ."), and thank the guest for appearing.

## ON A BOOK TOUR

Let us assume that you have written a successful or potentially successful book, and your publisher has asked you to go on a publicity tour. Up to this point, your time may have been spent in writing the book, and not talking about the material contained in it. However, you are now possibly recognized as an authority in your field, and you have the opportunity to transmit to the public the information contained in your book. All of a sudden, you have to appear on radio and television interviews and show up at bookstores for book-signing sessions.

Authors on book tours fare best when the publisher takes the responsibility for scheduling the talk-show appearances and itinerary. The publisher may hire an outside firm to make the necessary and complicated arrangements. Sometimes the task is assigned to the publicity department of the publishing company.

The basic procedure is for the publisher to send descriptive material and a review copy of your book to the various TV and radio talk-show producers in key cities. You will probably be booked for several appearances each day. The person setting up your tour will usually arrange for someone to accompany you to each studio or bookstore. This person will be familiar with the formats of each show and will help you understand what to expect. You will encounter a variety of formats and broadcast situations, and it is helpful to be briefed in advance for each one.

In order to conduct a successful book tour, you will need to assemble a travel wardrobe and look critically at your appearance, all the while thinking about the image you wish to project. Review chapter one on "Your Personal Appearance," particularly the section on selecting a travel wardrobe. Remember you will need only a few carefully chosen clothes, because you will never be seen twice by the same audience.

You will travel from city to city, from station to station, and from audience to audience. With luck, the scheduled appearances will not be too tightly scheduled, and you will have time between them to freshen up and collect your thoughts. It is important to arrive at each location relaxed and ready rather than visibly harried and tense.

Don't forget to carry a little emergency kit with you containing a fresh blouse or shirt, extra hose or socks, a snack of fruit or food bars for quick energy, and powder for your shiny nose.

Recently, I ran into a famous movie star at a TV studio whose book-tour schedule had been set up by an out-of-town person unfamiliar with the cities on the tour. She was promoting her autobiography—the result of several years of hard work. But instead of being able to *enjoy* her book tour, she was quite frantic, having to rush from interview to studio to book-signing party on an impossibly tight schedule.

She was tired, she'd lost her coat at one stop (it was a rainy day in early winter), she had the beginning of a run in her stocking, she had not eaten lunch, and she had a spot on her new silk dress that she found embarrassing. Instead of arriving at each site relaxed, in control, and "up" for the interview, she was rushing into each place slightly late, ushered in by an apologizing public relations person, and turning down requests to autograph her book by staff at the studio—all due to a too-tight, impossible-to-keep schedule of events.

Try not to let this happen to you. Get a copy of each day's schedule to approve before it is finalized. But if you do find yourself in a similar situation, do anything you can to minimize your reaction to the terrible schedule.

At some TV stations, your interviewer will come in with makeup, but no provision has been made for you to get made up. In such a case, hopefully, there is time for you to excuse yourself to apply your own powder in the restroom.

Once you are seated on the set, you will have to answer the same questions over and over on show after show. However, each time your answers must sound as fresh and interesting as if this were the first time you had been asked the question.

Don't get upset if your interviewer has not really read your book; often, he or she must do several interviews back to back and cannot possibly be as well prepared for each interview with book authors as you would like.

It may sound obvious, but during the interview, don't forget to mention the title of your book several times, and make sure that someone—you or the interviewer—holds it up to the camera.

Jot down hard-to-remember statistics on a card that you can keep in your pocket. Get to feel at home with cameras, microphones, crowds, and media confusion. Learn to ignore the distractions and concentrate on the information you wish to impart.

## BEING A SPOKESPERSON

To become a successful spokesperson for your corporation, congressional committee, or organization, you will need media experience and effective media skills.

The following are among the goals you should strive for in becoming an effective spokesperson: You will work closely with the officials and executives of your organization to determine company policy and to become an expert in your field. Members of the press will seek you out as a reliable news source, because they can count on you to be open, cooperative, and accurate. You will work to establish and maintain ongoing relationships with key members of the press who specialize in your area—such as politics, science, education, or business. Thus, when your press releases arrive, they will not be consigned unopened to the wastebasket. When you call a press conference, the press will attend and cover it. If the media needs an expert to appear on TV or radio, they will call you, knowing that you will be an effective guest. You will work long, hard hours to establish this reputation for integrity, but it will all be worth it.

If you are the president of a corporation, you may decide to become your own spokesperson. You may do some television or radio spots. However, do not yield to the temptation to put yourself out in front unless you and your associates are convinced that you are the best possible person available. Test tape your material in advance so that you can be honestly critical of your performance. Don't throw yourself open to criticism from your employees just because you have the power to put yourself on the air. On the other hand, there are many examples of the "fearless leader"—such as Lee Iacocca—who have become very successful in being identified with the corporate image.

## Corporate Crisis Planning

You may find yourself in a situation in which you have to respond to a crisis, such as a nuclear accident, chemical explosion, fatal accident, hotel fire, or drug poisoning. Anticipate the things that could go wrong in your individual situation, and formulate a plan for effective response.

Work out in advance the various roles your personnel will play; know your company policy and agree beforehand on what your basic response will be and who has the responsibility for checking the facts.

Do not make a public statement until you have correct information that has been checked and verified. It is better to say the information is not yet available than to make what later turns out to be a false or indefensible statement. Once news has hit the newsstand or airwaves, it's impossible to recall; corrections just never seem to have the same impact as the original news.

As you have further news bulletins to issue, don't delay in getting them to the press. Reporters appreciate your speeding updates to them, and this will help you to establish your corporation's and your own reputation as news sources sensitive to the needs of the press.

Also, during such crises, reporters appreciate your passing out any written materials as handouts—background information, policy statements of your organization, drawings or maps of a geographical area, press releases, or copies of the statement read by the spokesperson during a press conference.

Printed materials help reporters as they race to the phones to file the news with their news agency, newspaper, magazine, radio station, or whatever. For example, if you give them a written copy of a spokesperson's remarks, they won't have to take such extensive notes or transcribe audio tapes, but they can take notes in the margins of the printed copy and rush to the phones immediately. Your company is also ensured of more accurate quotes being printed in newspapers since they have been written down by you on the printed handouts.

## ACCEPTING AN AWARD

Some of the worst speeches are given at awards ceremonies. You may have wondered why a recipient is totally surprised into speechlessness. You may have cringed at the endless thanking of people the audience has never heard of and has no interest in. Somehow, the person receiving the award diminishes its stature when he or she makes an incoherent or self-serving reply.

If you are being given an award, write a well-crafted, well-thought-out, graceful, and *brief* acceptance speech or statement that expresses appropriate appreciation. Don't thank a long list of people who think they deserve to have their names mentioned over the microphone.

As an award winner, you have already achieved recognition for your talents. In your speech, you have a rare opportunity to be eloquent and effective and to add to the significance of the award. As a nominee you know in advance there is a chance that you will be the winner, so prepare a successful and graceful acceptance performance in advance.

Similarly, some of the most boring photographs are taken at awards ceremonies. Professional photographers groan when asked to take "handshake" and "holding up the plaque" or "passing the check" pictures during or after an awards ceremony. Many sponsors of an awards event want such pictures for the files, to send to you later on, or to make the boss (the one who is shaking your hand or handing you the check) in the picture happy. But only amateur newsletter editors are eager to publish such unimaginative, stiff pictures.

If you are asked to be in such photographs, go ahead and pose for the fake handshake or check passing. However, to help out such a situation, try to subtly suggest an alternative pose. For example, you and the other person could be talking to one another naturally, hands at sides or one of you gesturing as if in normal conversation. Or the two of you could be seated at a conference table, deep in an important discussion.

Anything is better than the faked handshake picture, except perhaps for one that later gets captioned: "_____ and _____ are doing _____, while _____ looks on. (More tips on being photographed are in the section called "Being Photographed.")

## WORKING WITH AN AGENT

As a successful public person, you may become so well known that having some kind of agent makes good sense.

A booking agent or agency can keep you constantly on the road giving speeches and making other public appearances or limit the appearances you make, according to your wishes. If you are to be paid for events, the agent will advise you on the best fee to charge. The agent can also negotiate fees for you—something you might be reluctant to do for yourself.

A literary agent can assist you in getting a publisher for your book or other writings. He or she may drive a harder bargain with the publisher than you would yourself because he knows the ins and outs of the publishing business.

Basically, hiring an agent is a business arrangement whereby the agent receives a certain percentage (often ten to fifteen percent) of your contractual earnings. He or she makes a living from your efforts, so that the arrangement has to be profitable for him as well as for you.

Obtaining an agent is a personal matter that you should not go into lightly. There are many horror stories of love-hate relationships between agent and client, as well as mutually profitable, longstanding arrangements.

Many very famous people use agents not only for booking or scheduling purposes, but also as a first contact and screening device for potentially bothersome phone calls or requests. In this way, your agent is also like someone protecting your privacy and screening you from unwanted interruptions or demands.

Such people, for example, are expert at saying such things as: "No, Ms. _____ does not give addresses at high school graduations"; "No, I don't give out her home telephone number"; "Yes, we'd be glad to send your sick niece an autographed picture"; or, "Yes, she may be interested in appearing at your charity's fund raiser—I'll get in touch with her and get back to you."

## BEING PHOTOGRAPHED

The public person is constantly being photographed in many different situations. Your picture may appear on the front page of the newspaper in black and white, in color on the front cover of a national magazine, on the TV news, or on a video-taped piece.

There are many things you can do to control the quality of the photography. First of all, remember that the photographer needs something fresh and interesting. Think in advance about what you might do to provide a good photo opportunity. Let us say you are going to be doing something with a bit of action, such as voting, moving about in a crowd, waving from a moving car, or showing something to the camera. Prolong the action long enough for the photographer to get his or her camera in focus. Sometimes the action cannot be caught the first time. Repeat the action if necessary, so the photographer can get a good picture.

A good photographer often tries to avoid a head-on mug shot that shows both ears. He or she usually tries to get a slightly skewed body angle. Never stand four-square into a camera; rather, give it a slightly advanced shoulder and a tilt of the head. If your face has a good side, habitually present it to the camera. As I've said before, it is good to remember that the distortions of lights and lenses often add several pounds and years to your appearance.

Try to find a "friendly" light, so you can avoid squinting into the sun. Move into the shade of a tree or building, or turn your body away from the harsh glare. Look up so that the camera can find your face. Seek an interesting, flattering background, if one is available. Avoid a distracting, moving, gaudy, eye-catching, or otherwise overpowering background.

While being photographed with a group, remember that the edges of the picture may be cropped, so move to the center of the shot, if possible. Short people should position themselves slightly in front of tall people, or they can move up onto a curb or steps to look taller. Heads of state and lawmakers automatically position themselves favorably because they have had much experience with bad and unflattering photography. Photographers love to catch you with your mouth open, or eating spaghetti, or in some other awkward pose.

Never let your hands or a hat come between you and the photographer. Take off your sunglasses so that your eyes can be seen. Never wear sunglasses that turn dark in the light or slightly tinted regular glasses when you are being photographed by a still or TV camera. Such glasses obstruct the viewer's contact with your eyes and often make you look like a criminal.

The most flattering pictures are taken when the camera is shooting from a slightly low angle. This tends to eliminate the circles under the eyes and to lessen the wrinkles caused by shadows. The higher you can position yourself above the camera lens, the lower and more flattering the camera angle will be.

If you are nervous when you are being photographed, here is a quick-to-use technique to help you relax. Press your heels into the floor so that your posture is erect and breathe deeply to enrich the supply of oxygen in your bloodstream. The purpose of this is to relax your body and have you look at the photographer as if he were your friend.

Keep in mind that one of the main objectives of relaxing is to eliminate the nervous smile that so many people paste on to their otherwise attractive faces as soon as a camera comes into their vision.

## TALKING ON THE TELEPHONE

The odds are that you spend a lot of time talking on the telephone. The telephone is a part of our daily lives that is taken for granted, but it should also be regarded as an important part of our media experience and opportunity.

When you talk to someone on the telephone, there is only your voice to express the real you. The listener will judge you and form a mental picture of your age, physical characteristics, personality, and abilities from your voice alone. On the phone, do strangers warm to you, or are they alienated?

I once witnessed a seminar on telephone selling techniques that dealt only with content and never once mentioned the qualities of a good speaking voice. The trainers of the seminar seemed to be telling the attendees that sales pitches and so forth are the only elements that sell merchandise. Experts, however, will tell you that a pleasant, well-modulated speaking voice itself is a very effective sales tool. At the very minimum, it may keep the listener on the phone a beat or so longer.

Try recording your telephone conversation. On playback, you may be amazed at what you hear. Remember that the telephone is an amplifying device that distorts the human voice and can enhance any undesirable qualities, which is similar to what a microphone does to the voice.

Analyze your voice and decide what is good and what you can change. Also, check your posture. Are you sitting at a desk all hunched over with arms braced in such a way that you cannot get air into your lungs? Do you slouch back in your chair with legs crossed—immobilizing your breathing?

You should use the same good posture that is habitual for effective broadcasting. That is, dig the heels into the floor, lift the diaphragm out of your belt, and fill the lungs with air. Let the telephone ring one more time, open your throat, and position your vocal apparatus "at the ready." Then, the first words you say will come out the way you intended. If you say your name or the name of your company, be sure it can be understood. Are you frequently asked to repeat or spell your own name? Note the clear, unobtrusive pronunciation of many persons at the phone company directory assistance service.

Call your own company to see what kind of an impression your receptionist or secretary is making on the public. What kind of a voice do you want your clients to hear? Contrast a cold, curt, unobliging telephone manner with a warm, obliging one. The diction must be clear and understandable, the consonants accurately voiced and pronounced. And it should go without saying that a staff person who answers the phone frequently should never, ever chew gum. Such little things make a big difference.

Your voice can transmit anger, illness, happiness, impatience, or enthusiasm. Young people in responsible positions are at a disadvantage when their voices are immature, yet they must inspire trust and confidence and authority. Even if you are a normal-size adult, have you ever had a caller ask to speak to your mother because your voice is tiny, high, or thin? A short, scrawny person may have a big baritone voice. In nature, big animals of the same species with big voices often become more dominant.

Quickening the pace of your conversation shows tension; slowing the pace is sensual. Learn to say what you mean directly and simply. Do not ramble on endlessly. Say what you want to say with conviction and meaning.

It is important to keep promises, appointments, and agreements. Your caller is constantly evaluating your sincerity, dependability, and emotion. Regard your telephone conversations as just as important and vital as a face-to-face meeting. Use that time on the telephone as an opportunity to practice your vocal skills. (Once again, see the chapter called "Your Voice.")

## Answering Machines

Most people hate answering machines, yet they can be a great convenience. To some people, the outgoing message may be nearly as important as a personal secretary. Record that message with care. First, throw away the suggested copy written in the instruction book, and write something original of your own that sets the right tone for you. Make the message concise and understandable. Rehearse it several times before you record it, or practice it on your tape recorder to see how it sounds. If you have a time limit on your outgoing message tape, use the sweep hand on your watch to time the announcement. When you make the recording, assume good posture, breathe properly, and pronounce the message clearly. Plan to do several takes, until you are happy with the results.

When you play back the messages on your answering machine, you have a good opportunity to be a voice critic. Do you like the placement of the voice? Does the caller talk so fast that you cannot understand the names and numbers? When you have to play the tape several times to get the message, your critical ear reveals details about the speaker.

When you leave a message on someone else's machine, it is a golden opportunity for you to practice your vocal skills. That message is a part of your public image. It is the only contact some people will have with you. They judge you by the impression that message gives, so make it a worthy reflection of you.

# FIVE

# APPEARING ON TELEVISION

A good chunk of my life has been spent in TV studios, going back to the days of black-and-white television. Since video tape had not been invented yet, programs were then live.

Shows went on the air back to back, of course, and the traumas of live broadcasting necessitated such things as lots of scrambling, off-camera activity during the ads. It also meant such curious phenomena as when one show was coming to an end, we would "lose" a camera when it had to truck across the studio to get into position to televise the opening of the *next* show.

In those early days we made up our guests as best we could, experimenting with whatever was available, including heavy theatrical makeup and black lipstick (!).

Today, the television industry is rapidly expanding, with the addition of cable, new network endeavors (such as the Fox network and the new Turner Network Television), the burgeoning syndication market, and new talk shows hitting the airwaves every week.

As a result, more and more individuals from different walks of life are appearing on TV, mostly as guests in the talk-show format, but often as expert analysts, interviewees on local and national newscasts, participants in teleconferences on every conceivable subject from fire fighting to surgical techniques, and people doing public service announcements (called "PSAs") for nonprofit organizations or causes.

So whether you are a teacher or the president of your local PTA, a new book author or a writer of magazine articles, an economist or a stockbroker, a physician or an attorney, you may find yourself asked to go on the air in one format or another.

Maybe you have never appeared on television before, and the thought makes you somewhat nervous or you really don't know what to expect.

Maybe you have already appeared on TV once or twice before, but didn't like (1) something about how you looked; (2) your gestures or body language; (3) the way you talked into the microphone; (4) your experience with a prompter; or (5) something about the format of the program that you didn't know about in advance (such as how many other guests would be sharing your interview time with you). So now you need some advice on how to do better next time.

Or you may be the veteran of numerous television appearances. If so, you just might find one or two helpful hints in this chapter to improve your on-air persona.

Appearing on television provides you with a valuable opportunity to reach a large audience. That's why television time is so effective—and expensive. A successful appearance can be beneficial; an unsuccessful one can have dire consequences. The stakes are high, and it behooves you to prepare carefully for your television experience.

Whatever your situation, this chapter will help you to become familiar with the process of appearing on camera, whether live or taped. So, after "The Johnny Carson Show," "60 Minutes," "Nightline," "Nightwatch," "The Oprah Winfrey Show," "The Morton Downey, Jr., Show," "Saturday Night Live," "20/20," "Face the Nation," or any of several dozen other programs with guests calls you, read this chapter before facing the cameras.

## PREPARING FOR YOUR TELEVISION APPEARANCE

Once you have accepted a commitment for a television appearance, you will need detailed advance information about it. Guests often appear at a TV station not knowing the name of the show they are booked for or even the name of the person who is expecting them (usually the booking producer). Such a guest may be detained unnecessarily by the security guard at the front desk because he or she lacks basic information about where he or she is supposed to be. Any security guard or receptionist working at the front desk of a television station can regale you with stories about lost or unprepared guests who show up in the lobby.

Among such lobby incidents that I have personally witnessed are (1) the guest who shows up for a live morning news show a half-hour after it has gone off the air for the day; (2) the guest who shows up at 9 p.m. for a taping session that was actually scheduled for 9 *a.m.* that morning; and (3) the guest who comes in and says he has to go on "in the next ten minutes or I'm leaving," when in fact he was not scheduled to go on the air for another hour or so.

Similarly, guests have been known to show up in a TV makeup room when they were scheduled to appear on a *radio* program aired in the same building. Or they may say to a makeup artist, "Why do I need makeup for a radio interview?" when the show they were booked for is actually a TV show!

Once at the studio, an unprepared guest may ask the producer the subject of the interview, whereupon he or she prepares a few hasty, last-minute remarks—which come off sounding like a few hasty, last-minute remarks. Or the file the guest has been given by a staff member may lack the very piece of technical information or statistics that he has been asked to discuss; someone told him to show up, and that's all he did.

All of this frustration can be avoided by careful advance preparation. You need to know the date, the time you are due at the studio—plus the on-air time if it is a live show—the name and exact address of the station, the name of the show, your station contact, and his or her office telephone number. You need to know whether the format of the show is an interview, a telephone call-in, or an on-camera "read," and whether it will be live or pretaped. You need to know how much time is allotted to your appearance—ninety seconds, six minutes, or a full hour. You need to know who else will be on the program with you, whether you will be interviewed by one person or a panel, and the subject(s) to be discussed.

If you are a celebrity who refuses to answer personal questions, you need to tell that to the booking producer in advance. If there is one person in the country whom you absolutely refuse to go on the air with, you need to communicate that fact. If you are wheelchair-bound, wear a hearing aid, or have any other special needs, that, too, should be told to the producer in advance.

Not long ago, I was working in a TV studio as the makeup artist for a network talk show, and we were expecting an advocate on veterans' issues. Because he called the station several hours in advance of his scheduled arrival time and told the producers that he was wheelchair-bound, the studio was able to remove some new electronic equipment that had been partially blocking the corridor to the studio for several days. If he hadn't called in advance, his interview would have been delayed while the equipment was moved out of the way.

Some government officials and members of the legal profession are barred from speaking about certain topics to the press. Among them are judges involved in important cases, Department of State officials involved in matters of secrecy, and Pentagon brass involved in national security. If you ever find yourself in similar situations, do warn the producers in advance that if asked certain questions, you can't answer them.

You should also find out if you will be reading prompter copy or if you are expected to supply any visuals either in advance or at the time of your interview.

In order to obtain all of this information, preliminary telephone conversations that you have with the booking producer should be carefully heeded. Producers will also tell you anything you should know about that show's particular format or what is expected from you as a guest. For example, there might be an opening question, to which a fifteen-second answer is expected. Failure to observe such a time limit may cause the director to stop the tape and do the opening a second time. Or you may be told that you will be going on the air with your arch-rival and that a gloves-off debate between the two of you is expected. Or you may be sharing your air time with others as one member of a large panel or roundtable.

If you don't pay attention to the producer stating such things over the phone in advance, you may be in for an unpleasant surprise when you arrive at the studio.

## A Preparatory Checklist

So now you are aware of the fact that in order to arrive at the right place at the right time, well informed, relaxed, and ready to go on the air, you should get as much advance information as possible about your television appearance. It also is a good idea to confirm all details the day before you are scheduled to appear.

The following checklist can help. You or one of your staff members should fill out a similar list for each TV appearance. This is particularly helpful when you are doing multiple television and radio interviews one after the other on the same day; you can review the checklist in the car between interviews.

- Name of program
- Date of TV appearance
- Expected time of arrival
- Time of taping or live broadcast
- Station or network name
- Station address
- Station switchboard telephone number
- Program contact or producer
- Producer's phone number
- Your interviewer's name
- Program format (such as hour-long live call-in show, pretaped interview with no edits, etc.)
- Subject(s) to be discussed
- Length of interview
- Names of any other guests
- Program is being taped in advance for broadcast on _____ date or
- Program is shown live
- Visuals or props to be provided by you, if any
- Will you be expected to read prompter copy? If so, will it be provided to you in advance?
- Travel arrangements, if any
- Remarks (may include such things as the following: the best way to get to the station; where to park; availability of a make-up person; what to wear; questions you might be asked; questions you would like to be asked in order to get your message across; or, the basic position your organization has assumed on a specific topic)

## Additional Advance Preparations

Make all of your other advance preparations before you get to the TV station, assuming that nothing can be done after you get there. This enables you to approach your television appearance with confidence and quiet authority, allowing you to relax and even enjoy the whole experience.

Prepare your notes in advance so that they can be referred to easily. Idea headings, direct quotes, or complicated statistics should be typed in capital letters, triple-spaced, on stiff notecards. (The cards should be pastel-colored rather than white so that they do not "bloom" on camera.)

If you are doing an on-camera "read," make last-minute changes on any script or prompter copy beforehand. Every TV producer has seen guests who keep the studio crew waiting while they fiddle endlessly with the script and political candidates and their advisers who cause unnecessary delays while they rewrite material which must then be retyped. In a television studio, on paid time, the clock is ticking away, often at a cost of thousands of dollars per hour.

Come prepared with questions you would like to be asked, which would permit you to give effective answers. This is especially appreciated by talk shows that do back-to-back interviews, with the host being only partially prepared; by interviewers who have not read your book (in the case of authors on a book-promotion tour); and by interviewers not expert on your technical or complex subject (superconductivity, the history of arms control agreements, relations with Latin American nations, medical breakthroughs, etc.). Thus, many interviewers are eager to get your sample questions. Keep in mind, however, that other interviewers don't want you to provide such questions and may even be insulted by your offering to do so.

Also be sure you know in advance how any visuals will be used— objects you intend to display, the cover of your book, illustrative pictures, or film clips that you may be supplying. Work out the details with your station contact so that you both understand what you plan to do. For an effective presentation, materials that require special handling need to be provided in advance to be viewed by the director. Pictures from your book can be duplicated a day or so in advance and cued into your presentation or interview. Slides need to be numbered in the sequence in which they will be shown. Indicate clearly on your script when the visuals will be used.

For example, if you are going to hold up a long chain of gold links recently recovered from the ocean floor where it had lain for several hundred years, a model of the human brain, a live snake, or an example of an unsafe toy, you should practice holding it up, if possible, before the actual interview. During the interview, the floor manager or director will tell you which camera will show a close-up of a given prop, and which camera you are to look at.

When possible, watch the program in advance of your appearance so you know what to expect when your turn comes as a guest. You will also have a chance to study your interviewer. Examples: If the interviewer constantly interrupts his or her guests, practice in advance using a polite phrase such as "Yes, but before I respond to that, let me finish my last point." If he asks shallow questions, pick out a sample question or two and, once on the set, say something like: "By the way, there's an interesting point that I could make about _____ if you asked me about it."

Television and radio deadlines are usually inflexible. Plan to arrive *at least* fifteen minutes early, so that you are relaxed and your hosts know their expected guest has arrived. Planning to arrive early gives you some leeway, in case you are delayed in traffic, you can't find a place to park, or you want time to freshen up. If you are coming from an airport, allow at least an extra hour for unforeseen delays.

If you are running even a few minutes late, call your producer-contact to tell him or her that you are on the way and give your estimated time of arrival without being too optimistic about it.

When you arrive late for a live TV interview, the staff members have already panicked, considered all of their alternatives, tried their best to repair the now-in-jeopardy schedule, and possibly have already replaced you with the next guest or with an evergreen interview from the tape bank.

On the other hand, never hurry on your way to the studio or run the last couple of blocks on a hot or rainy day. Arriving breathless shows you are not in control; uncontrollable perspiration may break out on your face after you go on the air, giving you a nervous or harried look, which is not the image you want to project.

Finally, it goes without saying that if you arrive drunk at the station you will never have to worry about being invited again.

I once did the makeup for a quasi-famous guest on a nationally televised talk show who showed up—wearing a tuxedo—so high he could barely walk. He had come straight from a formal party. Just before taping the interview, he went into the men's room and, unbeknownst to the producers, snorted some cocaine.

He pulled himself together enough to begin the rather short interview, except that halfway through, white powder began falling out of one nostril down onto the black lapels of his tux. Needless to say, not only was the interview never aired, that particular guest was never invited back to appear on that show. In fact, even though this incident happened several years ago, the producers of the program still talk about this sorry fellow in disbelief.

## AT THE TELEVISION STATION

By now, you have arrived at the TV station at least fifteen minutes to half an hour early, well dressed, relaxed, and well prepared.

Upon your arrival at the station, you should give the security guard or receptionist your name and the name and the telephone extension of your contact (again, usually the producer who booked you) at the station. This will avoid your being needlessly delayed in the lobby.

After you have been greeted, go over last-minute details with the producer or program host. To be certain that your host will give your correct name, title, and organization when you are introduced—and that they will be spelled correctly when they appear as a subtitle under your face—give the producer your professional card before the start of your interview. Don't be insulted if the interviewer asks you to pronounce your name a couple of times before air to ensure that he or she has it correct.

You will now, more than likely, be taken into makeup (see the section on TV makeup in chapter one) or be seated in the guest waiting room that is always called the "green room," no matter what color it actually is. Most network shows provide makeup services to their guests (but rarely the services of a hairdresser), while most local stations do not.

On major network shows, you may be asked to sign a routine release while you are in the green room. The release will request permission to use your name, face, likeness, and comments for broadcast. The basic purpose is to keep you from suing later on. Occasionally, a guest who is a lawyer will carefully examine the fine print. Sometimes a guest will cross out a word or sentence. But most guests sign the release without reading or understanding the contents. The basic release is harmless enough, and you should sign it or you probably won't be allowed to go on the air.

Before we get into the details of undergoing a successful interview and other on-camera tips, let's take a look at some of the technical aspects of the TV station itself, what you can expect, and how they relate to your television appearance.

## Television Terms

A complete list of terms used in the broadcasting industry would fill a small dictionary. This short list, although far from comprehensive, contains some of the more common terms that you might hear but not be very familiar with.

*Announcer copy.* Announcer's script for the open, close, or continuity of a program.

*Aspect ratio.* Relates to the ratio of picture width to picture height of a TV set; currently four to three (i.e., four units wide to three units high).

*Audio.* The sound portion of a television event. The audio technician is responsible for the mix and sound level control.

*Audio cart.* A cartridge housing magnetic tape usually containing the opening and closing music, etc.

*Audio check.* Testing the sound of the voice on the microphone for tonal balance and assurance that the microphone is functioning properly.

*Body turn.* Turning the top half of the body toward the person with whom you are sharing the set, leaving the hips in place; gives the illusion that you are looking toward the other person, but keeps the camera from getting a flat profile.

*Boom.* Projecting arm for support of the overhead camera or microphone.

*B roll.* The second tape needed to perform an edit when using two tape machines as sources for material.

*Bumper.* A shot (usually wide) of the set or studio designed to connect a segment of a program to a commercial break, and vice versa.

*Bust.* A term spoken in the studio by a technician or floor manager to the person being taped to indicate that a take has to be done over. Sometimes the videotape person will then ask the director or producer: "Save or burn?" When this happens, he or she is asking if he should save that take until a better one is made, or erase or record over it (burn it).

*Camera cable.* Umbilical cord to a camera from associated equipment.

*Cart.* Audio cartridge housing audio tape ready to be cued.

*Character generator.* Electronic generator of characters and type-faces available as graphics on the screen.

*Chroma key.* Device that generates a "hole" in a scene for the insertion of another image within the generated hole. The generated hole is dependent upon a selected color within a scene, usually blue or green.

*Colorbars.* Electronically generated test signal, displayed as different-ent colored vertical bars. Employed as a primary test signal for the assurance that color video systems are performing correctly, including proper monitor set-up.

*Control room.* The center of the creative and technical production process. The integration of various video and camera sources plus audio functions are performed in it.

*Cue.* A signal from the floor manager alerting a person to begin speaking or indicating another action. Most cues are related to time and are called "time cues."

*Daybook.* A final tabulation of news items and features assigned to remote crew coverage for inclusion in a day's news coverage.

*Dub.* Duplicate of a master tape.

*ENG.* Electronic News Gathering using portable cameras and/or VTR's on remote locations.

*Evergreen.* A timeless or undated show or segment that does not need to air immediately and can be held for future broadcast or rebroadcast.

*File tape.* Previously video-taped piece kept for future broadcast or archives.

*Gaffer's tape.* Special sticky-backed tape used for myriad purposes in the TV studio.

*Goodnight.* "Goodnight the crew" or "that's a goodnight" means that the segment, show, or taping is finished; similar to "that's a wrap."

*Green room.* A room for guests, actors, or broadcasters to wait in prior to their appearance on camera; it is, however, seldom painted green.

*Hard news.* Up-to-the-minute, fast-breaking news (see "soft news").

*High-Definition Television (HDTV).* High-definition television is a new technology that will provide viewers with a much clearer TV picture than they see today. It will be available in the United States in the 1990s. The new system will require the purchase of new TV sets to display the twice-as-sharp pictures sent by the high-definition signals. However, old TV's will still work and will be able to receive the new signals; the old sets will not display the sharper pictures. The present system in the United States has 525 horizontal lines, while the present European system has 625 lines. HDTV will have about 1,100 lines.

*In cue.* First words of a prepared piece (see "out cue").

*Line monitor.* Control-room monitor displaying the final product.

*Mini doc.* A small documentary, usually containing relevant interviews and follow-up information on news features of current interest.

*Mode.* Stereo or mono.

*Out cue.* The last few words of a prepared piece, such as a tape being rolled into the middle of a newscast (see "in cue").

*Paid media.* Purchased time for commercials or political campaign pieces.

*Phoner.* Term sometimes used for a telephone interview (i.e., the interviewee is interviewed using only the voice, with no video picture of him or her).

*Playback.* Replay of a video or audio tape.

*Post production.* Production done after a tape has been made to add visuals, captions, music, etc.

*Recap.* Recapitulation of items already broadcast.

*Remote.* Something being taped or broadcast live on location, away from the main studio.

*Rerack.* Rewind video or audio tape for replay.

*Revised script.* Rewrite of an original script.

*Room tone.* The natural sound of a studio or remote location.

*Satellite downlink.* The process of returning a broadcast signal from a satellite to an earth terminal.

*Satellite uplink.* The process of transmitting a broadcast signal to a satellite from an originating earth site.

*Script.* Text of a program with the left column indicating the video and the right column indicating the audio, plus timing cues.

*Soft news.* Documentary-type reporting, which gives background details and additional relevant information (see "hard news").

*Sound bite.* A short, video-taped piece, lasting several seconds or longer, to be edited into a news program.

*"Start your clocks."* Cue for starting stopwatches and timing devices in order to synchronize timing of a segment, interview, or program.

*Sweeps.* The quarterly measurement of a show's numbers of viewers and audience share. Advertising rates for each show and time slot are then pegged to the ratings.

*Talent.* Nickname for an anchor person, newscaster, or anyone else appearing on camera (usually a person paid to appear on camera).

*Tally light.* Red light just above the camera lens (with smaller versions of the main tally light appearing at the back and sides of the camera for the use of the technicians) that is lit when that particular camera has been selected for use by the director.

*Tease.* An introductory statement that previews the contents of an upcoming show; it is used to establish interest in what is to come.

*Tech.* Nickname for a technician—a technical person who operates equipment such as the camera, lights, audio, prompter, etc.

*Teleconference.* Televised conference transmitted by satellite to two or more remote locations.

*Time cue.* Finger or hand signals given by the floor manager to indicate the amount of time left in an interview or segment (i.e., two outstretched fingers usually mean that there are two minutes left).

*Two-way.* An interview whereby the interviewer is in one location (often the main studio), and the interviewee or other broadcaster is in a second, remote location (often a studio in another city, in an outdoor location such as during a "man-on-the-street" report, or on the White House lawn). The two sites are usually linked by audio and video (via monitors), incoming to the interviewer. The interviewee normally just hears the interviewer.

*Video.* The visual or picture portion of a program.

*Viewfinder.* Device that shows the camera person the scene his or her camera is shooting.

*Voice over.* A voice soundtrack to be played over visuals. An example in a newscast would be when pictures of an airplane crash are being shown and the sound is not of the crash but of the voice of the anchor describing what the viewer is seeing; or, the natural sound on the tape of the crash may be heard turned down very low, as the voice of the anchor is heard, too.

*VTR.* The Video Tape Recorder.

*Wireless audio prompter.* A device that enables the broadcaster to bypass prompter or cue cards and look at a product or in any direction he or she chooses. It consists of a small device hidden in the ear, which delivers previously recorded script lines from a small pocket tape recorder. The performer has recorded the spoken material in advance, and simply rolls the audio tape and repeats what he or she hears.

*Wrap.* "That's a wrap" means that the segment or program is completed (see "goodnight").

## The Physical Layout

*On First Seeing the Studio.* I remember clearly the first time I walked into a television studio (it was about 1950, believe it or not). I was escorting a couple of my children who were to go on a televised nursery-school show. I remember looking with fascination at all of the equipment scattered about. Of course, since those days the technical equipment in TV studios has been vastly improved and even scaled down. But things can still look cluttered and crowded, and you may well ask yourself, as I did that day, "Just what do they *do* with all of this stuff?"

Though this myriad equipment may at first appear confusing, in reality it is organized and necessary for the generation of a television program. You are aware of a kaleidoscope of scenery, backdrops, furniture, cameras, lights, monitors, microphones, and prompters. There may be technicians and a lot of other people milling around, checking lighting, adjusting equipment, asking questions, or giving instructions to each other.

Naturally, some studios are larger than others, depending on the type of shows that are routinely telecast from them. Interview studios need not be as large as ones used for dramatic productions or newscasts. Television studio sets range in size from a tiny set for interviews with perhaps only two chairs and a small table, to a single desk that may be part of a larger, working newsroom, to a huge studio from which major productions can be aired.

You may have to look where you are walking because of the many cables of different sizes snaking across the floor. Tied into various pieces of equipment, the most obvious cables are the large black sheaths connected to the cameras. I have counted as many as fourteen cables for a five-camera show.

A typical studio will have three or four cameras, some having certain distinguishing features, capabilities, and specific uses. Each camera has a large lens protruding from the front, plus a small red globe called a tally light, in addition to many little boxes and handles. Most cameras also have a square-shaped, mirrored prompter device in the front that enables you to read your script while looking at the camera lens.

You will notice that many lights hang from the ceiling, facing in various directions and at different angles. Some of the lights will be aimed at you—your key light is one of these—while other lights are aimed at the set, background, and environment in which you are being taped.

Experts who control the studio lighting have switches and other devices at their disposal that enable them to contribute to the creation of a picture containing proper "colorimetry."

The walls of the studio are usually lined with floor-to-ceiling drapes or cycloramas, which curve around the set and are used as a background. Desks, chairs, tables, podiums, plants, decorations, signs, logos, etc., comprise the rest of the set.

Television broadcasting facilities usually have the following elements in common: the control room; master control (often called "central control"); a section for editing, recording, and playback of video tapes; and at least one studio.

**The Control Room.** The control room, which is usually located near the studio, is where the key decisionmakers sit during a broadcast. As you walk through a station, you will notice that some of the key equipment for producing the broadcast is located in the control room, some in master control.

Seated in a row facing a wall full of monitors, clocks, and various other pieces of equipment are the director, the assistant director, and various technicians, usually the switcher and an audio person.

Producers also sit in the control room during a broadcast, usually behind the director. It is the producers who are in charge of the content and other creative aspects of the show.

The director is in charge of the production aspects of the show—it is she or he who calls the shots on such things as rolling tape, cueing people on the set when time is up, selecting camera shots and angles, fading lights or calling up theme music, and timing the show segments between any ads.

Most of the monitors that the people in the control room are looking at are black and white. There is a monitor for each facility, i.e., for each camera, video tape, remote location, etc. The few color monitors found in the control room show the program in progress from the studio. They also make it possible to preview an effect prior to using the scene.

A technician seated right beside the director is in charge of a piece of equipment called the "video switcher," which is embedded in a large desk and has a series of colored, lighted buttons. The switcher allows for the selection of the various signals appearing on the monitors. The technician (who is often called "the switcher," after the machine he or she is in charge of) also presses buttons that control such things as which camera is being used and the use of graphics.

During the program, the director gives a constant stream of commands to the switcher, such as "key," "matte," "camera two," etc.

The audio person sits in front of a console whose many knobs control the sound levels of microphones and music tapes.

Those involved in the technical aspects of the program wear headsets, which connect everyone together—the camera operators, lighting person, prompter operator, floor person, sound person, and directors. They can talk to each other, hear each other, and work together as a team, even though they are working in different rooms (such as the control room, studio, lighting booth, announce booth, etc.)

**Master Control.** The ultimate objective of all of the activity is to route the television program to various stations, or directly to air, or to record it on video tape for later broadcast or distribution. This is done in another nerve center of the station that is usually called "master control" or "central control."

It is from here that studio lights are controlled, color output is adjusted for proper skin tones, input and outgoing signals are switched from one point to another, etc.

## Back in the Studio

**The Set.** In the pioneer days of television, it was thought that the most flattering background was a black velvet curtain and spotlight-type lighting. While many set designers still like plain cycloramas as backgrounds, now we have the wonderful creative effects of modern lighting techniques made possible by advanced computers and sophisticated equipment. (An example would be the projection of clouds against a sunset-colored cyclorama that, unlit, is simply a plain, beige, muslin-type fabric drape pulled in place across the back of the set.)

The prime function of a television set is to create a suitable environment for you, the human being. The setting should not be so fancy that it overpowers your message. Some backgrounds are so ornate and busy that you can hardly see the guests who inhabit them. There may be so many plants, pictures, and brightly colored objects that the set itself is the star of the show. As viewers, we have all seen flower arrangements growing out of someone's head, props that are out of perspective, or objects that you puzzle over but cannot identify.

For example, I have missed many a funny line uttered by guests on "The Tonight Show" and "Late Night with David Letterman" because

I was so distracted looking at various parts of their busy background sets. On the Carson show, it often looks like a part of a large plant is growing out of guests' bodies.

Networks and individual television stations spend a lot of money on their sets—especially for morning and evening news broadcasts. Many shows are beginning to discard the old, ornate sets in favor of more neutral and realistic backgrounds.

The color of the set is very important because it affects the clothes you can wear. Obviously, a bright blue or red or plain black background makes it nearly impossible to wear any of those colors. This explains why the best color to wear is gray, and why good, strong middle-spectrum colors such as wine red, medium blue, or camel also look good on most sets. (See the sections on clothing in chapter one.)

One of the most important parts of the studio set is whatever it is that you will sit upon. This will determine your posture, your body language, and your ability to breathe.

The ideal television chair would be a small, hard, straight-backed one with no arms, which would permit you to sit straight from the center of your back and to tuck your heels under your shoulder blades. However, you will find few such chairs in the typical studio.

I remember once, when I was the producer of a talk show, that the chair provided for the guest seamed ideal—it was hard and straight-backed. The one problem was that it rocked. Just in time for air, I stuck a matchbook under one leg to stop the wobble.

Most of the chairs you will encounter will be upholstered armchairs, which you can easily cope with by sitting slightly forward on the front edge. Then there is the soft, fat, over-padded sofa, which can be a hazard in that it tends to swallow you up and overpower you. If you sit back in it and cross your legs, you will completely lose control of your breathing and speaking apparatus. You can overcome all that by perching as best you can on the front edge, ignoring the armrests and finding some way to anchor your body.

Swivel chairs promote busy-looking movements, so if you are seated in one, stabilize it into a fixed position.

At times, you will be fortunate enough to find a small, solid chair that permits interesting camera angles and good posture and gives you access to your voice box.

**Television Cameras.** Television cameras have unique capabilities. As mentioned earlier, today's cameras are greatly enhanced, which means that they show features the human eye normally would not see. As the camera approaches your face, or when your face occupies a major portion of the screen (a "tight shot"), it does not go out of focus at the point the human eye would lose clear vision. The camera or its lens keeps coming closer; therefore, it enhances, penetrates, and exaggerates your image. It reveals details that you cannot or would not ordinarily see with your naked eye; you have to check the monitor to see what the camera reveals. The lens flattens an image, and the lights cast shadows which the camera recognizes and displays. Thus, certain features are enhanced, such as circles under the eyes, wrinkles and beard, distorted colors, and reflections from shiny jewelry.

This explains why television makeup is essential—to help negate those pounds and years that the cameras add to your appearance and to compensate for the distortions caused by the overhead lights and enhanced cameras. (Again, see the sections on TV makeup in chapter one.)

The cameras also enhance gestures and movements—making them seem bigger than they might otherwise look. Only by looking at the monitor can the director or you gauge the relationship between objects on the set.

The camera has mobility, which allows it to go back and forth, up and down, or to pan right and left. The camera follows the performer, and you usually do not have to make any adjustment or concession to it. When instructed by the director, cameras can move in for a close-up or move back for wide shots. The focus or depth of field can be changed by lens adjustments.

Different makes of cameras exhibit different characteristics in colorimetry. For example, some tend to be on the warm side and have a tendency toward red, whereas others appear to favor blue and are called "cool." Some cameras have a tendency to make pictures appear hard, show excessive detail, and overshoot the borders surrounding an image. Many of these characteristics can be compensated for by lighting, makeup, and a knowledgeable staff.

Cameras mounted on a boom (tongue) or a platform called a "high hat" are capable of long-range, wide studio shots. Boom-mounted cameras are more flexible than floor-mounted ones and generate sweeping creative shots.

***The Floor Manager and Taking Camera and Time Cues.*** The floor manager, or floor person, wears a headset allowing him or her to communicate with the director in the control room. The floor manager responds to instructions from the director and lets him know what is going on in the studio. The floor manager (or someone such as the audio person or a camera person) will fasten your microphone on your clothes and tell you where to sit and which camera to look at. He or she will give you or your interviewer time signals and starting and stopping cues (see below). He or she will point at the camera that is about to go on you, and if necessary, tell you in advance how to move from one place to the other. He or she will also tell you when the studio is clear and the show is over.

The camera directly facing you is usually your principal camera. There may be times when you receive a cue to look directly at it, and other times you may be asked to look at a different camera, such as when you are answering a question from a listener. However, during a typical interview when you are the only guest, you will probably be asked to look at the camera only when you are being introduced and thereafter to ignore the cameras and speak to your interviewer.

The standard opening cue is a hand pointing to the lens, then a countdown of five seconds: five fingers, four fingers, three fingers, two fingers, one finger, and then a downward slash motion with the hand. The "five-four-three-two" second cues are often given orally as well as with the fingers, with the "one" second and "slash" cues being silent.

Or you may be given a starting cue by the floor manager saying "quiet in the studio," or "stand by," followed by his holding his hand under the lens of the camera that is to be used first, followed by the slashing motion described above. Thus, you will often not be given the "five, four, three, two, one" countdown.

In any case, when there are several cameras, the floor person will always cue you by pointing to the correct camera.

Time cues showing how much time is left in a segment or interview are sometimes printed on cards that are held up by the floor manager. The cards may also read "halfway" or "cut" or "wrap." Never acknowledge the cue by nodding. The floor person knows you saw the cue and expects you to automatically observe it. If you are given a "hard wrap" cue (either by a card or a circular finger-twirling motion from the floor manager), wrap up your sentence very quickly. In some studios, a slash gesture is also used to mean "cut."

Other cues you might see include a "broken finger" for a thirty-second cue; hands placed together then widened out horizontally for "string it out—keep talking"; or thumb and forefinger tapped together for "keep talking until the cut." The latter cue is often used as "please talk" when testing a studio mike for sound levels.

***Television Lights.*** In a television studio, almost all the lights are hung from the ceiling. They are aimed in different directions because each light serves a special purpose. "Key lights" are aimed at each person seated on the set. "Back lights" illuminate the background, while "fill lights" come from the sides to highlight various objects on the set. The lighting arsenal ranges from little "sun guns" to huge six-foot klieg lights.

Soft lights are flattering to the face but lack definition. As a result, they have to be used in combination with focused lights. Light reflected from umbrellas or shiny surfaces is used for special effects.

You can identify your key light as the one that is focused directly on you and blinds you when you look directly into it. It is synchronized with the direction of your camera and is angled so that it drops the shadow of your head properly down onto the scenery behind you. You can improve your image by turning your body slightly into your key light, shoulders straight and head up, so that the light hits under your brow bone. This reduces the circles under the eyes and helps smooth out any wrinkles. When you look down, the shadows cast by the brow bone can give you black "raccoon eyes." If you have heavy brow bones or deep-set eyes, keep your chin level with the floor. Remember that the viewers need to see your eyes, since eye contact is so important.

If you are about to appear on camera and some of your jewelry is reflecting light, you may be asked to remove it. A gold watch may be tucked discreetly under the sleeve, or a touch of dulling spray, creme makeup, or a bit of powder may be applied to a military insignia or whatever else is shining.

Much of how good you look will be due to the work of the lighting director or lighting technician. Such people range from the near-genius to the mad bomber. Geniuses try to make everyone look good, while others bombard their victims with harsh, unfriendly light that makes everyone look bad.

Lighting directors—especially very experienced ones—often develop their own identifiable styles; they develop a fondness for certain trademark lighting styles. They have to be tough in order to survive because they often take so much blame—it is easy to say that everything wrong with a picture is the "lighting man's fault." An old battle-scarred survivor is usually an expert lighting person.

Lighting can add years to your face because the enhanced cameras take pictures of the shadows cast by the overhead lights. Lighting can also wash out your skin tones or show up every little blemish and detail. (Another reason for wearing TV makeup is to help compensate for this.) Harsh light emphasizes the receding hairline or emphasizes the shadows cast by the aquiline nose.

Stay inside the space that has been lit for you. Moving in and out of the light can cast a bright reflection on the forehead. You cannot get up and move around unless the space has been especially lit for this.

**Television Monitors.** Television monitors are strategically located on the studio floor so that guests and "talent" (newscasters, interviewers, or other staff usually paid to appear on camera) can see the studio output. On live shows, those in the studio can see what even has preceded them and when they have gone off the air. The anchor can tell from the monitor when he or she is on camera, when the commercials are on, and when various film and video-taped pieces are cued into the broadcast.

Technical people, too, often need to use monitors to see what the cameras are seeing. By looking at the monitor, the lighting person can evaluate the lighting and make adjustments as necessary. The makeup person can see what distortions the lights and lenses are giving to faces.

As a guest, you can take a preliminary glance at the monitor before the show to see how you look, evaluate your posture, and make minor adjustments (such as removing a watch that flashes in the light when you gesture). After that, and throughout the show, do not look at the monitor because you would be looking sideways and losing eye contact with the camera or the person interviewing you.

Do not be disturbed by odd or unflattering color gradations that you may see in the studio monitors. For example, you might look pale or your blue dress may suddenly seem an odd greeny-blue on the monitor. No two monitors ever seem to match in color; in fact, even monitors on the wall of control rooms seldom match each other. On one, the face will be reddish; on another, the face will be pale, with the color of your clothes bearing no resemblance to what you are wearing. Never fear, the *main* monitor used in master control to adjust color output is accurate, and it is the only one that accurately shows what is being sent out on the air.

*Microphones.* There are many types of microphones and amplifying devices. As well as varying in size, they have different capabilities: Some are omni-directional, picking up sound from all directions; some accept sound only from the front; while shotgun mikes focus on one specific spot.

The best sound comes from a pair of small breastbone mikes clipped to your tie, jacket lapel, or blouse. This is the type of mike worn by most network anchors. When you see two mikes attached to the same clip, the extra one provides safety in case the other one fails.

The best placement for such mikes is about five inches below the chin, or about two shirt-buttons down. This maintains a maximum chest resonance and a uniform distance between mike and mouth.

Microphones are very sensitive—they pick up every sound, making a television or radio studio into one big sound stage. They pick up the sound of someone walking across the floor, of your fingers tapping on a desk, or the shuffling or turning of pages of your script. Sometimes a mike tucked under your tie or blouse will pick up the sound of rustling fabric. The sound of jangling jewelry—especially beads hitting the mike or bracelets banging into each other—is particularly distracting. When you touch a mike with your fingers, it makes an audible sound such as a scratch, pop, or click. Mikes can pick up the sound of a broadcaster's breathing as he or she fills the lungs with air between phrases.

Sometimes a technician will "dress the cord" of one of these small mikes by tucking it out of sight, beneath the jacket, tie, or blouse, and securing it with a tiny piece of gaffer's tape. For a stand-up presentation, he or she may pass the cord up the trouser leg, or conceal it in a skirt pocket or waistband.

You may be given an unmounted, hand-held mike, either cordless or attached to a long walking cord. This is the type of mike used by talk-show hosts who stroll through aisles taking questions from the audience, or during variety shows or telethons. Such a mike gives you the ability to move around freely. You have to gauge the correct distance from mouth to mike, and keep it a uniform distance—usually six inches is ideal. You can anchor your elbow against your body to keep the mike steady. If you have to walk with a cord, tuck it into the back of your belt, with the cord positioned behind your right leg. It is thus possible to walk without tripping over the cord, which will follow easily behind you as you move.

Boom mikes are used on location, in movie sets, or in large studios or sound stages where movement is required. They are always out of camera range. Large directional mikes may be used at press conferences and public functions.

Another type is the podium or table mike, which is fixed at an angle, either on a movable stand or attached to a table. (This is the kind of mike used by radio announcers.) You can usually raise or lower such mikes by their goosenecks to the best height or angle for you. Once you have established a comfortable position, maintain a constant distance from the mike and do not turn away from it. The audio person will "ride the gain," adjusting the sound level if necessary, but if you move too far away, there is little he or she can do to keep the sound level constant.

You may be asked to wear a self-contained, power pack audio system with a battery pack that clips to your belt and is concealed in the small of the back under your jacket, or may be strapped around the waist under your clothes. A tiny mike is placed under the blouse or shirt or on the lapel. Singers, actors, and dancers frequently use these sophisticated sound systems, which are often called wireless microphones.

A newly refined sound system consists of a battery of receivers, each equipped with its own foot-long antenna. These receivers are tuned to the mike which the performer wears concealed under the clothes. The performer moves freely, drags no cords, and there is no distortion of the human voice. This neat little system has to be insured for about $30,000 when in use.

It pays to get acquainted with your mike. All audio systems amplify the human voice, especially in the upper ranges. Use the lowest voice range that is comfortable for you. There is no need to speak loudly or use excessive volume. Resonance in the lower range sounds best on any microphone. Use a one-on-one conversational tone. To keep your voice fresh, lively, and pleasant-sounding, smile into the microphone. Sound friendly, instead of grim or pompous.

Remember that once the audio is turned on, you are live, and someone will hear every word you say. Assume that your mike is always live and never dead, and that what you say into it never dies.

***The Cue Earpiece.*** When you appear on a telephone call-in show, moderate a panel, or appear on a remote telecast beamed from another location, you will probably be asked to wear what is called a "cue earpiece." Such an earpiece enables you to hear the incoming telephone calls, the person talking at the remote location, and any instructions coming to you from the control room.

At first, you may be confused by the various voices coming through your earpiece if you are, at the same time, trying to answer a question or carry on a conversation. But with a little practice, you will understand the purpose of wearing it.

The little button which fits into your ear may be made of soft molded plastic, sized for comfort and connected to a curled plastic audio wire. The sound technician or floor manager will fit the button into your ear, then hook the cord up, over, and behind your ear and to the back of the neck, where the whole thing is anchored out of sight on the back of your jacket with a metal clip or a piece of sticky gaffer's tape. The wire is then run down your back, under your jacket, and plugged into an outlet that is tucked out of sight on the back of your chair, a desk, or behind the set. Check to see that the whole arrangement is comfortable for you, and make sure that you can move your head freely. Once the earpiece is in place and you are wired up, remember not to move suddenly or try to stand up, or your earpiece may pop out.

If the earpiece does not work temporarily, simply say that you cannot hear what is being said. Someone will come to the rescue and tell you what to do. They may repeat the information you could not hear and tell you to keep talking.

Your interviewer is accustomed to wearing the earpiece device. She or he has probably learned to read the prompter, take cues, listen to the control room chatter, and carry on a conversation—almost all at the same time.

## The Prompter

A prompter is a device that through reflection and magnification of a typed script enables you to read it while looking directly at the lens of the TV camera. Your script, which has been specially typed for the prompter, appears on the prompter's face no matter which camera you look at. The prompter copy is reflected upward onto a glass surface mounted at an angle in front of the lens. The viewer sees your eyes as if you were looking into the lens, when in reality you are reading the script. Your eye contact with the camera will automatically be correct.

The prompter operator will advance the copy as you speak, keeping the line you are speaking above the middle of the screen. The words will scroll upward at the pace you are speaking, as the prompter operator matches your speed.

Double prompters are sometimes used for news conference statements and long addresses. The copy is projected onto right and left glass stands, which resemble music racks. These are invisible to the cameras and to the audience unless one knows how to detect them in the long camera shots. Double prompters enable the speaker to establish natural eye contact with the audience, making it possible to look from side to side, with the copy always directly over the camera lens.

**Preparing Prompter Copy.** Prompter copy has to be prepared in advance on a special typewriter using large type and wide margins. Only a few words will fit on each line. The script that is to go on a prompter should be submitted well in advance to allow time for the material to be retyped properly to fit the particular prompter machine being used.

Prompter copy paper has vertical lines which indicate the margins. All of the copy is typed between these narrow lines, to fit the prompter limitations. The pages are numbered, and the prompter copies are joined together with tape to form a continuous strip. The paper is then rolled up and run through the machine in one seamless piece. Copy for a three-minute broadcast might be six or eight feet long before it is rolled up.

When no prompter is available, "idiot sheets" or "cue cards" may be used. These are huge cards—nearly poster sized—with handwritten copy. They are held as close to the lens as possible, but it is difficult to read them without shifting the eyes.

Every seasoned newscaster uses copy that has been painstakingly written and timed to the second. The viewer often has the illusion that the broadcaster is speaking spontaneously, when, in fact, he or she is reading from the prompter words he may have spent hours writing. The viewer also has the illusion that the broadcaster is talking only to one person. The prompter has thus eliminated the need to look down at the copy and then look up into the camera lens.

**Marking Up Prompter Copy.** You will probably find it helpful to mark up the prompter copy before you read it on camera. There are so few words on a line, within the narrow margins, that it is hard to see to the end of a sentence and to know when you will be able to take a breath.

I remember once when the late Hubert Humphrey was a senator, he was asked to tape a response representing the Democratic Party's point of view concerning an important political issue. When he got to the studio, he was handed a script he had never seen before. I, along with the rest of the crew, ended up having to wait while he spent about thirty minutes marking up the prompter copy to fit his famous personal speaking style. But once on tape, the script sounded like it was his own spontaneous words.

To mark up your copy, first underline the words you wish to emphasize. Draw in a wavy line underneath the words of long, difficult titles and proper names that have to be read together. Re-emphasize the commas, periods, and other punctuation marks with a heavy black pen, so that they can be easily identified. Mark phrasing and pauses with slash marks and / or a series of dots (". . ."). Usually, one slash mark indicates a pause; two slashes indicate a longer pause; and three slashes indicate a paragraph. Indicate qualifying phrases by using parenthesis marks. Use heavy quotation marks before and after quotations. Some broadcasters add asterisks to show where they can take a breath.

Develop a system that works for you. Mark your copy in such a way that the main points and buzz words leap out at you. As you become more experienced, you will automatically prepare your original script to include markings that you understand. Experienced broadcasters can gallop through prompter copy with varying speed and emphasis, easily interpreting the meaning of the material in a natural, conversational manner.

***Rehearsing Prompter Copy.*** Always rehearse reading your prompter copy in advance. You have to know what to expect, and the prompter operator needs to gauge your pace and style. You need to feel confident that the operator will maintain the right speed for you. Remember, the operator is supposed to keep the line you are reading near the middle of the screen. There is a small arrow on the monitor that indicates the line you are reading, so both of you can anticipate what is coming next.

The prompter operator wears earphones that connect him or her to the director in the control room. He can thus be helpful to you if there is a problem. For example, you may have a bright light shining in your eyes that makes it difficult to see the copy without squinting. The prompter operator can tell this to the director. Or the prompter may be positioned too close, too far away, too high, or too low.

As you rehearse, practice pronouncing any foreign or difficult words, or proper names with which you may be unfamiliar, asking for help if you are questioning any pronunciation. Look for tongue twisters, onomatopoetic words, or words you habitually mispronounce. Now is also the time to change any grammatical mistakes that have crept into the copy, or sentences that are too long or convoluted.

After rehearsal, you may wish to make last-minute corrections on the final roll of copy. Be sure the corrections are easy to read and not confusing because of crossed out words and miscellaneous markings. Use a heavy black pen, and make the corrections the same size as the print. Rather than risk an unreadable script, cut the corrected piece out, and replace it with accurate copy.

***Reading Prompter Copy.*** Your goal is to read the prompter copy as though you were saying the words in a conversational manner. It is easy to sound dull, monotonous, and stilted on camera. Understand that the prompter is not your master; it is only a helpful device that eliminates the necessity to memorize your material. It supplies you with words, and *you* give them their meaning. *You* employ the principles of good speech, such as changing the pace, pitch, and range of the voice, plus pausing in the right places.

As mentioned previously, you should keep a copy of your script in front of you the entire time you are on camera. This enables you to anticipate the next piece, to glance at it in its entirety to gauge its length, and to check the timing sequence, as necessary. Also, if the prompter should fail during the broadcast, you can rely on your own script copy in the emergency to continue the program. Thus, you should turn over the pages you are reading from the prompter as you finish with them, so that if the prompter fails, you can find your place on the script as quickly as possible.

You may feel that you develop a glassy-eyed stare when you read prompter copy for a long period of time. To avoid this, occasionally shift to your written script. Look down and purposely read from your written script, then look up at the prompter once again, looking into the camera's lens.

Some people have difficulty reading prompter copy convincingly. I once worked with a prominent judge who was doing a series of video-taped lectures. Even when he used transcripts of his own speeches, he could not make them appear to be natural; the process of having to "read" the copy verbatim eliminated the spontaneity of his own natural, informal speaking style. As we discussed this problem, I found out that when he gave a speech, he didn't read a typed speech, but instead spoke using only a few notes. We finally solved the problem of reading from the prompter by putting his own brief notes on the prompter, and merely giving him time cues via hand signals to maintain the time constraints.

Now that we have covered some of the more technical aspects of the TV studio so that you will be familiar with it before you go onto the set, we will go back to the actual interview process.

## Being Interviewed

*The Interviewer.* Try to learn something about the person who will interview you. Hopefully, he or she will be well informed, intelligent, and will ask relevant questions. A good interviewer will be sensitive to the pertinent information in your message. He or she will move logically from one point to the next and give you an opportunity to say what needs to be said. The interviewer's body language will indicate that he or she is interested.

Even though he or she has prepared a list of questions in advance, the good interviewer will be sensitive to your answers and will follow up on them.

However, it is possible to be interviewed by a person who is uninterested in what you have to say. He or she may not have read your book or done the homework necessary for an understanding of you and your message. The interviewer may be a stellar personality with a big ego and a quirky style of conducting interviews.

On a comedy show, he or she may try to get a laugh out of the situation, whether or not it is appropriate or in good taste. He may be thinking of what the audience might find funny or fascinating.

An interviewer may have a research file on you that contains derogatory information with which he hopes to embarrass you. Or he may be paying more attention to the time cues than to the content of your answers.

If you find yourself in such a negative interview situation, try to control the situation as much as you can by bridging from the questions to the important point you need to make, presenting the information you want the audience to remember.

*Interview Tips.* The first time you mention your corporation or organization, give its full name. After that, you can use the initials.

Call your interviewer by name when appropriate.

Concentrate on the key points you will want your viewers to remember. Repeat those points, when appropriate, for emphasis.

If you are a newsmaker, and you are aware of some "news-in-the-making" that may occur tomorrow or soon thereafter and your interviewer may not know about it, he or she will appreciate your mentioning it before you start the actual interview, giving him or her the opportunity to ask you about it. He or she will also be happy about this since you may be breaking some news before the rest of the press hears about it.

Listen carefully to the phrasing of the questions, turning them to your own advantage. Use them as an opportunity to say what you think should be said.

When you do not know the answer to a question, say so.

Strive to say something memorable.

Do not dispute details of an erroneous statement at great length. Simply give the correct facts.

Don't mumble, use too many "ahs" or "wells," fiddle with your notes or a piece of jewelry, cross and recross your legs, stroke your beard, constantly adjust your tie, or otherwise come across as ill-at-ease.

*Other General On-Camera Tips.* Television needs constant action to be interesting, and the director will constantly cut from one camera to another without your being aware of it. There might be quick reaction shots that catch you unawares. The cameras need to keep moving from close-ups to wider group shots to long shots and possibly even overhead camera shots.

For example, if you must cough, adjust a lock of hair that has fallen in your eyes, or pat sweat off your upper lip with a handkerchief, do so discreetly and with dignity as if you were on a podium or dais or at a head table during a dinner with all eyes upon you.

If you have been told to ignore the camera altogether during the actual interview, look your interviewer in the eye most of the time, listening carefully to what is said and reacting directly to your interviewer.

On a show in which viewers call in to ask you questions, you may be instructed to look at a certain numbered camera (such as "Camera 1" as opposed to "Camera 3") that gives the illusion that you are talking directly to the viewer.

On some television programs, you will find that you are not in the same room or even the same city with the person who is interviewing you. (When you are in a different city from your interviewer, this is usually referred to as a "two-way.") You may see the interviewer on a special monitor, which is usually mounted low, out of camera range. When you look at this monitor to hear the question, keep your chin up, so that it will not appear as though you are looking down. When you answer the questions, you will be instructed to look up at your assigned camera lens.

Also in such instances, an earpiece will be placed in your ear to hear the program audio. This technique is more desirable than listening to speakers on the floor, since there is then the tendency to lean toward the speaker for better listening power.

Never walk in front of a television camera without asking the floor manager if it's okay to do so. The director may cue a camera on at any time, without notice. Walk behind the camera, or duck low underneath the lens.

Since an accidental flash of a mirror into a lens can put an expensive camera out of commission by causing a burned-in flare in the lens, always keep mirrors faced away from the lens—cupped into the palm of the hand. If you are using a powder compact in the studio, cover the mirror beforehand with masking tape. Never use a two-sided mirror in the studio.

## More about Appearing on Camera

*Looking Pleasant on Camera.* You may be told that you look sad, grim, or downtrodden on camera. When you see yourself on the monitor, you may think that you look stern, depressed, and ten years older. You may be asked to smile, but you feel uncomfortable doing so.

To help counteract this, practice in a mirror to discover how far you can go to "half-smile" and lighten up your facial expression. Lift the brows. Part the lips and push them forward slightly and expectantly, just as you start to speak. Keep your gaze turned slightly upward, not downward. Keep your posture erect and elongated.

When you smile, your voice smiles too. Keep the voice alert and interested.

Professional actors and entertainers often keep a fixed grin on their faces as they hear the countdown to the air time. In this way, when they receive the camera cue, the back of the throat is open, and their first words come out properly placed. The audience never sees the contrived smile, only a pleasant expression as the cameras roll.

In sum, make the whole experience an "upper" instead of a "downer." Picture yourself as kindly and genial.

***How to Talk to a Camera.*** Some people can talk to an audience, but find it difficult to talk to a camera because they normally depend on the audience's reaction.

You really cannot overcome this by pretending to talk to the camera operator, since you cannot see his or her face and he is looking through the viewfinder or listening to instructions from the control room and will not respond to your remarks.

So who can you talk to? Look at the camera as if you were fond of it. Regard it as a close friend.

Or you might try to visualize that you are talking to a single listener who is eager to hear what you have to say. Even though you may be heard by millions of people, you are actually communicating one-on-one with that single, involved listener.

***Gestures on Camera.*** Keep the framework of the camera's viewer in mind—the area is the size of a television monitor, with a roughly four by three ratio. This means that your gestures have to remain close to the body, with the elbows held fairly close to the rib cage. Your gestures should stay in the area between your chin and your chest. The hands should never be in front of the face or advanced toward the camera, as they will be overly emphasized and enlarged.

Never touch your face except to do something meaningful, or possibly to remove your glasses.

Use welcoming gestures with the palms turned outward, rather than rejecting gestures with the arms crossed close to the body. As a viewer, you may well recall seeing interviews in which two hostile people sat with arms folded and chins jutted forward. Remember that all gestures on camera are magnified—high gestures reveal tension, and wide, wild gestures are lost.

In an interview situation, when your principal camera is on your right, direct your gestures toward the left, toward your interviewer. By putting the hands away from the camera, the gesture stays in proportion. If you gesture right, to a camera on your right, your hands are magnified and distorted.

Practice in front of a mirror to see which of your gestures are effective and relevant to the meaning of your material. If possible, arrange a practice session in front of a camera, and study the video tape. When you are a guest on a talk show, ask the producer for a copy of the video tape, and study it later. Use it as a learning tool. (Also, see the section called "Be a Television Critic" in this chapter.)

## APPEARING ON CAMERA IN A REMOTE LOCATION

As you become more well known in your field, a TV crew may one day come to your office, home, or another site to record a brief statement or sound bite for a TV news program. In such a case, keep your remarks brief and concise to prevent them from being edited out of context. Be prepared for such a set-up to take more time than you may expect.

If the crew is taping in your office, it will bring technical equipment such as cameras, lights, monitors, and sound gear. The technicians may clean off your desk, move flags and furniture around, darken the windows, and rearrange your treasures. Trust them. They are searching for a certain look, and will usually end up with a suitable framework for the taped piece.

When using your office for an interview, the remote crew members will need an adequate electrical supply. Unless they bring their own power source, they will look for your electrical outlets. To keep them from overloading the circuits, they may use power from several different rooms or hallways. Know how to call your electrician if there is trouble, and know where any electrical fuse box is located. It may pay to alert your building's electrician in advance.

After an on-location, one-camera interview, it may be necessary to do reverses. The camera, which has been focused on you, will be reversed to focus on your interviewer. He or she will repeat the questions with a pause in between, so they can be edited into the finished sequence.

If you agree to do an outdoor stand-up, allow extra time for extenuating circumstances. Street noise or overhead aircraft can require an extra take.

Never cancel a remote location shoot at the last minute unless it is absolutely unavoidable. A great deal of advance time, coordination, and money is involved in assembling a remote crew.

Location film and video tapes are put together in a series of tries called "takes." You may be proud that you can do a short segment in one take, but producers and directors rarely want to stop with the first one. They may ask for different body language or emphasis, or there may be flaws in the camera's technical moves or focus. Do not take the request for extra takes personally, because in the end you are all striving for the best possible piece for broadcast. Even professional actors do many takes before everyone is satisfied. Conserve your body strength, relax, and pace yourself. When the director finally says "that's a keeper!" or "print that one!" you realize that this group effort has accomplished what it set out to do. You will have a piece that you can be proud of when you see it later on the air.

I remember a famous actor who was doing a remote shoot in front of the White House. The piece was only twenty seconds long, but he was having an off day. The tourist crowds on the White House tour had to be detained and quieted during thirty-nine seemingly endless takes. When I eventually saw the final perfect piece aired on TV, I realized the viewer seldom knows what is involved in such a production.

Longer pieces and commercial films offer their own set of problems. For example, outdoor lighting is a real challenge when shooting commercial films. Gaffers may unload truckfuls of lights, stands, filters, scrims, and gels. Available light or sunlight may have to be matched to artificial light. The natural lighting levels will change as the day progresses. The scouting team may have incorrectly calculated the glare of the sun on white marble or other reflective surfaces. Rather than be photographed in the bright sun, seek some shade in the shadow of a building or under a tree. Otherwise, you may find that you can't help squinting into the sun, the picture will be washed out by too much light, and shadow lines in the face will be exaggerated.

Uncontrollable noise can also be a major source of frustration to a film crew. Any number of sounds can ruin a good take—crowd noise, an ambulance siren, passing planes or buses, a lawn mower, or a crying baby. Curious crowds will surround a film crew in hopes of seeing a celebrity. Pedestrians will often stroll unawares across the camera field. Their conversation may ruin a take because their voices were picked up on the sensitive sound systems being used.

Location shooting always seems to take more time than anyone anticipates. Allow ample time for travel from location to location. When on location, never count on catching a plane or getting to an appointment or a social dinner on time, unless the producers know of your time constraints in advance.

## THE INVESTIGATIVE TV UNIT

If you are a very high-profile person, you may be sought for a feature story by an investigative TV unit such as "60 Minutes."

If such a program is interested in interviewing you, you will probably first be contacted by a researcher. Once preliminary conversations yield enough information, a producer will then be assigned to the project. Finally, you will be interviewed at a given location (usually in a nonstudio situation with a film crew). It may all be done in one location in one interview, or in multiple locations over several days or weeks. After the producers have reviewed your interview(s), you may be called back to set up one more taping so that they may ask additional questions; this is especially true if the news changes as your segment is being produced.

Both positive and negative information may be used, and you must assume that you will have no control over the final edited material. You may have spent hours of your time being interviewed, and they only use thirty seconds of it. Or what they use may seem to be unfair and out of context. Only you can decide if it is worth it to you to be interviewed by an investigative TV unit. Often, the ensuing publicity for you and your message is worth the trouble and risk.

## BE A TELEVISION CRITIC

Now that you have read the sections on your appearance (particularly on clothes and makeup) in chapter one, voice placement in chapter two, and can understand the distortions caused by camera lenses, overhead lights, and amplifying devices, you can begin to see how easy it is to make innocent mistakes when you are appearing on TV. You begin to see with the eyes of a person who has worked behind the camera for years.

It's fun to be a television critic. Sit down some evening, pen and paper in hand, and flip the dial between competing network or local evening news broadcasts and perhaps some of the entertainment shows that follow. Make a list of all of the things you see that detract from the message the news correspondent or performer wishes to transmit.

The following is a sample list of some of the on-camera distractions—both visual and spoken—that we have pointed out previously and that you may now notice as you watch TV:

- a bold striped or patterned tie that shimmers with a moiré effect
- a plaid jacket
- a striped shirt with a white collar
- a black suit, white shirt, and/or too-red tie
- a gold watch that catches the light
- a shiny lapel pin or insignia
- a woman in an overpowering red-and-white-striped sweater
- a black-and-white printed dress
- a red dress or jacket that bleeds outside its true borders
- sparkling sequins on a dress
- a blouse with a large, bright, printed pattern
- crossed legs in a tight skirt that hikes up and is too short
- earrings that dangle and move and catch the light
- shiny earrings larger than the earlobes
- beetle blue or green eyeshadow
- a slash of bright red lipstick covered with gloss, which almost makes it look like the madeup mouth moves independently of the natural one
- a performer who fidgets constantly with the hair
- hair on a man or woman that constantly flops down over the forehead and eyes
- an obvious hairpiece or wig
- a mustache that obscures the upper lip line
- a scraggly beard
- big bare ears that pull the eye away from the face
- the broadcaster who shifts the eyes slightly off-center while reading prompter copy
- body language that expresses hostility
- a turned-down, negative facial expression
- excessive facial or head movements
- hand gestures outside the TV screen ratio
- someone who slouches over a microphone
- an interviewer who asks four- or five-part questions that are impossible to answer

- a harsh or too-shrill nasal placement of the voice
- a person who says "uh" or "well-ah" in every sentence
- a fast talker who ignores pronunciation of the consonants
- pronunciation of the soft "a" through the nose, in words such as "fact," "Africa," "matter," and "action."

At the end of the evening look at your list to see how you have become a knowledgeable critic of what looks and sounds good on TV. No doubt you will have added some pet peeves of your own. You will marvel at how seldom you see the perfect media image on the TV screen. People who have mastered sound media techniques are among those who endure and become highly acceptable as on-camera personalities.

# SIX

---
---

# SURVIVING
# PUBLIC LIFE

---
---

A s a public person, the odds are that you normally maintain a strenuous schedule. You may be constantly exposed to stress, pressure, and heavy responsibilities. You may experience a lack of privacy and rehabilitating downtime. The vicissitudes of public life require extraordinary coping skills and a strong physical constitution. All of this means that you need to take extra good care of yourself in order to meet the requirements of an active life.

Former president Ronald Reagan is a man who has survived public life with flying colors. Despite being America's oldest president to date, he survived eight years in the White House in apparent good health and good humor. Mr. Reagan did this despite a potential assassin's bullet, several bouts of illness, and a number of stressful events that occurred during his terms in office.

One reason that he may have weathered his years in the White House so well is that he understood the benefits of downtime—insisting, for example, on small but frequent periods of relaxation. Although some members of the press may have criticized his frequent trips to Camp David and his California ranch, he *may* have actually improved his ability to withstand the rigors of the presidency by such activities.

This chapter will discuss briefly some of the factors that affect your health, including smoking, food and drink, dealing with stress, and travel fatigue.

No matter what the nature of your career, if you are in the public eye you probably cannot afford to be ill, since your voice and body language reflect the state of your health. When you are bone-tired, bad habits may tend to reassert themselves. When you are exhausted, you take a chance that you will say or do something in public that you will later regret and that the press—and the public—will not easily forget. These incidents take on a life of their own.

Everyone can recall some event, such as how a famous actress looked and talked when coming down the courthouse steps after going through a painful divorce, or when a politician blew up at the press after losing a key election, or the government official who wept in public with the TV cameras rolling. These images can haunt an individual during the rest of his or her life. Such an incident will be brought up over and over again by interviewers, and any existing video tape will be shown for years to come.

As a public person, you cannot say, "I'm sorry, I don't feel too well today because I had too much to drink last night." Or "After a cattle-car flight and three packed-house presentations yesterday, I got to bed at 4 a.m., so I'm exhausted today." Or "I have the flu and a temperature of 102, but I am nevertheless here to make this stupid speech."

Instead, you must look relaxed and remain calm and in control. Uncertainty can have a negative effect on you, your staff, and your audiences. Try to manage your schedule of appearances so that you have time to survive. When you can, let your staff work to protect you from losing your sense of well-being. However, only you can say "no" to a schedule overload, since the final decision is yours.

Some public figures enjoy their work immensely, like to work long hours, are good at what they do, and accomplish a great deal. However, others cross a line and become workaholics. They reach a point when they work for the sake of working and maintain debilitating schedules without regard for their health. They are often unable to continue to be productive. Once stress and fatigue become a part of their daily existence, productivity suffers and there is a danger of emotional and physical burnout.

If you find yourself fitting increasingly into the workaholic category, it is important to pace yourself and to keep your workload at an achievable level, so that when the spotlight moves upon you, you can handle the challenge. This is especially important for the political candidate on the campaign trail.

Be kind to yourself. Do not waste time feeling bad about things that cannot be avoided, minor delays or negative incidents, innocent mistakes that you may have made, or something critical that was said about you. Since your role is so important, you deserve some self-given loving care.

How you handle a crisis often depends on your emotional makeup. When you believe in yourself, your opinions, and your work, it is easier to rise above the instabilities of your personal and professional life. Regard adversity as a challenge that you can conquer.

## AVOIDING ILLNESS

Do everything you can to avoid getting a contagious illness from other people. Since you are constantly subjected to crowds, develop your own ways to protect yourself. If you have to shake hands with everyone in a crowded room, wash your hands before touching your face or eating. Wash your hands after touching stair railings, elevator buttons, and doorknobs.

Distance yourself from people with coughs and colds. Turn your head unobtrusively when someone sneezes or coughs. Ask your doctor about getting flu shots for your own protection. Some people believe that relaxation techniques can increase immunity to colds. Certainly, when you are overtired and your resistance is down, you are more vulnerable to infections.

## SMOKING

These days, everyone is more aware of the ill effects that smoking can have on one's health. Even airlines have recently banned or limited smoking on flights both short and long.

Smoking is often directly related to the use of your voice. The accumulation of tobacco tars inside your lungs can limit your ability to breathe. Also, nicotine constricts your blood vessels so that your heart has to work harder to get enough oxygen to your brain. Instead of quieting your nerves, it can increase the tension in your body. The heat of the cigarette irritates the sensitive lining of your lungs and throat, which may account in part for a cigarette cough.

It has been said that smoke from a smoldering cigarette in an ashtray may contain more harmful ingredients than the smoke that is inhaled by the smoker.

Thus, before you make a speech or other public appearance, avoid a smoke-filled room, and move away from people who are smoking.

Public figures who are smokers should seriously consider quitting. Another reason not to smoke is that if you are meeting the public, as a smoker you cannot conceal your "smoker's breath" and the odor that permeates the hair and clothes. This odor is particularly noticeable clinging to wool suits. Smoking can irritate nonsmokers, and in general, is a highly unpopular habit right now.

## GETTING EXERCISE

Just before your public appearance, it is a good idea to keep moving around so that your brain can receive an adequate supply of oxygen. Even if you have to sit or stand for long periods of time, you need to keep your circulation going.

Coaches often advise athletes not to stand still before a game, but, rather, to keep moving. As a platform person, you can use this knowledge to great advantage.

Walking is a great exercise, since you can do it anytime, anywhere, and anyplace. Before your speech, you can stroll the corridor, move around the room to keep the circulation going, or possibly walk around the block. Walking can help to reduce tension, keep you calm under stress, and make you sleep better; it is also a safe form of exercise for people of any age.

While sitting, you can do unobtrusive heel-to-toe exercises. You can do such exercises behind the speaker's table or on a long plane ride. One such exercise is to twist and rotate your feet around and around to activate the muscles in the backs of your legs.

When standing at the podium, you can occasionally shift your weight from one foot to the other or step slightly forward or backward. The simple act of walking up on the stage or approaching the platform can become a pleasant, mildly invigorating experience.

People who must stand long hours on their feet—such as teachers, store clerks, chefs, nurses, and security people—often use various techniques to help keep the circulation going. They do nearly invisible exercises with various muscle groups, or they slightly shift their weight to the outside of the shoe, as though to turn the toes inward. You can do the same thing.

Another exercise you will find most helpful is to stand on your heels with the toes up as far as they will go. Rock forward on the toes. Do this for one leg at a time—walking in place, so to speak. You will be able to feel your muscles working for you to keep your circulation going.

# FOOD AND DRINK

The food you eat can make a critical difference in your overall health as well as in your public performances. What you eat can influence your energy level, mood shifts, and mental alertness.

Before you make a major speech or give an important interview, go into training much as an athlete would. Decide in advance what you will eat and drink. Develop a routine of your own that works well for you. Some speakers eat at home, and ignore the banquet fare. They know from long experience the proper balance of proteins, carbohydrates, fats, and sugars that gives them a feeling of well-being and contributes to a good performance.

Avoid overeating just before your speech or other public appearance. Heavy, rich, highly spiced foods can rob you of your energy. If you are the banquet speaker, you may choose to ignore the big steak, and opt instead for the salad, vegetables, and baked potato.

At a cocktail party, patronize the raw vegetable tray. Eat the apple from the cheese tray, even if it was meant as a decoration. Remember, you can eat anything you want when your speech is over.

Avoid suspicious-looking foods such as mayonnaise-based salads, shellfish with no ice, or meat-based canapés that have changed color. There is no need to eat the food just because it is there.

Some performers have favorite preshow pick-me-ups. They include a slice of lemon to cleanse the vocal cords, herbal tea with perhaps honey and lemon, fruit, yogurt, pasta, or granola.

The public person has to remember to drink enough water to avoid dehydration. Normal sources of water are often not a part of public life. Try to sip water all day and take a drink every time you pass a water fountain. Don't substitute soft drinks, beer, coffee, or tea for the water that you need. When traveling, devise ways to constantly replenish your water intake. One way to do this is to carry small bottles of mineral water with you wherever you go.

Caffeine can constrict the blood vessels. Since it is found in soft drinks, coffee, tea, and even chocolate, you should avoid these as much as possible. Consuming several cups of coffee, particularly if combined with nicotine and alcohol, is not a good idea just before your public appearance.

Alcohol is a depressant that is metabolized at roughly one drink per hour, depending on your body weight, how much you've eaten, and other factors. (A glass of wine, a beer, and a normal-size mixed drink all contain a roughly equivalent amount of alcohol.) The effects of alcohol are enhanced under hot lights or in a hot room. Alcohol impairs your ability to regulate your internal temperature; one drink before you speak under certain circumstances may carry the jolt of two or three. Beer really does not cool you down, because you cannot get enough liquid volume to regulate your body temperature.

In short, the public person should consider carefully before drinking alcohol either before or during a public appearance. Certainly, a public person's reputation can be ruined by even one episode of being, or even *appearing* to be, inebriated in public.

## STRESS

As a public person, you are certain to find yourself in stressful situations; they go with the territory. Most certainly, you will at times encounter circumstances which demand more than you feel capable of dealing with. You have to expect them and learn ways to control stress.

Many good books exist that deal with the subject of handling stress, and it is not my intention here to write in great detail about what has been so well covered elsewhere. I simply want to point out some of the ways that stress can particularly impact on the public person.

Many famous people are felled by heart attacks and illness that may be indirectly related to stress. Others suffer through personal tragedies related to a stressful life-style. Still others develop mental disorders or abuse drugs or alcohol in response to the particular stresses of public life.

Negative stress can take its toll on your immune system, making you vulnerable to colds and infections. Excessive stress places an added load on your heart and blood vessels. It can affect your sleep patterns, sexual function, and physical stamina.

Some people experience a decline in personal productivity, possibly endangering their careers and upward mobility. Too much prolonged stress can lead to burnout, which can have long-range consequences.

Learn to gauge when you are functioning at the peak of your abilities. Recognize the signals that tell you you need to cope with stress. If you feel depressed, alienated, defensive, always tired, short-tempered, or frustrated, do something to reverse the pattern.

Recognize the problems caused by an overloaded schedule. Be aware of your own limitations, and set boundaries on taking further responsibilities beyond which you will not go. Delegate trivial tasks to someone else and save yourself for the important things. Divide such tasks into manageable segments, which can then be accomplished one at a time.

Devise your own time-management plan, making a daily list of priorities and anticipating your deadlines.

If possible, try to surround yourself with support people who understand that you must face stressful situations. They should be professional, considerate, efficient, and unobtrusive. Such staff members can take care of routine requests or off-the-wall demands on your time that would sap your energies if you had to take care of each one yourself.

Schedule downtime for yourself when you can do the things you really enjoy. Streamline your wardrobe, workplace, paperwork, and reading material.

Have a hobby or sport that you thoroughly enjoy, be it tennis, golf, fishing, woodworking, gardening, or a collection. Develop a sense of humor, and see changes in your life as a challenge.

In your day-to-day life in the public eye, concentrate on devising ways to ease stress. For example, change the pace of your work or travel schedule by taking mental and physical breaks—anything to bring about a cessation of the constant pressure. Take a series of minivacations rather than waiting for one long one. Take naps whenever possible. Eat your lunch outdoors on a park bench, where the phone does not ring. If an appointment gets canceled unexpectedly, don't read more memos; instead, get out and visit a museum or do something else that you would enjoy and allow you to recharge your batteries. If you have a difficult problem, set aside a short period of time to lean back and relax, letting your thoughts wander. This is often an effective problem-solving method. Find the relaxations, even the small ones, that restore your sense of well-being and replenish your inner resources.

On the other hand, a certain amount of stress can have positive manifestations. It forces you to perform at peak capacity. It temporarily increases your efficiency. It stimulates you to meet new challenges. For example, responding to the stimulus of a live audience is a positive experience. A manageable amount of stress causes your body to release a hormone which gives you a feeling of mild euphoria, well-being, or exhilaration. You will be more alert and motivated to a higher level of endeavor.

This kind of stress has been termed "good stress." Some people who love a challenge, competition, or functioning on the edge of danger (race-car drivers or downhill ski racers, for example) seek it out. You may even come to depend on that good stress to enhance your public performances.

## TRAVEL FATIGUE

Travel can have its own uniquely stressful situations. When spending long hours in a plane, get up and move around at regular intervals. Use the exercises described above to keep your circulation going and your muscles relaxed.

Unexpected delays, changes in schedules, and unaccustomed situations bring their own frustrations. If you possibly can, arrive at your destination a day early to acclimate yourself to a different climate, different food, and maybe different time zones or altitudes. Similarly, if at all possible, plan to stay an extra day after a particularly strenuous conference in order to rest and recuperate. Allow some leeway in your schedule to meet any unavoidable delay or emergency.

When long, boring delays are inevitable, create your own relaxing environment that will make the time enjoyable. Bring along a good book or some reading material you haven't had time to enjoy before, and a personal tape player with a good supply of your favorite music; schedule an hour for a professional massage; or select a favorite restaurant and look forward to eating dinner there.

When you cross several time zones, your body clock can become confused. You might forget what time it is, what city you are in, when to sleep, and when to eat. In such situations, a special light diet and a relaxed time schedule can be helpful.

On most airlines, special meals are available to you when ordered in advance. Remember not to become dehydrated—carry a travel cup or plastic bottle and drink water during the trip.

In any case, know how much is too much fatigue, so that your energy level is not dangerously depleted. As much as possible, arrive at your destination as refreshed as you can, so that you will be prepared to participate effectively in the event to which you are committed.

## THE BOTTOM LINE

"To thine own self be true."

Everyone has heard this line and maybe thought how trite it sounds. But is it?

The bottom line is that as a public person you have received advice from everyone from your own teenagers to expert consultants . . . with coworkers and friends, perhaps, somewhere in between.

And by now you will have examined and assessed the main points in this book about your personal appearance, your voice, your message, and techniques available to you to use in transmitting that message.

Now, *you* have to take all of the disparate elements of your public self—all of those things that you have been putting together—and you have to join them with the best of the advice that has been presented to you. During this process, you will be discarding those elements that make you uncomfortable or are simply wrong for you.

In addition to the expertise that you possess in your field, you have now added a professional polish that helps you to meet the challenges inherent in being in the public eye.

As a public person, you know you simply cannot come across as false in any way. You cannot be somebody you are not.

You are the person responsible for your life, and you have to live with yourself long after all of the tumult and shouting are over and the others have gone home. In the end, *you* must visualize how hindsight and history will regard you and your accomplishments.

# FOR FURTHER READING

Bartlett, John. *Familiar Quotations.* 15th ed. Boston: Little, Brown and Company, 1980.

Bliss, Edward, Jr., and Patterson, John M. *Writing News for Broadcast.* 2d ed. New York: Columbia University Press, 1978.

Carnegie, Dale. *The Quick and Easy Way to Effective Speaking.* Revised by Dorothy Carnegie. New York: Pocket Books, 1962.

Ehret, Charles F., and Scanlon, Lynne Waller. *Overcoming Jet Lag.* New York: Berkley Books, 1983.

Lustberg, Arch. *Building Podium Power.* Washington, D.C.: U.S. Chamber of Commerce, Association Department, 1988.

Martel, Myles. *Before You Say a Word: The Executive Guide to Effective Communication.* Englewood Cliffs, N. J.: Prentice-Hall, 1984.

Matthews, Christopher. *Hardball: How Politics Is Played—Told by One Who Knows the Game.* New York: Summit Books, 1988.

McGinniss, Joe. *The Selling of the President.* 20th anniversary ed. New York: Penguin Books, 1969.

McKenzie, E. C. *14,000 Quips & Quotes for Writers & Speakers.* New York: Greenwich House, 1980.

*NBC Handbook of* Pronunciation. 4th ed. New York: Harper & Row, 1984.

Norfolk, Donald. *Executive Stress.* New York: Warner Books, 1986.

Peale, Norman Vincent. *The Power of Positive Thinking.* New York: Fawcett Crest, 1956.

Rizzo, Raymond. *The Voice as an Instrument.* 6th ed. New York: Macmillan Publishing Company, 1985.

Rogers, Natalie H. *Talk Power: How to Speak without Fear.* New York: Dodd Mead & Company, 1982.

Uris, Dorothy. *A Woman's Voice: A Handbook to Successful Private and Public Speaking.* New York: Barnes and Noble, 1975.

Van Dusen, C. Raymond. *Training the Voice for Speech: A Guide to Voice and Articulation Improvement.* New York: McGraw-Hill Book Company, 1953.

# INDEX

voice (*continued*)

good voice characteristics,
67–68

importance of, 62–63

improvement, need for, 67

lazy lips, 86

listening to voices, 75

mannerisms, 75

muscular activity, 66

nasality, 70, 75, 77

one voice for all situations, 79

phonetics, 85–86

pitch, 71-72

placement, 70–71

polyps or nodules on vocal
cords, 82

posture for speaking, 66

practicing with tape recorder,
81, 88

projection, 73

public speaking. *See* public
speaking

relaxation exercises, 82–83

resonance, 69–70

self-improvement, 77–79, 87–88

sinus irrigation, 82

space between teeth, 85

speech therapy, 79–80

structure of, 63–66

stuttering, 81

on telephone, 169–71

timbre, 73

tone, 74

volume, 72

Walters, Barbara, 61

Watergate scandal, 134

Webster, Daniel, 5, 98

West, Mae, 61

Wilde, Oscar, 97

women

accessories, 25–26

clothing for, 20, 21–24, 178

color coordination for, 23

emergency kit for, 28

fabrics worn by, 23–24

grand entrances, 29

gray clothing on, 20

hairstyle and color, 53–55

hands, 58

jewelry for, 24–26

makeup for, 34–45, 48

purses, 24

shoes for, 26–27

television makeup, 48

travel wardrobe for, 27–28

World War II, 131–132